PROJECTING CANADA

Arts Insights, a new series from McGill-Queen's
University Press, showcases current research in the
social sciences, humanities, and social work.

Arts Insights, an initiative of McGill's Faculty of
Arts, brings together research in the Social Sciences,
Humanities, and Social Work. Reflective of the range
of expertise and interests represented by the Faculty
of Arts at McGill, Arts Insights seeks manuscripts
that bring an interdisciplinary perspective to the
discussion of ideas, issues, and debates that deepen
and expand our understanding of human interaction,
such as works dealing with society and change,
or languages, literatures, and cultures and the relationships among them. Of particular interest are
manuscripts that reflect the work of research collabo-
rations involving McGill faculty and their colleagues
in universities that are part of McGill's international
affiliation network.

Arts Insights will publish two titles a year in English.
The editors prefer original manuscripts but may
consider the English language translations of works
that have already appeared in another language.

SERIES EDITORS
Nathalie Cooke, Richard Schultz, Wendy Thomson

Projecting Canada
*Government Policy and Documentary Film
at the National Film Board*
Zoe Druick

Projecting Canada

Government Policy and Documentary Film

at the National Film Board of Canada

ZOË DRUICK

McGILL-QUEEN'S UNIVERSITY PRESS
Montreal & Kingston • London • Ithaca

© McGill-Queen's University Press 2007

ISBN 978-0-7735-3185-7 (cloth)
ISBN 978-0-7735-3259-5 (paper)

Legal deposit first quarter 2007
Bibliothèque nationale du Québec

Printed in Canada on acid-free paper.

This book has been published with the help of a publishing
grant from Simon Fraser University.

Photos used with permission of the National Film Board.

McGill-Queen's University Press acknowledges the support of
the Canada Council for the Arts for our publishing program.
We also acknowledge the financial support of the Government
of Canada through the Book Publishing Industry Development
Program (BPIDP) for our publishing activities.

Library and Archives Canada Cataloguing in Publication

Druick, Zoë
Projecting Canada: government policy and documentary film
at the National Film Board of Canada / Zoë Druick.

Includes bibliographical references and index.
ISBN 978-0-7735-3185-7 (bnd)
ISBN 978-0-7735-3259-5 (pbk)

1. Documentary films – Social aspects – Canada. 2.
Educational films – Social aspects – Canada. 3. National Film
Board of Canada – History. 4. Documentary films – Canada –
History and criticism. 5. Educational films – Canada – History
and criticism. 6. Canada – Cultural policy. I. Title.

PN1993.5.C3D78 2007   070.1'80971   C2006-905188-7

This book was designed and typeset by studio oneonone
in Sabon 10.5/13.5

CONTENTS

ILLUSTRATIONS

ACKNOWLEDGMENTS

This book began as my PHD thesis in the Department of Social and Political Thought at York University. It evolved in the years following my graduation according to new finds I made in the archives, new developments in the field, and new perspectives I developed while teaching communication studies in the English Department at Wilfrid Laurier University, the Cultural Studies Department at Trent University, and the School of Communication at Simon Fraser University, where I now work. I would like to thank the members of my PHD committee, Peter Morris, Scott MacKenzie, and especially my senior supervisor, Barbara Godard, for their support. Peter Morris was very generous with documents in his possession from the John Grierson Archive (Stirling, Scotland) and other information about the National Film Board, for which I am grateful. Thanks also to Michael Dorland for his comments on the thesis.

I am grateful to my colleagues in the School of Communication for sharing their ideas with me, reading my work, and giving me practical advice for being in the academy. My thanks to Fiona Jeffries, Pablo Mendez, Catherine Murray, Ira Wagman, Yuezhi Zhao, and Rachel Zolf for their comments on the manuscript at various points. Editors and anonymous manuscript readers at McGill-Queen's University Press helped bring forth the book from the thesis.

I would also like to acknowledge Bernard Lutz of the National Film Board Archives, Claude Lord of the National Film Board Photo-thèque, and the staffs of Library and Archives Canada, the British Film Institute, the Vincent Massey Archives, the Public Record Office (London), the League of Nations Archives (Geneva), the John Grierson Archive (Stirling, Scotland), the Media Library at Simon Fraser University, and the Sound and Moving Image Library at York University, especially Kathryn Elder. Media history is only as good as the archival sources that sustain it, and I have been lucky to work with so many dedicated people.

I acknowledge with thanks funding received from Simon Fraser University Discovery Parks Fund for travel to archives. The book was buoyed up by a generous grant from the Simon Fraser Publications Fund at a crucial moment.

Sections of chapter 1 were published as "'Ambiguous Identities' and the Representation of Everyday Life: Notes Toward a New History of Production Policies at the NFB of Canada," *Canadian Issues* 20 (1998): 125–37. Parts of chapter 5 first appeared as "Documenting Government: Re-examining the 1950s National Film Board Films about Citizenship," *Canadian Journal of Film Studies* 9 (Spring 2000): 55–79. My thanks to these journals for allowing me to republish aspects of this work here. Special thanks to the NFB for providing the images for the book.

On a personal note, I would like to thank the many friends and family members who have provided so much support and sustenance over the years. Through their example, my parents Don Druick and Cheryl Sourkes taught me both to assume the value of art and to realize the material conditions of its production, lessons that have filtered into the framing of this study. My heartfelt thanks go to my partner, David Layton, who has seen this process through many stages and provided a joyful companionship while also valiantly trying to teach me to see the pleasure in rewriting.

ZOË DRUICK
Vancouver, B.C.

ABBREVIATIONS

BFI   British Film Institute
CAAE   Canadian Association for Adult Education
CCCC   Committee on Cooperation in Canadian Citizenship
CCEC   Canadian Council for Education-in-Citizenship
CIIA   Canadian Institute of International Affairs
EMB   Empire Marketing Board
FAO   Food and Agriculture Organization
CGMPB   Canadian Government Motion Picture Bureau
GPO   General Post Office
ILO   International Labor Organization
IRT   Imperial Relations Trust
JGA   John Grierson Archive
LAC   Library and Archives Canada
NATO   North Atlantic Treaty Organization
NAUK   National Archives (United Kingdom)
NFB   National Film Board of Canada
NFBA   National Film Board Archives
NFS   National Film Society of Canada
UNESCO United Nations Educational, Scientific, and Cultural
        Organization
UNRRA   United Nations Relief and Rehabilitation Administration
WHO   World Health Organization
VMA   Vincent Massey Archives

PROJECTING CANADA

Documentary and Cultural Policy

As a result of the coordination and centralization effected through the creation of the National Film Board, new fields of usefulness are being developed in connection with governmental film activities. Of these, possibly the most significant is the entry of the government into the production of documentary and realist films.
– Department of Trade and Commerce, *Annual Report*, 1939–40

In two realms of cultural output Canada has been unsurpassed as a producer: documentary film and cultural policy (not to mention policy analysis). This book began as an exploration of how these subjects converge in the topic of documentary film production at the National Film Board of Canada.[1] The subject of realist representation of the population at a state-funded agency seems to lend itself to a study of the place of cultural production in the relation between citizen and state, in short, of governmentality. But the road was not as direct as I supposed.

The 1990s saw a plethora of critical studies of cultural policy as an aspect of population management. Following on from Foucault's work on governmentality and a set of related publications, Ian Hunter, Tony Bennett, Toby Miller, and others made the connection between culture as a site of the management of well-tempered subjectivity and government policy.[2] In Canada, this mantle was taken up by Michael Dorland in both his edited collection *The Cultural Industries in Canada* (1996) and his study of feature film policy, *So Close to the State/s* (1998). All of this work encouraged a rethinking of the place of arts and cultural policy as a subject of study and a possible site of intervention in cultural studies. Governmentality, Foucault's reformulation of the problematics of state power articulated by Louis Althusser in his famous work on ideological state apparatuses, extended and rearticulated his theory of biopower as a problem inherent in modern states that nonetheless exceeded the state paradigm. Defined as the "conduct of conduct," governmentality is an ethos of management operating at the level of daily routines and crystallized in social institutions.[3] The articulation of culture to government in critical studies of cultural policy made for a logical extension of Foucault's work in this area.

According to this approach, cultural policy is taken as a citizen-building technology. "Cultural policies produce and animate institutions, practices, and agencies. One of their goals is to find, serve, and nurture a sense of belonging, through educational institutions and cultural industries." In a word, they are a "means of governance."[4] Yet they are also opportunities for citizens to map the social world.[5] This compelling link between government and representation seems tailor-made for understanding the citizen-building work of the National Film Board (NFB), and indeed it has not been entirely overlooked. In the introduction to his *Cultural Industries in Canada* anthology, Michael Dorland positions the NFB and its animating legislation as part of Canada's "symbolic environment." According to him, the symbolic environment has "defined the rules, terms, conditions or turns of language by which players are authorized to enter and play the cultural industries 'game' in the Canadian context."[6] But no matter how significant the NFB may be in terms of Canada's symbolic environment, however, because it is not a cultural industry, its analysis has not been part of the governmental turn in cultural policy studies; it does not merit a chapter in Dorland's anthology.

So, perplexingly, studies of the governmental agenda of culture did not seem quite to apply to the documentary films of the National Film Board, which were, for the most part, not seen to be either "cultural" in the high art sense or "popular" as the discourse of the cultural industries demands. NFB films seemed, if anything, to be governmental in a different way – in terms of their relationship to social science. I began to explore the history of government information and was intrigued by the connection between documentary film and the state's production of information about the population, especially statistics. According to Ian Hacking, Bruce Curtis, and others, statistics, or the production of abstracted, categorical information about the population, has been linked since the nineteenth century to the development of probabilistic models of management and control.[7] Statistics, rather than culture, seemed to provide the basis for a novel way of thinking about documentary and government.

From here my thinking turned toward the documentary movement and its connection to state objectives of producing probabilistic narratives about the population. Documentary film emerged as a state project in England, continental Europe, and the Soviet Union at the end of the 1920s and developed in the United States during the 1930s, finally reaching Canada in 1939, where it flourished in the 1940s. Given the importance of the documentary film in the state objectives of the period, it seemed likely that documentary film could be epistemologically connected to other forms of government information and education of the period. For example, the interwar years saw the rise of social scientific method, with its array of visual technologies, from graphs and maps to photographs, and this was also the time when the cementing of social science and government occurred, especially in liberal democracies. My entry point was the question of how population studies were linked to documentary film, both conceptually and visually, and what, if anything, this had to do with the life of the NFB.

Documentary film's claims to reality are often likened to the scientific emphasis on objective observation.[8] Yet, as the history of documentary has shown, unmediated observation of the world is far from what documentary is about.[9] The interpretive frameworks of social science are more relevant to documentary than pure science is. Not only does documentary mirror ways of knowing that have been pioneered in the social sciences, but the development of the form of documentary film can be seen to be related to its institutional role in representing the population in order to help predict and manage it. The links are clear, for instance, between the use of the case study and the generalization of particular information to claims of social typicality. Also, the use of the interview, arguably one of the mainstays of documentary film on and off screen since *Housing Problems* (1936), is perhaps the most important form of social scientific data gathering after observation. According to the social science historians Andrea Fontana and James Frey, in-depth interviewing and participant observation often go hand in hand.[10] Another significant similarity is the power relationship inherent in social science and documentary alike, and the way it is connected to the material production of knowledge. As theories of knowledge and power have changed, so have both social science and documentary.

Social science, both quantitative and qualitative, emerged in the twentieth century as a way to study human group life in modern societies. Encompassing sociology, economics, anthropology, psychology, political science, and some forms of social history, social science has gone through massive changes in the past century. In a recent comprehensive survey, Norman Denzin and Yvonna Lincoln divide the twentieth century history of social scientific study into the following periods:[11]

1900–1950, traditional, positivist social science
1950–1970, modernist, the golden age of postpositivist social science
1970–1986, blurred genres, postpositivist crisis of representation, characterized by self-reflexivity and the introduction of structuralism, semiotics, phenomenology, cultural studies, and feminism
1986–1990, exacerbated crisis of representation, high levels of self-reflexivity
1990–1995, postmodern period of experimental and new ethnographies, the narrative turn, emphasis on literary and rhetorical tropes
1996–present, postexperimental inquiry.

It is instructive to compare this taxonomy of social science with Bill Nichols's widely cited timeline of dominant documentary film forms in *Blurred Boundaries* (1994):[12]

1930s–1950s, expository: didactic, directly address the real
1960s, observational: eschew commentary, observe things as they happen
1960s–1970s, interactive: interviews utilized to retrieve history
1980s, reflexive: question documentary form, defamiliarize the other forms
1980s–1990s, performing documentary: stress subjective aspects of a classically objective discourse.

One can see clear parallels between the two lists, especially in terms of a questioning of traditional method from the 1960s and a turn toward reflexivity in the 1980s. But despite the links between the modernist and postmodernist moments in social science and documentary filmmaking,

Nichols, like most film theorists, addresses these changes in documentary as though they are purely reactions to previous forms of film truth.

One clear point of comparison between documentary and social science concerns the "voice of god" narration of early documentary films (epitomized in 1940s NFB films by Lorne Greene's booming, disembodied voice). It is commonly posited that the narration-free observational cinema of the late 1950s and the 1960s was developed as a response to the overbearing authoritarian narrator of 1930s and 1940s films. Yet in social science history there was a very similar reaction against what Michael Angrosino and Kimberly Mays de Pérez have called "traditional ethnographic reportage [that] favored the supposedly objective third-person voice, emanating from the 'omniscient narrator.'"[13] Similarly, Mary and Kenneth Gergen write that part of the purpose of reflexive social science is for "the investigator to relinquish ... the 'God's-eye view' and reveal ... his or her work as historically, culturally, and personally situated."[14] Lincoln and Denzin assert that "recent understandings in the social sciences now convince us that there is no 'god's eye view'; there is no 'voice from nowhere,' no 'voice from everywhere.'"[15] In other words, documentary is not the only discourse that has rejected its earlier forms of authoritative knowledge production. Observational documentary resisted expository documentary form; both mirrored the form of expression favoured by social science at the time of their inception. This link is even more significant when one considers the use of both social science and documentary by government.

Documentary film materialized in the way of expressing knowledge that was dominant in the social sciences in the 1930s and 1940s, and it was challenged in similar ways in the 1950s. These practitioners of golden age social science "put in place a tragic and often ironic view of society and self," write Denzin and Lincoln. This is redolent of the voice-overs of the NFB in the 1950s, often read by Stanley Jackson, which Peter Harcourt has characterized as asking more questions than they answer and revealing themselves to be questions of "leisured, unharassed, middle-class culture," presenting their subjects with an "abstract and slightly rhetorical air" and a "boyish sense of wonder."[16] Similarly, the turn toward reflexive films in the 1970s and 1980s mirrors the shift during the same period from participant observation to the "observation of participation" and an emphasis on the process of writing, according to autoethnographers Carolyn Ellis and Arthur Bochner.[17] The emphasis on first-person films and representatives of marginal communities in the 1980s and 1990s parallels a shift in ethnography from outsider to "bi-cultural insider/outsiders, native ethnographers [who] construct their own cultural stories (often focussing on their own autobiographies), raise serious questions about the interpretations of others who write about them, and use their dual positionality to problematize the distinction between observer and observed."[18] Although documentary film may be examined as a representational strategy unto itself, it makes some sense to think about its parallels with social science as well. In Canada, documentary film production was enabled by a cultural policy that created the NFB. Inspired by governmentality theory and the field of critical cultural policy studies, my goal in this book is to shed some light on the complex relationships between cultural policy, social science, and documentary film.

OUTLINE OF THE BOOK

In an influential 1986 essay, Maurice Charland posited that Canadian broadcasting had been shaped by a discourse of "technological nationalism" that "ascribes to technology the capacity to create a nation by enhancing communication." However, according to Charland, technological nationalism leads only to a false civil society and an "absent nation": communication is pursued for its own sake, but its substance remains secondary, even absent.[19] In reference to feature film policy, Charles Acland referred a decade later to the "absent audience" for Canadian feature films. He contended that the audience in studies of film was always deemed to be truant, missing, rather than recognized as pursuing tastes different from those of the elite educational state.[20] The films of the National Film Board seem to be betwixt and between these two absences. They were used to create limited and temporary publics, not the public sphere ascribed to broadcasting. These publics, or audiences, have been targeted and limited – not the absent mass audience, but the specialized, need-based community. In this respect, too, NFB documentaries are more closely connected to social science than to either political theory (public sphere) or the popular culture/high art debates of fictional film. What are deemed absences in other discourses – the absent nation or the absent audience – have not been the significant terms through which documentary cultural policy has been articulated.

Documentary film has been a privileged site of production in Canadian culture, providing a way of seeing the nation. This policy has challenged both the absent nation and the absent audience theories of Canadian media. The documentaries of the NFB show the nation, subdivided into the categories of government and social science, back to itself. Institutions such as the NFB are important parts of Canada's symbolic environment, as Dorland suggests; they provide the frames in which cultural products are made and disseminated. The focus of this book, then, is the complex interconnection between documentary film form – a notion of everyday life as the subject of governmentality and documentary alike – and the cultural policy mandate given to the NFB, as well as the way it has been interpreted and changed over time.

This book undertakes an examination of the emergence of both a cultural institution and a mode of communication. In my desire to bring context to text, I have combined archival and historical research with film analyses. This is not a study of film in the traditional sense. Rather, it is a study of visual culture, the semantically productive quality of aesthetic texts, the dialogic aspect of documentary communication, and the role of cultural institutions in nation building. Each chapter examines a distinct historical situation and attempts to consider the specificities of social policy in relation to the cultural formations that were engaged with the NFB in each era, ranging from educational lobbies to cultural nationalists and new social movements. As I shall explore in what follows, documentary cinema – its form, its institutionalization, and its audiences – is an exemplary site for seeing how communications media were given the task of putting into practice the modernizing policies of industrial societies. This philosophy emanated from the British context in the dying days of empire, but it was equally rooted in the social scientific development of public relations in the United States. John Grierson, the famous father of the documentary, straddled both worlds, and his work provides an important coalescence of these philosophies.

Chapter 1 gives the history of the National Film Board and outlines its histriography. In each era, discussions of the NFB's future, and therefore its history, have been fraught political subjects. The politics that have clouded discussion of the NFB have tended to ignore the institution as it actually was, focusing instead on what it has been or what it might have been. I present a framework of governmentality and propose thinking about the NFB as it has operated. In chapter 2 I consider

the relationship of Canadian communication models to empire communication. I contend that the NFB may instructively be placed in relation
to British practice, which early on adopted film for its colonial and domestic governance. In chapter 3 I explore the relationship between documentary film, government information, and social science. John Grierson
was an intrinsic link, I argue, between British government film and
American social science, the latter becoming an important part of government through the Chicago School's connection to the New Deal.
Chapter 4 examines the connection between non-theatrical documentary,
nationalism, internationalism, and education in mid-century Canada,
including the place of the Massey Commission in the cold war Canadian landscape. This discussion continues in chapter 5, in which I explore
the issues of citizenship and security in the cold war context and examine a number of films in relation to this social and political backdrop.
In chapter 6 the legacy of oppositional filmmaking is considered in relation to the new forms of citizenship being struggled over in the 1960s
and 1970s. I attempt to demonstrate that this celebrated, radical moment in the NFB's history needs to be considered in relation to a shift in
government social policy toward new forms of citizenship. The new social
movements of the period became the sites of filmmaking experimenta-
tion. The turn to self-reflexive filmmaking and marginal communities in
the 1980s and 1990s is the subject of chapter 7. Here I argue that the
crisis of the state that accompanied the rise of neoliberal free-market
ideology was paralleled by crises in both social science and documentary film. I attempt to tease out the logic that ensured the continuation
of the NFB in this tumultuous period. In the conclusion, I sum up the
implications of considering the NFB as it is and was, rather than as it
might have been, and I look at its films and policy as tactics of governmentality. Throughout the study I try to attend to the nuances of films
and filmmakers working within this paradigm. One of the things I did
not expect to discover was the extent to which the element of struggle
or dialogue between competing voices and claims on documentary truth
remains embedded in NFB films.

FILM ACTS

The NFB policy, I argue, is rooted in interwar theories of empire marketing, social science, the administered welfare state, and mass and adult

education that encompassed both film form and modes of audience formation. In the book, I examine the ways in which this logic of bringing coherence to a divided polity has continued throughout the existence of the National Film Board, even during its most "radical" moments. In other words, film *acts*.

The National Film Board of Canada was established with the National Film Act of 1939. Modifications to the act followed in 1950 and 1985. In a basic sense, these acts have been the policy that gave the NFB its mandate and its life – an injunction to act. But in another sense, the legistlation facilitated the production of films that are themselves utterances or acts of speech, instances of meaning making. As with any utterance, documentary films are constrained by rules of discourse – what the Russian literary critic M.M. Bakhtin has called speech genres.[21] In the case of NFB films about the everyday life of the population, these film acts have attempted to bring about a kind of cognitive – and sometimes affective – activity about the meaning of various social policies in Canadian life.

Although I deal extensively with government policy in this book, I avoid the language of propaganda, except where it is used in a source I am quoting from, such as Grierson's wartime writings. Film has been linked with propaganda since its outset, and the interwar period when documentary film got its start was the heyday of the political mobilization of film. There are many reasons to use the term, one being the connection between documentary film and the development of marketing, public relations, and mass education in the same period. These are powerful associations. However, the term comes freighted with early-twentieth-century social scientific assumptions about the passivity of the audience and the unidirectionality of communication, which are still contentious and in fact require more data about audience response than actually exist. I hasten to add that my reticence concerning the term "propaganda" does not render me a supporter of a free marketplace of ideas approach, by default. Just as the propaganda model gives too much power to the producers of messages, so the marketplace of ideas gives too little consideration to the unequal relations of power that shape communication production, distribution, and reception.

The approach that I find much more satisfying, though perhaps harder to apply, is one that considers communicative acts as struggles over meaning making. No film is ever the final word on a topic. As long as humans continue to signify, final words do not, by definition, exist. Utterances are, as Bakhtin suggests, a contribution to a larger dialogue, tacitly responding to previous utterances and anticipating future response, "a link in a very complexly organized chain of other utterances."[22] This dialogic perspective on government documentary film made in liberal societies can illuminate the pedagogic role of film in various social projects. But it also can account for the films' excess of meaning. Films made on the subject of everyday life inevitably exceed official intentions.

The National Film Board has served as an important training ground for generations of Canadian filmmakers. Many have spoken, both on and off the record, about their frustrations in working their film projects around and through government objectives. The dialogic or, in Julia Kristeva's terms, intertextual approach allows the analyst to approach these films as engagements with state policy objectives, rather than as crude mouthpieces for them.[23] Media productions are different from policy papers in this way, and this is precisely what makes them such interesting objects of analysis. For example, all visual forms of communication are fundamentally ambiguous, open to multiple readings, their meanings changing over time. I believe that the concept of film as utterance, as speech act, provides a new and potentially rich way to read films in relation to their production contexts, as well as taking into account their unfinalizability.

Documentary film – "the creative treatment of actuality," in Grierson's still unsurpassed definition – is an outstanding site of intertextuality. Documentary filmmakers use images, sounds, stories, and actors from the "real world" to craft their films. In watching documentaries, the viewer is formally suspended between having access to reality and having an awareness of the filmmaker's enframing, as well as other limitations and constraints on the interpretation being shown. In NFB films, a third term woven into the film's conception and realization is the relationship to state policy. More or less easily, more or less successfully, NFB films tell stories about Canadian society in its ongoing formation. This process-based orientation is ultimately what makes the films openended. And unlike broadcasting or feature films, process has been built into the function of NFB documentaries. Process, not absence, therefore makes the most sense as an analytic frame.

No story about reality is innocent of power. Bakhtin's analysis of the centripetal forces at work in any heterogeneous dialogue is a strong reminder that all discourses occur in contexts informed by power relationships. According to Bakhtin, the centripetal forces of official culture attempt to move opinion together even while a centrifugal counterforce moves them apart.[24] Even powerful interests must constantly struggle to control meaning. All texts can therefore be said to contain productive contradictions to a greater or lesser degree. There are never guarantees that meaning will be transmitted uniformly, especially when the stories are about an everyday world experienced by large numbers of people. One of the interesting features of documentary film is that it is a form of cultural production that is often concerned with everyday life – culture in the anthropological sense. In this regard, analysis of documentary film policy, which facilitates the audiovisual expression of state social policy, challenges the frameworks of cultural studies and political science, from both of which it is often categorically excluded.

In this way, documentary film bears a family resemblance to other documentary discourses, such as law and history. The social historians Natalie Zemon Davis and Carlo Ginzburg have each drawn attention in useful ways to the quest for the individual voice in official or otherwise typifying records. In her book *Fiction in the Archives*, Davis indicates the narrative strategies that characterize standard pardon tales of sixteenth-century France, showing both how certain strategies were shared in the quest for exoneration and how the legal system required narrative retellings of events.[25] For his part, Ginzburg demonstrates how apt state forces can be to document deviance. In official church documents produced in sixteenth-century Italy, he was able to find the verbatim representations of ordinary people's words – so long as they were seditious or blasphemous.[26] Both Davis and Ginzburg have been able to find the voices of ordinary folk, however stylized, in the moment when they transgressed official regulations. NFB films depict aspects of the population that must, like Davis's pardon tales, be organized into available templates for representing reality. Nevertheless, as in Ginzburg's inquisitor's records,[27] a trace of the voice of the accused must be presented in quotation marks, if only because exact words were the basis of the charges.

Similarly, even as everyday life is being reflected back to the population, it is often altered in its enframing by a series of "experts," including voice-overs and on-screen text, not to mention editing. This intervention returns the image of Canadian life and citizenship to the people in a slightly altered form. Images of Canadian life on film are rare enough; and undoubtedly at different times in different communities they have served as powerful lures to an audience used to American domination of movie screens. Looking at the familiar must have been a form of validation for many viewers, even while it was presented in highly mediated ways. With more than sixty-five years of uninterrupted state-sponsored filmmaking, the National Film Board of Canada provides an exceptional opportunity to think about how the state, cultural institutions, filmmakers, filmgoers, and film itself are all participants in a complex dialogue about the social world. Documentary film in this case is both the result of cultural policy and, in another sense, an interpreter of the state's policies as they operate at the level of everyday life, or culture. Documentary, culture, and policy are connected in a myriad of complex ways.

What follows is best described as a narrative about Canadian society, citizenship, and communication. The National Film Board, an institution committed to these projects, is a place where these governmental ideas crystallize – in policy, production, scripts, films, and viewing locations. But the NFB is only ever part of the story. And since its story has been written many times, I rely on the reader to refer to other sources for other perspectives on this complex aspect of Canadian cultural history. In order to examine the particular dialogue about social science, population, and government heard in and through the production of NFB films, I have had to sacrifice or marginalize some other perspectives. As with any discourse about reality, this one is partial. However, the argument herein is not frivolously made. I take it to be of the utmost importance for readers – citizens – to reflect on the role of cultural funding and its connection to social policy. Cultural policy does have concrete effects. This book attempts to examine the relationship between policy, films, and citizens in what has been one of Canada's most productive areas of cultural output.

The National Film Board and Government

Documentaries always were forms of re-presentation, never clear windows onto "reality"; the film-maker was always a participant-witness and an active fabricator of meaning, a producer of cinematic discourse rather than a neutral or all-knowing reporter of the way things truly are.
– Bill Nichols, "The Voice of Documentary"[1]

Political administration has come to depend heavily on statistical knowledge of population ... Official statistical knowledges of population are essential components in the technologies of risk management and insurance that shape many of the ways in which contemporary social life is understood and governed.
– Bruce Curtis, *The Politics of Population*[2]

As far as filmmaking institutions go, the National Film Board of Canada, a state-sponsored filmmaking institution specializing in short non-theatrical documentary films, has an almost mythic status, both in Canada and abroad. Thousands of films have been made under its auspices since its inception in 1939, and they have been screened widely across Canada and around the world. In the current configuration of the global film industry where free trade in commercial cinema is the main priority, the NFB seems to represent an anachronism, a remnant of a socialist alternative to the capital-intensive rationalized systems of global Hollywood, Mumbai's Bollywood, and even Nigera's Nollywood. So how to explain the existence of the National Film Board?

In this book, I argue that we must begin our consideration of the National Film Board not from its present status, which may seem to be a utopian throwback, but in the context of its emergence and sustenance – in the nitty-gritty of government policy and discourses of intelligibility that were mobilized in each of the many crises that the NFB has faced since its inception. Against sustained opposition from the private sector and members of the Conservative Party, usually in their role as government opposition, the NFB's biggest advocates have not in fact been socialists, by any stretch of the imagination; rather, they have been modernizing social reformers aiming to use the medium of film as a communications technology for consolidating middle-ground opinion in Canada and about Canada. Although "documentary" has a series of associations with social mobilization on the left, as I shall discuss below, the British documentary movement out of which the National Film Board emerged was specifically organized to appropriate realism's more radical potential and apply the form to the liberal nation-building project. As I shall try to show, documentary in this tradition embodies the same contradictions as the welfare state alongside which it developed. Its seemingly subversive elements developed as a response to the foundationally radical socialist challenge that was being posed to capitalist societies. Yet official documentary film and welfare state administration both relied on an instrumentally predictive model of social control that ultimately served to undermine their seemingly radical trappings.

One obstacle to the understanding the NFB in this way has been the canonization of its exceptional films as essential aspects of Canadian national cinema. Over the past sixty-five years the NFB has produced approximately ten thousand films.[3] Of these, there is a small canon of films, mostly by well-known Canadian directors, that are brought up whenever the NFB's aesthetic achievements are discussed. NFB auteurs include such luminaries as Norman McLaren, Arthur Lipsett, Pierre Perrault, Gilles Groulx, Denys Arcand, Claude Jutra, Michel Brault, Don Owen, Wolf Koenig, Roman Kroitor, Kathleen Shannon, Tom Daly, Alanis Obomsawin, Colin Low, Michael Rubbo, and Nettie Wild. It is an impressive list and demonstrates not least the historical significance of the National Film Board in providing a training ground for some of the nation's most important filmmakers. But collectively these filmmakers and producers have been responsible for only a small fraction of the total output of the NFB. As well, many of them made mundane sponsored films. Does anyone appreciate Arthur Lipsett's psychology series, for example, or Denys Arcand's study of volleyball? Significantly, most of the award-winning and critically acclaimed films made by these directors – these exceptional, canonical films – have been theatrical successes. Yet as I will show, for the bulk of the NFB's output the emphasis has been on non-theatrical distribution methods. Although the NFB has acted as a training ground for great filmmakers and has produced many excellent films, this has never been its stated policy objective. Rather, one might say, the NFB's artistic accomplishments have been a welcome by-product of a different cultural objective.

In this book, I do not attempt to examine all of the films produced by the NFB. Even if such a project were possible, I am not sure that it would produce the most desirable results. The most recent book-length study of the NFB, Gary Evans's *In the National Interest* (1991), provides an exhaustive chronology of the board in the postwar period and still covers only a fraction of the overall output. Donald Bidd's massive NFB *NFB Film Guide: The Productions of the National Film Board of Canada from 1939 to 1989* gives a brief synopsis of all the films produced by the board during its first fifty years. There are also descriptions of most of the NFB's films on its website (www.nfb.ca). These are resources to look at for a detailed description of NFB films. Here, I set out to accomplish something different. Rather than looking at the NFB films as a configuration of isolated texts, I attempt to examine the political and policy rationale for the National Film Board over its lifespan. It is my contention that the NFB represents a rarified site for examining the use of new communications technology (in this case, film) and a new film form (documentary) for education, nation building, and the governmental project of an administered welfare state. I examine dozens of representative films, those well known and forgotten alike, that help illuminate the way in which the National Film Board operated as a technology for seeing the social side of the Canadian state (see filmography). Before I lay out my thesis, however, a brief review of the existing literature and received opinion on the history of the National Film Board is in order.

HISTORY OF THE NATIONAL FILM BOARD

The National Film Board of Canada was established by the passage of the National Film Act in May 1939, just months before the outbreak of the Second World War. The Film Act described the make up of the National Film Board and provided the famously vague mandate for the production of films that would "help Canadians in all parts of Canada to understand the ways of living and problems of Canadians in other parts."[4] The NFB grew exponentially during the war, taking over the government information and propaganda filmmaking activity from the pre-existing Canadian Government Motion Picture Bureau in 1941. By the end of the war, the NFB employed upwards of seven hundred people and was making hundreds of short films, many of them for two successful newsreel series: *Canada Carries On* and *World in Action*. The NFB organized travelling film circuits in rural Canada as well as in factories and trade union halls, massively expanding the non-theatrical audience for films. After the war, in 1945, the film commissioner, John Grierson, was implicated in the Gouzenko Affair, which was considered the first spy scandal of the cold war.[5] The NFB came under attack from the private film industry for its unfair advantage in securing government contracts and from the business press and the Conservative opposition for its allegedly politically dubious connections to communism. Grierson left under ambiguous circumstances and the NFB had its budget cut back severely.

Yet in the late 1940s and early 1950s, when facing what seemed to be almost certain death, the NFB was granted a reprieve in the form of cold war national cultural policy articulated in the *Report of the Royal Commission on National Development in the Arts, Letters, and Sciences* (1951) (the Massey Commission). The NFB remade itself as an educational film provider in the 1950s, and it was also the site of technological and stylistic innovation by Unit B and the French section, both of which pioneered poetic cinéma-vérité documentaries without the voiceovers that had become the NFB signature in the 1940s.

In the late 1960s the NFB embraced new technologies such as IMAX and portable video, as well as pioneering community media process videos through its *Challenge for Change* and *Société nouvelle* programs. In the 1970s it established Studio D, the women's studio, and in the 1980s and 1990s it focused on supporting emerging filmmakers from minority and First Nations communities. At the present time, the NFB supports a massive website and continues to fund documentary and educational films.

HISTORIES OF THE NFB

The first history was a manuscript written by longtime NFB employee Marjorie McKay.[6] Written to mark the twenty-fifth anniversary of the NFB in 1964, it remains unpublished. The following year, Peter Morris, who at that time was working at the Canadian Film Archives, published a pamphlet entitled NFB: *The War Years*, in which he anthologized a collection of articles about the NFB that had been published during the war. He also compiled a selected index of films made between 1939 and 1945. In 1979, he edited an issue of *Cinema Canada* devoted to the National Film Board, which included articles by Gary Evans, Kirwan Cox, Piers Handling, and Pierre Véronneau, among others. C. Rodney James published the first book-length study in his 1977 work, *Film as a National Art: NFB of Canada and the Film Board Idea*. In 1981 D.B. Jones published *Movies and Memoranda*, which became the standard text on the subject. Tending toward rhetorical hyperbole, Jones posited that "Grierson's ... relationship to the Film Board was like God's to the world: he created it such that it *would* get out of hand."[7] Historian Gary Evans has published two volumes on the NFB: *John Grierson and the National Film Board: The Politics of Wartime Propaganda* (1984), which considers the war years; and its companion, *In the National Interest: A Chronicle of the National Film Board of Canada from 1949 to 1989* (1991), which presents a less interpretive history of the postwar period. *John Grierson and the NFB* (1984) is the published proceedings of a symposium held to honour Grierson in response to a policy recommendation to dismantle the NFB. With the exception of Morris's two collections, each of these histories celebrates the NFB and eulogizes Grierson, who died in 1972, as a charismatic leader who left an indelible mark on the institution's aims and methods and who was, therefore, a formative force on the Canadian arts landscape.

It was not until Joyce Nelson published *The Colonized Eye: Rethinking the Grierson Legend* in 1988 that the received history of the National Film Board's early years was questioned in any systematic way. Nelson situated Grierson within his international connections with big oil companies and Hollywood studios as a "champion of emergent multinational capitalism."[8] Around the same time, articles by Peter Morris and Kathryn Elder in different ways further challenged the pious sanctity usually shown to Grierson and the National Film Board.[9] Almost simultaneously, Pierre Véronneau published his history of French production during the NFB's first twenty-five years, *Résistance et affirmation*, in which he plumbed the irony of nationalist Québécois filmmaking thriving in a federalist institution.

Histories of the *Challenge for Change/Société nouvelle* era are harder to find. The most sustained study of the period is Rick Clifton Moore's unpublished PHD thesis, "Canada's Challenge for Change: Documentary Film and Video as an Exercise of Power through the Production of Cultural Reality" (1987). Janine Marchessault and Scott MacKenzie have written provocative analyses of the program, and there is a 1999 special issue of the journal *Wide Angle* devoted to George Stoney, who headed the program in the late 1960s. Elizabeth Anderson provides the most sustained critique of Studio D, which in many ways inherited the *Challenge for Change/Société nouvelle* mandate.[10]

With the history of this institution thus substantially written – and revised – a series of studies on the NFB have recently been published with very different aims. D.B. Jones's *The Best Butler in the Business: Tom Daly of the National Film Board of Canada* (1996) provides a much-needed study of NFB staff other than Grierson, as do books by Jim Leach and David Clandfield on Claude Jutra and Pierre Perrault, respectively.[11] Graham McInnes's memoir of the NFB during the war years was published in 2004. Robert Babe included Grierson in his selection of ten "foundational" writers in *Canadian Communication Thought* (2000), sandwiching him between Harold Adams Innis and Dallas Smyth.[12] Brian Low's NFB *Kids: Portrayals of Children by the National Film Board, 1939–1989* (2002) thematizes the representation of Canadian children and discusses the films in terms of their connection to educational theory. *Candid Eyes: Essays on Canadian Documentaries* (2003), edited by Jim Leach and Jeannette Sloniowski, offers a rare opportunity to read in-depth textual analyses of a selection of NFB documentaries. In his study of cold war Canada, *Plateaus of Freedom: Nationality, Culture, and State Security in Canada, 1940–1960* (2003), Mark Kristmanson offers an insightful new reading of *Neighbours*. Tom Waugh, in recent articles, has deconstructed the queer subtext in *Neighbours* and other 1950s NFB films.[13]

GRIERSON, DOCUMENTARY, AND MEDIA STUDIES

Outside Canada, Grierson's work in Canada is seen in an international perspective, and the Canadian film board is not given much attention. Grierson's biographers, Forsyth Hardy and Jack Ellis, who are also his bibliographers, have set the reverent tone with which Grierson and the documentary film movement are usually approached. Hardy, a colleague from Scotland, who edited the two published collections of Grierson's writings, *Grierson on Documentary* (1946) and *Grierson on the Movies* (1981) (the separation is of course significant), also published *John Grierson: A Documentary Biography* (1979). Jack Ellis, whose momentous *John Grierson: Life, Contributions, Influence* (2000) is the culmination of a lifetime of work on Grierson, earlier published *John Grierson: A Guide to References and Resources* (1986).

In its vast sweep, *Grierson: Life, Contribution, Influences* represents the most valuable text for putting Grierson and his ideas back into their international and often institutional context. But although the National Film Board of Canada is called his most important accomplishment and the peak of his career, it is confined to only one of the book's fifteen chapters, albeit one of the most substantial. All told, Grierson's connection to Canada constitutes approximately one-quarter of the total book (many of Ellis's interviews were with members of the early NFB establishment). But we are clearly shown the connection of Grierson's Canadian work with that done in England before and after the war, as well as that done throughout the Commonwealth (Australia, South Africa); with that done in the United States (where, aside from his well-known stints in New York studying tabloids and in Hollywood studying film audiences, he was apparently offered the head of public affairs at CBS television after the war); and with his work for UNESCO in Paris.

Although there are devotees of the documentary film movement wherever the subject is discussed, as a rule, Grierson and the movement have been treated much more critically in England than in Canada. Paul Swann's *The British Documentary Film Movement, 1926–1946* (1989) and Ian Aitken's *Film and Reform: John Grierson and the British Documentary Film Movement* (1990) both situate the documentary film movement within its social and political context, tracing intellectual and governmental trends in England. Aitken is more of a traditionalist than

Swann, however, and it is significant that he has gone on to edit the anthology *The Documentary Film Movement* (1998), which includes a sixty-eight-page introduction lauding the movement's accomplishments. Far from celebrating this school of production, Brian Winston's studies of documentary, including most explicitly *Claiming the Real: The Documentary Film Revisited* (1996), condemn Grierson for shutting down the possibilities of non-fiction film.

Nicholas Pronay of the University of Leeds, a noteworthy example of someone who knew Grierson after the war but was not seduced by him, has written the most searing indictment of the successful public relations behind the Grierson legend: "There is nobody else in the history of the non-written media whose influence and legacy is at once so pervasive, so much in need of re-examination in the light of the record – and yet so suitable to be set down in print. For, of course, he was a man of words not of pictures."[14] Pronay summarizes the Grierson pattern with a bluntness found nowhere else: "Looking at the Grierson record, there seems to be a curious pattern of brilliant promise and great initial success, followed by failure to actually achieve his goals while at the same time achieving solid successes in jobs and tasks which were not those he really set his heart on."[15] According to Pronay's analysis, Grierson's success in Canada was of little comfort for the man who wished to succeed in Britain.

APPROACHING THE NATIONAL FILM BOARD FROM A NEW PERSPECTIVE

With so much already written about the National Film Board, one might well ask, What more is there to be said? It is the contention of this book that the National Film Board provides an important case study of the use of visual media in general and documentary film in particular for liberal government. Liberalism is a political philosophy characterized by its support for minimizing government and emphasizing individual freedom and the ability to act reasonably. According to Foucault's analysis of power, freedom is the precondition for the operation of governmental reason. These are the forms of discipline that we impose upon ourselves and that define proper and acceptable behaviour in social institutions. As Barry, Osborne, and Rose put it, "Freedom, in a liberal sense, should thus not be equated with anarchy, but with a kind of well-regulated and 'responsibilized' liberty."[16]

The discourse of liberalism characterized the middle-way politics of the interwar period when the British Documentary Movement began. It was the dominant philosophy of the League of Nations, the New Deal, and the Empire Marketing Board. I shall attempt to show that documentary film as it developed in the West during the 1930s reflected the technologies of the liberal democracy that it was developed to support. Not only was documentary intimately bound up with the democratizing projects of mass and adult education, but it also embodied social scientific techniques, such as the interview and the representative sample, which were foundational to the development of new techniques of governance such as the opinion poll. This is the style of filmmaking and the technology for knowing and regulating the population that I term "government realism."

Although governmentality is not limited to the state, according to Foucault, modernity has been the process of the increasing governmentalization of the state. Since the 1940s, as the federal state has adopted more and more responsibility for labour, the assimilation of immigrants, the promotion of official languages, the facilitation of spaces for oppositional groups such as youth and First Nations, the accommodation of feminist demands for equality, the recognition of multiculturalism, the acknowledgement of alternative sexual practices, and so on, the NFB has found ways to represent these social shifts on film. The priority in the first twenty-five years of the NFB's existence (1939–64) was the representation of the process of urbanization, industrialization, and the establishment of the welfare state. Even the anthropological films of this period were made to produce a record of practices that would inevitably disappear in the wake of modern life. From the mid-1960s, the NFB has been engaged with representing the variety of resistance movements that emerged to question the metanarratives of progress promised by modernization.

Dealing in public information in general and films about citizenship in particular, the NFB presents an excellent site for reading narratives of ideal citizenship, strategies of government in the Canadian welfare state. Hundreds of NFB documentaries depict average, typical citizens in moments of contact with government agents or services, such as schools, hospitals, and employment offices. Government documentary film is, in this way, a technology of social science, which in turn is the technology of liberal democracy. The National Film Board has become an outstanding archive of this process. A brief discussion of governmentality theory and the history of the link between statistics and documentary should clarify this perspective.

GOVERNMENTALITY

Foucault defines governmentality as the range of practices organized around conducting the conduct of self in society. Colin Gordon has elaborated this concept and connected it with Foucault's work on biopower to designate "forms of power exercised over persons specifically in so far as they are thought of as living beings: a politics concerned with subjects as members of a population."[17] In his work on the Canadian census, *The Politics of Population*, Bruce Curtis has made the link between governmentality and technologies of observation, of which, he posits, statistical studies are a part. "Population," he writes "is not an observable object, but a way of organizing social observations."[18] Methodologically, this means "that we hold consistently to an understanding of 'population' as the variety of ways in which social relations are subjected to authoritative categorization and configuration by state agencies."[19] According to Curtis and others, the census and its cognate statistical studies are productive ways of categorizing and thereby seeing the population.

In welfare states, social life becomes a field of government intervention. Colin Gordon puts it this way: "In modern liberal societies the social is, characteristically, the field of governmental security considered in its widest sense; the register of government forms, in return, the surface of the inscription of the security problems of society."[20] Graham Burchell explains that "the principle of government requires of the governed that they freely conduct themselves in a certain rational way."[21] These actuarial methods of "social insurance" are predicated on the gathering and studying of statistical data. As Curtis has observed, "official statistical knowledges of population are essential components in the technologies of risk management and insurance that shape many of the ways in which contemporary social life is understood and governed."[22]

According to this technical understanding of governance in liberal societies, the process of category making is intrinsic. Social categories, the basis of the census and other statistical research and an essential part of documentary films, are themselves epistemological and policy decisions, yet they pose as social fact. In other words, measuring – or indeed documenting – the population may actually help to produce it. Paul Starr has observed the constitutive power of such categorizations: "Classes acquire common interests and become manifest in part through the category choices of official agencies."[23] The foundation, then, of the nation-building particular to Canada has been the subdivision of the population into manageable groups.

In order to assess the population, especially in terms of national projects, the concept of representativeness – different in important ways from the "average" – had first to be conceived. After years of debate by the International Institute of Statistics, the concept was finally accepted in 1934. In order to determine probabilities, categorization and measurement were essential prerequisites; qualitative decisions about how to classify had to be made. This is the process that Ian Hacking has called "making up people."[24] According to Hacking, by the end of the nineteenth century "a new type of law came into being, analogous to the laws of nature, but pertaining to people. These new laws were expressed in terms of probability. They carried with them the connotations of normalcy and of deviations from the norm."[25] Two related results of these material and conceptual shifts were the consolidation of national statistic-gathering agencies (in place of the parish and social reformer) and the development of the modern welfare state. Coeval with the development of statistics was the development of the means of visually representing the information in the form of patterns or representative types. Thus, bar and line graphs, maps, photographs, and films are all intimately linked to the conception of the population as an aggregate of different classes and groups with a variety of regulatory civil needs.

This delineation and taxonomy of the social requires a point of view. In the first fifty years of the twentieth century, the governmental point of view being developed with regard to the social was "a general statistical point of view."[26] With the advent of population management came statistical practices. The Dominion Bureau of Statistics and the Canadian Government Motion Picture Bureau – two apparatuses for the visualization of the population – were housed in the same department, Trade and Commerce. It was Minister of Trade and Commerce W.D. Euler who proposed the National Film Act that brought the NFB into existence in 1939. The development of both actuarial technique and mathematical logic combined with governmental concerns about order to accelerate the adoption of widespread gathering and representing of statistics. The production of social categories and the compiling of records, on the one hand, and the assessment of probability, on the other, were important parts of creating modern states and modern citizens.

NFB: TELLER OF STATISTICAL TALES

As I hope to show in the following chapters, the National Film Board adopted non-theatrical distribution from empire communication theory, and its narratives of typicality and risk from American social science. State documentary film, as pioneered by the British movement of the 1930s and arguably brought to its full realization only in Canada, can be characterized as the telling of statistical tales. The narrative strategy used in many films parallels that of statistical production itself. Starting with the distillation of facts and opinions from the population, usually through the efficient means of the representative sample, these facts and numbers are subsequently combined and superimposed onto the story of a typical person or place, whether "real" or "fictional."

The close connection between social policy and documentary narrative becomes apparent in the controlling "voice" of NFB films, although there are often conflicting voices and some resultant ambiguity.[27] While Canadian Government Motion Picture Bureau films were often geared to attract tourists or promote trade, NFB films about everyday life have consistently been concerned with social types. Several analytic categories essential to the birth of the managerial welfare state may be found in NFB films about the everyday life of ordinary people:

- *mental and social hygiene*, a preoccupation of eugenics found throughout the political spectrum in the first half of the century, including nutrition, fitness, racial integration and housing;
- *labour-management cooperation*, the much-touted "middle way" where social concessions are made to labour in return for political acquiescence;
- *national security*, perhaps the prevailing concern of cold war Canada;
- *education*, the watchword of the documentary film movement and the point of contact with citizenship training. Not only are most NFB films made for a pedagogical purpose, but many also depict people in institutional educational settings. The NFB made its place

in the postwar world in the realm of education, especially with regard to integrating difference and promoting multiculturalism.

These themes and tropes characterize what I am calling government realism. Realism has been characterized as a "styleless style."[28] Yet nothing demonstrates documentary realism's stylistic conventions so much as a survey of how they have changed over time. The most common narrative strategy in early NFB films was the enactment of a typical story. This might entail the use of either a scripted "real" person or an actor.[29] Such stories were manifest in one of two styles: dramatic re-enactment or the observational style of cinéma-vérité. By the late 1960s the edited interview had become prevalent. The use of interviews, often intercut with archival footage and with or without authorial voice-over, is still typical of the NFB style. In the 1980s and 1990s a fourth style emerged, which resembles what Bill Nichols has called "performing" documentary. In these films the focus is on the filmmaker's subjective response to historical and social events.[30] In NFB films, this style is often combined with the invitation to filmmakers from "marginal communities" to tell their own stories. Despite the many changes in realism's style, documentary tends to follow in the modern tendency of realism to treat the "representative as typical" and therefore the opposite of the symbolic.[31]

Realism has long been associated with a radical political position. Using unspectacular style to focus on the world ignored by Hollywood has been associated with a range of political philosophies, including Soviet realism of the 1930s, Italian neorealism in the 1940s, kitchen-sink realism of British postwar dramas, and Third Cinema. Yet although the NFB philosophy does situate Canadian official cinema in opposition to Hollywood and utilizes realist style, these aesthetic decisions have been yoked to a less radical political platform. Despite changes in documentary style and government objectives for the NFB, issues of labour, health, education, and assimilation have consistently been depicted in narratives about quasi-anonymous individuals. In government realist style, by and large, typical individuals representing a range of population subcategories from different regions and cultures are depicted as members of class and occupation identities. At times they even provide feedback or criticism of government programs deemed representative or "typical" of their group. However, almost every film at least implicitly endorses either the federal system or the social policy process by which group identities must be securely fixed before they can be recognized and supported within the larger national context. Remaining true to the prevailing ideas of government and social science, NFB films about the everyday life of ordinary people show a consistent pattern of statistically probable stories about the population. Although they partake in the realist aesthetic, they are not part of a radical political program.

Having laid out the parameters of government realism, I turn next to the British government's film program, which had such a strong effect on Canadian documentary film policy. Although most Canadian histories of the NFB play down the influence of Britain on Canadian cultural formation, I propose that, by looking at Britain's use of film and communication for empire building, we can develop a better understanding of the international currents at work in the formation of Canadian cultural policy and the widespread use of film for government in the 1920s and 1930s, the period just preceding the establishment of the National Film Board.

TWO

Empire Communications
and Documentary Film

The film, without question, has a great deal to do for this country, because of its great need for reorientation of sectional sentiments. The Committee on Information is already now getting down to work and I believe it may find the war situation an admirable opportunity for doing much of more lasting importance to Commonwealth relationships than day to day promotion of war mobilization.
– John Grierson, letter to Stephen Tallents[1]

The first flush of documentary in Britain was sustained by such practical realities as the drive to a new conception of Commonwealth relations after the Statute of Westminster, the swift growth of modern international communications, the growth of international interdependence on scientific levels and of course by the wave of social reconstruction in Britain which in the thirties affected government policies no matter what party was in power.
– John Grierson, "Documentary"[2]

The establishment of the National Film Board has clear connections to Britain, not least because of its founder, John Grierson. In this chapter I argue that the connections go deeper – to a way of seeing the population and conveying information visually that connects to the middle-way politics of 1930s England as well as to aspects of its colonial and educational policies. As many NFB histories have been written as salvos in a debate about Canadian cultural nationalism, this seems an important piece of the puzzle to re-establish. Indeed, I argue that the documentary film movement cannot be thought of without considering its connections to imperial communication strategies for both trade and empire sentiment. The archival evidence shows more clearly than current histories that Grierson was sent to Canada to expand the "imperial preference" mandate of Britain's international communication strategy in the interwar period.

I further posit that Canada was interested in this British imperial model because it answered some of the problems facing the federal government with regard to film – namely, provincial control over the regulation of both theatrical distribution and education. A national film board might be applied to some of these regional problems in much the same way that empire communication theory attempted to overcome its own regional divides and imbalances. In fact, Canada had greater hope on this front than the empire as a whole. Moreover, Canada was well placed – next door to the United States – to open a front in the information war against the U.S. film and newsreel industries for the hearts and minds of British (and recently British) subjects everywhere.

To this end, the Canadian education lobby – a powerful group with nationalist sentiments and international allegiances – of which Vincent Massey was a part, was instrumental in articulating popular sentiment to government policy around the National Film Board in the 1930s, 1940s, and 1950s. Many of these cultural nationalists were also empire men, educated in the United Kingdom and steeped in British traditions. Although many of them supported Canadian film as art, the limited funds and the conflation of government and education forces appear to have led to the delimitation of film production to government realism.

In this chapter I trace the connection between theories of empire communications and practical funding decisions, and examine how these played themselves out in the Canadian context. Referring to both Canadian and British government documents, I bring an international framework to the story of the establishment of the NFB. The point is not to minimize the specifically "Canadianness" of the NFB but rather to situate this Canadianness as the product of a variety of historical conjunctures, rather than as an essential Canadian trait. Further, I posit that the ideas of empire governance and communications put forward by the Empire Marketing Board, the British Film Institute, and the Imperial

Relations Trust in the 1930s helped set up a model of communication and multicultural governance that Canada would absorb into its own cultural policy and that would help sustain the NFB after the war. I trace the Canadian side of this story in chapter 4.

FROM LONDON TO OTTAWA

The first activity toward the establishment of a Canadian film board began in London. In 1936 Vincent Massey, Canada's high commissioner to Britain, sent a memorandum, written by his private secretary Ross McLean (later assistant commissioner to Grierson and then film commissioner himself in the mid-to-late 1940s),[3] to the secretary of state for external affairs.[4] In it McLean, who had met Grierson at a London film screening, recommended that Grierson be invited to conduct an "independent and exhaustive survey of Canadian publicity film activities."[5] According to most Canadian stories of the NFB, it was on the basis of this report that in 1938 John Grierson, Scottish film theorist and the founder of the British Documentary Movement, was invited to Canada to advise on government film production. He so impressed Canadian politicians that his visit was followed by an invitation to write the Film Act that would establish Canada's National Film Board. Finally, Grierson was invited to become the NFB's inaugural commissioner, at first temporarily and then permanently, a situation that lasted for the duration of the war (1939–45).

It is understandable that boosters and detractors alike see Grierson through the lens of developing Canadian national identity. Many of the studies of the NFB summarized in the last chapter were published in the 1970s and 1980s, a period in Canadian cultural history when there was a widespread move to establish a national cultural identity distinct from that of either Britain or the United States. But as the quotations at the head of this chapter show, there was an imperial aspect to this story. Grierson had been sent to Canada on behalf of the British government a couple of times during the 1930s, when he also travelled around the United States, as well as visiting various parts of the British Empire. His first official visit to Canada took place in 1930–31, when he came to study the work of the Canadian Government Motion Picture Bureau.[6] His famous 1938 trip was funded by a grant from the Imperial Relations

Trust, which had earlier channelled some funding to Canada's National Film Society and through which Grierson had already exerted considerable influence on the formation of the Canadian film scene.

Even a closer look at the Massey-McLean report makes the imperial connection unquestionable. The "Memorandum on the Use of Canadian Films in the United Kingdom" sets its tone from the outset by insisting that the need for better filmmaking from Canada was felt acutely in Britain: "As part of a broad policy aimed at improving Canadian publicity and propaganda in the United Kingdom it is scarcely possible to over-emphasize the importance of an effective use of films. There are still abroad in this country flagrant misconceptions of conditions of life in Canada, and a deplorable ignorance of the present stage of development and potential resources of the Dominion ... There is only one effective way of combating this misunderstanding, by presenting to the widest possible audience an adequate pictorial record of the many phases of Canadian life."[7]

The report specified the need for the development of documentary film services in Canada in order to improve trade: "There is no sounder basis for the expansion of trade than a deeper and wider knowledge of differences in taste and modes of life. These can be conveyed most effectively by interpreting in a wider sense the functions of the Motion Picture Bureau, by improving the quality and enlarging the quantity of Canadian films, and by adapting them more consciously to the demands of the British public."[8] Beyond using the empire framework, McLean also displayed an awareness of the educational theory of non-theatrical distribution, suggesting the use of different films for different markets: "The right type of film for different types of audiences implies a wider variety of films and a more conscious adaptation for different needs than the work of the Motion Picture Bureau so far presents."[9] This rereading of the founding document of the National Film Board seems to justify the investigation of the connection between empire communication and Canadian film. The Empire Marketing Board provides one clear link.

IMPERIAL CONFERENCES AND THE EMPIRE MARKETING BOARD

In the 1920s and 1930s the British government convened a series of conferences to discuss trade and imperial citizenship (1926, 1930, 1932).

Film was an important topic at these meetings. Its powers of propaganda and persuasion, in the words of the time, were feared to be enormous, and despite reluctance to fund the arts with public money or to intervene in laissez-faire trade policies, it was widely agreed that its powers needed to be used for the benefit of the empire. As the Prince of Wales laconically put it, "Trade follows the film."[10] Film, it was believed, could aid in "positive" incitement to empire identity and consumption, based not on coercion but on patriotic choice – the so-called imperial preference.[11]

In preparation for a more productive political use of empire films, a "secret" discussion paper entitled "Exhibition within the Empire of Empire Films" was circulated before the 1926 Imperial Conference. The document stressed the power of film both in education and in advertising nations and their products:

A position in which so powerful an influence as that of the Cinema, reaching as it does all classes and all ages of the community, is exercised throughout the Empire almost wholly by non-British producers is obviously a dangerous one. It is not suggested that foreign films are the medium of intentional anti-British propaganda, or that, except in a very small proportion of cases, they are open to positive objection; the influence exercised is indirect and for that reason more difficult to deal with. It is clearly undesirable that so very large a proportion of the films shown throughout the Empire should present modes of life and forms of conduct which are not typically British, and, so far as setting is concerned, tend to leave on the minds of untutored spectators the impression that there are no British settings, whether scenic or social, which are worth presentation. However, [sic] good the foreign films may be in themselves, there is still a need for the shewing of more home-produced films; however good foreign education may be, we should still feel that if we sent our children to be educated exclusively in foreign countries they would miss something important in their education.[12]

Reiterating the themes of the pre-conference discussion paper, the general economic subcommittee of the 1926 Imperial Conference included the following observations on the importance of film in its report: "The importance and far-reaching influence of the Cinema are now generally recognized. The Cinema is not merely a form of entertainment but, in addition, a powerful instrument of education in the widest sense of that term; and, even where it is not used avowedly for purposes of instruction, advertisement, or propaganda, it exercises indirectly a great influence in shaping the ideas of the very large numbers to whom it appeals. Its potentialities in this respect are almost unlimited."[13] Focusing on the concern about film as inadvertent commercial publicity, the authors continued, "moreover, it is an undoubted fact that the constant showing of foreign scenes or settings, and the absence of any corresponding showing of Empire scenes or settings, powerfully advertises (the more effectively because indirectly) foreign countries and their products."[14]

In terms of theatrical fiction film, the discussions of the first Imperial Conference contributed to the establishment of the British quota system introduced in the 1927 Cinematograph Films Act. Hollywood studios, with their branches in Europe, had been making it difficult for British producers to break into the theatrical market for fiction films. It was hoped that a quota at the level of exhibition would correct the problem. In terms of the non-theatrical side of distribution, the conference helped lead to the establishment of the Empire Marketing Board (EMB). Established in 1926 to publicize the empire with techniques taken from both advertising and modern education, the EMB targeted school children, workers, and female consumers with messages about the coherence of the empire.[15] Showing people films in alternative venues could mean careful segmentation of the audience (into children and adults, labourers and housewives, for example) and could also teach audiences a different set of expectations for the filmgoing experience – from thoughtless entertainment to thoughtful consideration of films for various kinds of education and cultivation. This development was connected to a move to create film libraries (or "clearing houses," as they were often called), of suitable educational and empire films, many of which were circulated to these venues free of charge.

The EMB's mandate to "bring empire alive" to British citizens was fairly vague. A central objective of the EMB publicity department was to alter the associations with the word "empire." The word's connotations had to be shifted from those of economic exploitation to those of the common good, "the economic development of the Empire bringing benefits to all its citizens not merely profits to businessmen."[16] To this end, broad-ranging EMB publicity presented "a vision of Empire as a system of cooperative development bringing mutual benefits in which the image of the family had a moral as well as economic dimension."[17] Further, the prospect of empire was tied not to warfare and oppression, but to international peace, a message thought to appeal to women as the majority of consumers.[18]

By the late 1920s the Empire Marketing Board was making films. Sir Stephen Tallents, head of the EMB, who later played a prominent role in the General Post Office (GPO) film unit, the BBC, and the wartime Ministry of Information, published in 1932 a pamphlet entitled *The Projection of England,* which summarized his views of film and the politics of empire cohesion: "In the cause of good international understanding within the Empire and without it, for the sake of our export trade; in the interests of our tourist traffic; above all, perhaps, in the discharge of our great responsibilities to other countries of the Commonwealth of British peoples, we must master the art of national projection and must set ourselves to throw a fitting presentation of England upon the world's screen."[19]

Its first two cinematic productions reflected the widely divergent philosophies competing for prominence in promoting the imperial ideal. *One Family* (1930), made Walter Creighton, head of the first film unit, was a fable about "the gathering of the ingredients for the royal Christmas pudding from all parts of the Empire as viewed through the eyes of a small boy, with society ladies personifying the Empire's colonies and the Dominions." It went well over budget and was, by all accounts, a great flop. Grierson's first film, *Drifters* (1929), a derivative Soviet-style documentary-drama of the North Sea herring fishery, seemed inexpensive and innovative by contrast.[20] Grierson replaced Creighton as film officer in 1930.

Grierson used the EMB as a platform to launch the British Documentary Movement, which remained closely bound up with the philosophy and methods of imperialism. As Grierson wrote in 1933, "[The EMB's] principal effect in six years (1928–1933) was to change the connotation of the word 'empire.' Our original command of peoples was becoming slowly a co-operative effort in the tilling of soil, the reaping of harvests, and the organisation of a world economy. For the old flags of exploitation it substituted the new flags of common labour; for the old frontiers of conquest it substituted the new frontiers of research and world-wide organisation."[21]

ADVERTISING IMPERIAL PREFERENCE AFTER
THE EMPIRE MARKETING BOARD

According to most historians, after the demise of the EMB in 1933, the documentary film movement continued in the GPO film unit, where Grierson worked until 1937. While GPO films such as *Song of Ceylon* (1934) and *Night Mail* (1936) address the role of communications networks in national and empire cohesion, I would argue that the subject of empire cohesion and film diverged at this point to the British Film Institute. In the study *The Film in National Life* (1932), which recommended, among other things, the establishment of the British Film Institute, it is clear that the standards set by other countries and through the League of Nations Institute for Educational Cinematography at Rome were compelling enough to inspire the British quietly to agree to intervene in the market and support the development of the arts.[22] One of the ways to justify this expense was to use the language of empire communications.

Both the British Film Institute, formed in 1932, and the British Arts Council, formed in 1934, had an imperial aspect to their mandates. Both used the imperial preference concept, and both aimed to consolidate British national culture for promoting positive associations with Britain at home and abroad. The following quotation from *The Film in National Life* makes this connection clear:

A film has a national conception and an international life. If it is more than a piece of hack-work, it will express the national tradition and outlook of the country which made it, no less surely than that country's painting and books. But increasingly and irresistibly, the film public is international to a degree unimagined in literature, and difficult to realize with works of art which are bulky, fragile or precious. We have to think internationally, therefore, in the sense that we want to see the best work from other countries freely admitted to our own, and nationally in that we want British peoples to see life in terms of British culture. No nation which produces films and no nation which imports the films produced by others can afford to ignore the cinema, and any society of nations such as the British Empire or the League of Nations must look on the cinema both as an international force and as an international problem.[23]

In 1934 the British Film Institute established the Dominions, India and Colonies Panel, which met regularly until 1939, and under its auspices Grierson wrote his "Notes for English Producers." Minutes from this committee show sustained interest not only in the reception of British culture abroad but also in the support for dominion-made films to be brought to England and shown around the empire. Film was essential to empire cohesion: "Films have generally been advocated as a means to make the parts and peoples of the Empire better known to each other ... A man has generally little knowledge of the life of one colonial branch of his own family. But he can none the less feel strongly enough for them when occasion arises, and for others of his political allegiance in time of danger, irrespective of blood and race. It is not knowledge but feeling that inspires unity and impels action, though feeling without knowledge is blind and likely to blunder."[24] In the very first meeting, on 5 May 1934, the chair of the committee, Dr Drummond Shiels, commented that "it was essential, if the work of the Panel was to fructify, to have the full support of the territorial Governments. It was hoped that the Departments concerned would report the endeavour that was being made by the Institute to their respective Governments and ascertain their views as to how the development of the film for educational and cultural purposes can best be accomplished."[25]

The committee made a clear distinction between the colonies and the dominions and noted that in the dominions the governments had control over native populations much as the British did in India and the colonies. Although the minutes show that Canada was mentioned at almost every meeting, the film activities that interested the committee were those oriented toward empire relations, such as those of the Overseas League, various provincial education programs, and the National Film Society. The Canadian Government Motion Picture Bureau was never mentioned.

By 1938 there were twelve British agencies and committees "concerned with the promotion of Imperial unity through the film."[26] the most important one for Canada was the Imperial Relations Trust Film Committee (IRT), but all of them served to reinforce the need for nontheatrical empire film production, distribution, and exhibition. The IRT had been founded in 1937 when gold baron Sir Henry Strakosch, a lifetime colonial administrator in India and South Africa,[27] granted

£250,000 to the government for the purpose of "strengthen[ing] the ties which bind together the Dominions and the United Kingdom."[28] The IRT "allocated limited funds for the encouragement of educational and cultural film services between Great Britain and the Dominions."[29] Grierson had been shut out of most of the committees, according to Paul Swann, except for the British Film Institute's panel on the colonies and dominions.[30] However, working as the technical adviser to the IRT gave him the most leverage to take his ideas abroad.

Grierson was sent to investigate the state of Canadian filmmaking in 1938 under the auspices of the IRT. One of the first things the IRT did was to provide funding for a film and education conference in Canada to encourage the consolidation of amateur film distribution activities under the National Film Society of Canada (NFS), a national coordinating group. On the basis of Grierson's recommendations, the executive committee of the NFS was granted £1,750, primarily to acquire British films for circulation among educational film societies in Canada.[31] Grierson explained to his British bosses: "This new organization, representing as it does, all the national organizations, apart from Government departments, interested in the education and cultural uses of the film is a valuable development. It provided organizations in Great Britain with an ordered access to Canadian audiences and an instrument through which they can, with economy and efficiency, operate in Canada. It gives the Canadian Government valuable aid in developing Canadian audiences for films of national educational value. It may, therefore, be expected to play a considerable part in breaking down the sectional outlook now prevalent in Canada."[32]

Although the IRT's mission was clearly to solidify empire sentiment, it was thought that using the auspices of the indigenous NFS would allay suspicion of "propaganda from the outside."[33] Echoing sentiment from the imperial conferences, Grierson wrote, "The interchange of films between different parts of the Empire has until now been largely piecemeal and uncoordinated. The possibility of systematized development is now becoming apparent. Much good would be done if the Dominions Office found it possible to participate more directly than it has done in the past in a valuable development."[34] In a confidential memorandum written in 1939 recalling his visit to Canada, he wrote:

In June 1938, I was invited by the Film Committee of the Imperial Relations Trust to make a survey of film developments in Canada. The Imperial Rela-

tions Trust had allocated certain limited funds for the encouragement of educational and cultural film services between Great Britain and the Dominions.
Its Film Committee required further information on which to base its recommendations. At the same time, I was invited by the Canadian Government to
make a survey of the film activities of the various Government departments
and particularly of the operations of the Canadian Government Motion Picture Bureau, with a view to developing the supply of Canadian films to Great
Britain and improving the distribution machinery at Canada House.[35]

Records of the IRT meetings show that the Canadian film scene had
been a subject of much interest for the group. Although the IRT was
specifically interested in how Britain was projecting itself in its colonies
and dominions, it was also keen to know how people in the colonies and
dominions were perceiving each other. Repeated discussions at their
meetings demonstrate the degree to which they were concerned about
American dominance of film screens in both fiction and newsreel genres.
A report on the "Distribution of Empire Films in Great Britain and of
British Films in the Dominions and India" made the point that empire
films were required and that "much could ... be done to improve the position [of empire films], if the regular production of news and interest
items were stimulated in the Dominions."[36]

Grierson wrote to Canadian Minister of Trade and Commerce W.D.
Euler, in 1938 in order to stimulate anxiety about the fate of Canadian
trade if Canada maintained its conspicuous absence from the world's
newsreels. "The international circulation of news reels today," he stated, "is one of the most powerful and important media by which a country makes itself known across its borders ... Australia has many times
the representation of Canada in British news reels by reason of superior
quality and efficiency of supply." Anticipating his contentious suggestion
for references to Canada in American films in the 1940s, Grierson suggested that unless Canada could produce and distribute its own newsreels, it would be best to get more coverage in American newsreels,
because of their extensive global distribution.[37] Significantly, Euler went
on to be the minister who proposed the National Film Act in the House
of Commons.

Although in Grierson's writings on documentary he often used the
newsreel as his rhetorical whipping boy – the antithesis of the documentary movement – one of the NFB's greatest achievements during the war
was in fact the production of two newsreel series, *Canadian Carries On*

and *World in Action*, which saturated Canadian screens. *World in Action* films were shown in India, South Africa, Latin America, and the United States, fulfilling to some degree the empire dream of decentralized information services to rival American news.[38]

In his report about Canadian film activities submitted to the IRT film committee in August 1938, Grierson clearly stated that the end of the empire quota system, which had been deleted from the 1938 version of the Cinematograph Films Act, had struck a "death blow" to the production of Canadian features.[39] Grierson's report – developed after extensive fact-finding trips around Canada in which he spoke to several government ministers and newspaper editors, among others – had the overall aim of improving "production policy, personnel and creative service" in the Canadian film industry. The report contained extensive recommendations on how to increase circulation of empire films in Canada and of Canadian films in the United Kingdom – at the time, the best way to Canadian screens was through films produced for "quota purposes" by American companies in England. Following the British position since the Imperial Conference of 1926, Grierson took the view that non-theatrical distribution was the way forward for empire communication. Non-theatrical distribution in Canada was "in a very unsatisfactory state, particularly from a British point of view," he wrote. Moreover, the supply of non-theatrical films was largely American: "Schools are increasingly getting their educational films in American patterns and even the Department of Labour uses American films in connection with its juvenile training work." After establishing the Canadian weakness and American strength in every aspect of film production, distribution, and exhibition, Grierson recommended "a central organization which would co-ordinate demands and through which the Canadian Government and British and Dominion film interests could work." This vision was to take shape in the form of the National Film Board.

Grierson's research in Canada showed that one of the political concerns in the dominion was regional divides. He decided to sell the idea of a centralized film agency in terms of this local political reality: "I considered it unlikely that the fullest support in the co-ordination of the non-theatrical field in Canada would be forthcoming unless it was association with definite and contemporary Canadian needs. I therefore, in all my discussions, associated the improvement of film supplies with, in the first place, the need for breaking down Canadian sectionalism. There is no question but that this would help to focus attention on the role which the film might play in Canadian public life and secure backing for the development of the non-theatrical field."

Instrumentally, he advised on using the dynamics of the existing educational and governmental scene to push through an empire agenda. This section is worth quoting at length:

It would seem wise ... to avoid direct association with "propaganda from without" and particularly with any movement which is suspected of hindering the natural development of Canada as an independent Dominion, or reaffirms a statement of Empire relationships which, in common opinion, is outmoded ... This means that we should work with and through Canadian organisations of the highest national authority. We should avoid setting up separate organisations for the showing of British and Dominion films. It might even be wise, when the time is ripe, to discourage separate work by the Overseas League, and encourage it to work entirely through native organisations. We should associate our work with the needs of the Canadian field. The non-theatrical field in Canada will be developed because Government and other national authorities will quickly learn that the film is a means by which different parts of Canada may be brought alive to each other, international relationships taught, and sectionalism diminished. We should associate ourselves with this development and on the good grounds that until sectionalism is diminished, a clear statement of the Dominion's relationships with Great Britain and the other Dominions cannot be articulated. We should associate ourselves with, and wherever possible, give leadership to, the various efforts that are being made to use film in connection with such fields as adult education, child welfare and public administration ... It is my proposal that in our film work in Canada, we should make these native considerations the key to our activities. Help Canada to organise a system of film distribution which it patently needs for its own good health, and the cause of Imperial relations would benefit in two ways. It would be associated with a development which is of prime interest and importance to Canada itself; and it would help to create a path to Canadian opinion which is now lacking.

Whatever Grierson's reputation for hyperbole and overstatement of his knowledge and power, the report is significant for demonstrating the intense empire interest in the Canadian film scene. And even if Canadian organizations were simply using this interest for their own ends, it nevertheless had a direct effect on the establishment of coalitions of elites prepared to stand by and support the need for Canadian and empire documentary film. As I shall discuss in chapter 4, these film societies would prove to be instrumental in vocalizing support for the foundation of the NFB in 1939 and for its perpetuation in 1949.[40]

EMPIRE COMMUNICATIONS IN CANADA

On its creation in 1939, the National Film Board's initial role was to coordinate all government film activities, including those of the Canadian Government Motion Picture Bureau. However, in 1941 the bureau was absorbed into the NFB. Echoes of empire communication are readily apparent in the National Film Act, which states that the commissioner's role is to "advise upon the making and distribution of national films designed to help Canadians in all parts of Canada to understand the ways of living and the problems of Canadians in other parts."[41]

Descriptions of the films to be made in Canada during the war (and presumably for distribution abroad, as well) echo theories of empire communications. For example, Grierson suggested the use of a film for interviewing Canadians of different racial origins (including German) to present Canada as a nation united by the "democratic cause."[42] He also suggested "a film in French designed to foster British-Canadian sympathy in Quebec."[43] In an early report to Sir Stephen Tallents (three weeks after Grierson's appointment as film commissioner), he announced, "We have scheduled for immediate production two films in the larger documentary class. One is on the people of Canada which I think [Evelyn] Spice will direct. It ought to give a fresh sight of the different peoples and economic groups involved in this melting pot and bring about, particularly in the United Kingdom, a better understanding of the different problems of statesmanship here."[44] In another report to Tallents, Grierson outlined Canada's film objectives during the war. They included military and war films and films for peace. The latter include films on "the human geography of Canada for schools at home and overseas," "films for general civic education," and "special developments in Canadian life, ie., problems of Canadian citizenship." He added, "Films on the people of Canada and on Canada's North American relationships are still in the course of scripting." Paradoxically, the French-speaking population, which had been the subject of various policies of assimilation, now began to be seen as the bulwark against Americanization in Canada:

Canada's economic necessity is supported by her natural habit of thought and her natural desire. She is a country of many races, but closer to Russia than the States in her method of relating them. She has not subscribed to the melting-pot idea and today has two official languages. One third of her people are French-speaking. They have no sentimental regard for England, and sometimes the opposite. Yet paradoxically, for fear of losing their separate language and separate culture, they would be the ultimate barrier to absorption of Canada into the United States and the ultimate defence of the Commonwealth tie ... No nation except Russia has, in her own form and character, pursued more imaginatively the conception of diversity in unity.[45]

Grierson adapted to the Canadian case the strong emphasis on education that he had used in his work in England. He strategically used the information services of federal ministries to bridge the gap between province, region, and nation. Writing to Tallents soon after the outbreak of the war, he desribed the liaison system he had established with Prime Minister William Lyon Mackenzie King, "which leaves the actual doing of things to existing machinery."[46] If his suggestions were acted upon, he explained, "what may transpire is the nearest approach to a Ministry of National Education which the Dominion Government can have under the British North America Act; for it may mean that the system of contacts with the more important media can be deliberately used to build unity in Canada and provide a service of propaganda which remembers the terms of peace, as well as the terms of war."[47] Three and a half years into the war, Grierson was still reporting to Tallents that his schemes for government provision of information, "tied to some extent to common ends," would be more of a Ministry of Education than anything else.[48]

Many federalists recognized in the National Film Board an opportunity to produce films with national themes as a way of superceding provincial powers over education. For example, one MP, Joseph W. Noseworthy, commented in the House of Commons on 12 May 1944, "I am particularly anxious to see the film board take a much broader and more active part in the educational programme conducted in the schools throughout the land. I know that in that field we immediately run up against provincial prejudices."[49]

As the NFB was rooted in an empire communications strategy dating back to the mid-twenties, it is no wonder that the British remained interested in its progress after the war. Many in England regarded the National Film Board of Canada as the greatest institutional accomplishment of the British Documentary Movement. The Dominions Office expressed interest in the direction of the NFB after Grierson's departure in 1945 (and relief at the appointment of Brooke Claxton).[50] A 1947 report on educational film in Britain, entitled *The Factual Film*, includes a ten-page appendix on the NFB which, seemingly without need of any explanation, includes Canada's National Film Act in its entirety as well as a concise history of the NFB and its programs of theatrical and non-theatrical films.[51] For many in England, the National Film Board of Canada was an example of how the dominions could answer to the call for empire communications. Even the production of stronger national sentiment in Canada would serve the purpose of turning hearts and minds away from America and Hollywood and thereby possibly contribute, if indirectly, to fostering imperial preference. I shall return to the imperial connection to Canadian cultural policy and documentary film practice in chapter 4.

In the next chapter, I examine the theories involved in interwar American social science in order to situate Grierson's theories of documentary in relation to his social and political theories. State-sponsored documentary film in Britain and Canada developed a style that was indebted to social science and its related techniques of sampling, public relations, and opinion polling.

THREE

Government Documentary Film and Social Science

Dig back to where the files become cases and the cases become people and there is no lack of the substance of cinema.
– John Grierson, "The Eyes of Canada"[1]

The British documentary group began not so much in affection for film per se as in affection for national education. If I am to be counted as the founder and leader of the movement, its origins certainly lay in sociological rather than aesthetic aims.
– John Grierson, "The Course of Realism"[2]

The [Canadian] government is taking films seriously and ... the film is going to play a big part in public opinion in Canada.
– John Grierson, confidential memorandum[3]

In her discussion of John Grierson's connection to ethnographers such as Alfred R. Radcliffe-Brown, anthropologist Anna Grimshaw notes that like structural-functionalist anthropology, Grierson films emphasized the wholeness of modern society: "Its different work processes, its different classes and genders, its different spaces ... there is a marked emphasis on the normative – society is conceived as a 'moral order.' Its individual parts exist only as experiences of the whole."[4] Moreover, Grimshaw connects this with documentary as a new form in the 1930s: "The emergence of new subjects of study – people understood in the context of their own lives – stimulated innovations in documentary method analogous to those emerging in the new fieldwork-based ethnography."[5] One of the clearest methodological links to anthropology, she posits, was the overwhelming presence of "types."[6] Grimshaw's observation is redolent of Brian Winston's argument that documentary always claims a certain generalizability from its representations: "On the screen, every last Inuit, industrial worker, and deep-sea fisherman comes to stand both for themselves and for a class of persons of their type." Winston reasons that this is linked to the documentary's connection to social science and its theory of probability: "Implicit probabilistics allow for any particular account of an event or person, if presented as being of social significance, to be received as evidence of whole classes of such events or persons. Probability leads to synecdoche and synecdoche thus becomes critical for documentary film 'actuality.'"[7]

Both Grimshaw and Winston agree that documentary film of the Grierson school of the 1930s links social types to a vision of a manageable social whole. However, neither of them discusses Grierson's own schooling in social science, specifically the social surveys of the Chicago School. Grierson studied at the University of Chicago during the mid-1920s, just before he began work at the Empire Marketing Board. This chapter considers the development of social science and documentary from the mid-1920s to the mid-1940s, a period that parallels the rise and fall of empire communications. I contend that American social science provides some important discursive background to the establishment of the National Film Board as a kind of welfare state institution, as well as demonstrating the connection between Canadian documentary and social science.

Widespread unemployment in the 1930s, followed by extensive use of civilians as soldiers and industrial workers in the Second World War, combined to bring Western governments round to the idea of controlled economies and administered welfare societies in the 1940s. In the United States, the "surprising" move toward the welfare state was a "pragmatic" result of the major economic failure of capitalism that had resulted in the Great Depression.[8] In the United Kingdom, the Beveridge Report of 1942 "established a virtually unlimited role for the state in welfare."[9] Leonard Marsh's *Report on Social Security for Canada*, presented to the government in 1943, proposed a wide slate of welfare services, including income security, housing, family, and health policy.[10] Perhaps most importantly, the Marsh Report gave credibility to a national coordinating system of social insurance, if not the grounds to nationalize formerly provincial powers over health and welfare, an issue analysed in the *Report of the Royal Commission on Dominion-Provincial Relations* (Rowell-Sirois Commission), which was released in 1940. It fell to the federal government to "assume responsibility for maintaining full employment and a stable economy."[11]

In Canada, Britain, and the United States alike, governments began to take over social functions that had formerly been provided by family, church, and community. Welfare historian Norman Barry writes: "What is peculiarly modernistic about welfare philosophy is the elevation of what many writers such as Burke have called the 'lower responsibilities' of government to a position equal in importance to the preservation of law, order, continuity and social cohesion. Following on from this is the almost natural claim that government action is condemnable should it fail to meet the demands of the welfare imperative. From this perspective the roots of the welfare philosophy are primarily utilitarian: the value of welfare measures is obviously linked to certain sorts of consequences."[12] The introduction of institutionalized national forms of welfare was thus a utilitarian response to conditions that threatened the operation of capitalism, rather than a concerted move to socialist ideals. Welfare used theories of risk aversion to insure society against radical change – or radical collapse. Social science and statistics were the basis of this move into extensive administration.

This new involvement of the state in the everyday life of individuals was based on the theory of eugenics, or the link between individual development and health and corporate social health. Eugenics, which may be defined as biosocial engineering, has variously taken the form of "ethnic cleansing" and progressive utopianism. In either case, because of its reliance upon questions of blood and belonging, eugenic projects have been most successful when they have been affiliated with national governments. As Angus McLaren has shown in *Our Own Master Race*, in Canada in the first half of the twentieth century, social concern was often articulated through eugenic discourse.[13] Although harmed by association with Nazism, eugenics arguably sustained itself in different discursive form after the Second World War in the concept of the welfare state. Such a project required new methods for measuring the populace, and social sciences emerged to fit the bill.

THE DEVELOPMENT OF SOCIAL SCIENCE

In the early decades of the twentieth century, American universities began to receive large endowments from the private sector to develop new techniques with which to study modern society. The hope was that through this research, new techniques for governing and marketing could be discovered and applied. The rise was precipitous: "In 1921 one hundred foundations granted slightly over $180,000 for research and advanced education in the social sciences and history. By 1927 that benevolence had burgeoned to almost $8 million."[14]

The ideas prevalent in this new scientific study of society included a modified Darwinism that focused on the effect of the environment on the labour and life of the community; an emphasis on empirical studies that produced measurable results and could, in turn, be used to devise plans of intervention; a growing mobilization of the anthropological conception of "culture" as the fount of beliefs and opinions; and an emphasis on education as the democratic method of integration. Based in large part on the kind of studies of the population carried out by governments in the census, social scientists, journalists, and statisticians banded together – often with largesse provided by private donors such as the Rockefeller Foundation and Carnegie Corporation – to discover the effects that competing messages could have on behaviour.[15] Coinciding with the rise of mass society and the mass media, these studies were focused on the organization of mass populations and economies as well as the conduct of individuals.

Throughout the 1920s and 1930s, pollsters and social scientists strove to perfect scientific sampling techniques, such as random, stratified, area, quota, and pinpoint. Far and away the most important technique developed was the representative sample, by which a small group could stand in for a much larger, equally proportioned group.[16] A corresponding realist aesthetic emerged across many media during this period. For example, writing on social issues in the 1930s was characterized by an emphasis on facts presented in general terms, abstractly quantified (statistical), and on specific facts that made claims to be representative (descriptive).[17] Descriptive methods included the case study, the participant-observer report, and the informant narrative.[18]

The epistemological experiments in the social sciences and arts laid the foundation for narratives and other formal elements being deployed by the newly invented documentary film form. Documentary of the 1930s was characterized by its attention to anonymous types, as well as the limited advent of the use of the on-camera interview (for example, *Housing Problems* [1936]). Many documentaries relied on scripted re-enactments of typical activities, often "acted" by ordinary people. The social scientific ideas to which Grierson was exposed at Chicago help explain more than his commitment to film and public education. Closer examination helps us understand the narrative strategies of British and Canadian documentary films themselves. Films made under the influence of Grierson are concerned with anonymous individuals who are typical of particular population or occupation groups. They resemble the statistical method favoured by sociology and political science. Forsyth Hardy thus accurately notes that "for [Grierson] documentary was never an adventure in film-making at all but an adventure in public observation."[19]

Social science found its first home at the University of Chicago: "Formed in 1892 as the Department of Sociology and Anthropology, Chicago's was the first sociology department to be established anywhere in the world and, until the late 1920s, some would argue 'Chicago sociology was, in effect, American sociology.'"[20] Grierson was brought into contact, in the mid-1920s, with the architects of the New Deal at the University of Chicago, where his studies were funded by a Rockefeller Foundation fellowship. Pursuing his master's degree in sociology and political science, his initial subject of study was "immigration and its effects on the social problems of the United States," a popular subject at the Rockefeller Foundation.[21] After working with his supervisors Charles Merriam and Robert Park, two of the most influential social scientists in America,[22] his subject was modified to "Public Opinion – Social Psychology" and "Newspaper Psychology."[23] Even after his interest in film and democracy was piqued by Walter Lippmann,[24] Grierson's writings show clear affiliation with the social scientific and managerial government ideas of his academic milieu.[25]

JOHN GRIERSON AND THE CHICAGO SCHOOL OF SOCIAL SCIENCE

The work of Grierson's supervisor Charles E. Merriam is exemplary of the Chicago school of thought, which bridged the private sector, the university, and the government. Hired as a political scientist at the University of Chicago in 1900, Merriam was active in Chicago municipal politics, formed the Social Science Research Council in 1923, and became the president of the American Political Science Association in 1925.[26] Merriam was thus well situated to become vice-chairman of the Rockefeller-funded President's Research Committee on Social Trends, initiated by President Hoover in 1929 with the goal of "survey[ing] social changes in this country in order to throw light on the emerging problems which now confront or which may be expected later to confront the people of the United States."[27]

Throughout the 1920s, Merriam oversaw an international comparative study on citizen training, which produced individual reports on the Soviet Union, Italy, Great Britain, Germany, Switzerland, Austria-Hungary, the United States, and a "primitive" tribe, the Duk-Duks. In his overarching synthesis, *The Making of Citizens* (1931), Merriam postulates that the most pressing question for modern society is what makes affiliation to groups come about and what makes it disintegrate. In his words, what are "the essential elements in the texture of group cohesion?"[28] An examination of his ideas in this seminal international study of education and citizenship sheds light on ideas propounded by Grierson.

According to Merriam, political science must come to grips with how loyalties, values, and even individual characters are developed in mass democracies. To this end, he maintains that civic training is an ongoing project; if it lapses, old allegiances may crop up again.[29] This is particularly the case with immigrants, for although all other social groupings potentially compete with the state ideology, the "shifting allegiances" of immigrants are a particularly worrisome "terra incognita" of political life.[30] "What," he asked, "is the relative strength of the ethnic groups and the political and economic groups? How do they fare in cases of conflict when the individual must choose between race and country? How do these deep-seated but competing loyalties stand when placed upon the field of competition?"[31] Government, for Merriam, is thus the site of the orchestration of networks of influence: "So far is it from being true that politics has nothing to do with economics and social forces, these are the very materials out of which the governmental is woven, and without which it has not vitality or value."[32] The end result of Americanization should be a homeostasis of ethnic traditions overseen by modern organizational values. However, he believed that this equilibrium was never achieved once and for all.

In Merriam's view, the cornerstone of the modern state is the reliable and efficient citizen: "Vigorous citizenship rests upon soundly constituted types of personality, and the nature of this fundamental soundness is an important part of the making of the future citizen."[33] In this regard, civic education figures prominently: "The process of a politicization begins far down the scale both in organization and in years. The point of departure for civic education is the child, and the goal may be that no one escapes the formal educational system with a disintegrated, disordered, or unbalanced personality, of a type that will obstruct the processes of orderly human relations in the field of the political."[34] Healthy bodies are as important to citizenship as normal personalities: "It is possible to build the citizen from the ground up, using as a point of departure the controls of body and mental balance now emerging from scientific studies to revolutionize our knowledge of political nature and our ability to deal with it successfully. An admirable beginning has already been made in the development of medical care for school children, but it will be necessary to extend this to cover new types of attention based upon new studies of the human constitution, physical and mental; and to adjust the organization of civic training to this new basis in the new realism."[35]

In this view – which bears no small resemblance to the eugenic engineering of national biological and reproductive health – the mental and physical "hygiene" of the individual is tied to the health of the nation. For Merriam, education and citizenship training rely on the sound basis of managed health. With their obvious role in modern communication, the mass media are given a prominent place in Merriam's thought: "Millions of persons are reached daily through these agencies, and are profoundly influenced by the material and interpretations presented in impressive form, incessantly, and in moments when they are open to suggestion. Unquestionably, here is an agency of prime importance which will have very large place in the future development of the educational process."[36]

Grierson reportedly kept a copy of Merriam's *American Political Ideas* handy until the end of his life, and the influence on Grierson's technique and theory is readily apparent.[37] Merriam's instrumental ideas about civic education and his emphasis on the need for social scientific study of the population to assess loyalty and devise plans for building national sentiment can be traced clearly in Grierson's work. Grierson used these ideas to sell the idea of documentary film as an empire-unifier to the Empire Marketing Board and, subsequently, to convince the Canadian government that public education through film could produce both Canadian unity and a sense of distinction from the United States.

In a 1945 letter to Brooke Claxton, Grierson remembered the clash in 1927 of his new ideas with the prevailing mentality in the British civil service:

(1) The inevitable trend is away from laissez faire toward Government planning, Government co-ordination, Government leadership in all matters affecting the economic and social life of the Nation; (2) With the new initiative imposed upon it by Parliament must come, of necessity, the duty of explaining plans, securing co-ordination and giving the information etc., which are of the essence of leadership; (3) Modern governments cannot, therefore, forego [sic] their duty on the educational plane, which is the common basis of national thought; (4) Nor can they forego [sic] their duty on the imaginative plane where sentiments are crystallized and patterns of interest and loyalty are created; whence their especial and direct interest in the imaginative media; radio, films, posters etc.[38]

Grierson's ideas about representativeness, which can be clearly seen in the anonymous types that populate British and Canadian documentary films, correspond to the ideas of his other supervisor, the widely influential Robert Park, often considered the "architect of the Chicago School."[39] Park's work was characterized by his use of ecological metaphors for human culture. Social groups, not individuals, were his focus: "All social problems turn out finally to be problems of group life, although each group and type of group has its own distinctive problems."[40] In fact, in Park's view, "culture" was to "personality" as groups were to individuals.[41] Moreover, culture, which perpetuates social life through education,[42] is diffused "in a manner analogous to that in which, in a plant community, an existing 'formation' is broken up by the invasion of alien species."[43] Thus, in North America at least, cultural relativism and determination was already being adapted in the theory of the 1920s into human ecology – more or less at the same time that the language of "race" was being phased out; environments, not essential qualities, were the raw material of modernization projects.

Sharing with Merriam an interest in how group behaviour affects the society at large, Park explored social groups "in order to discover methods of analysis that are applicable to the study of all types of groups."[44] Park's quest for typical groups resembled his search for a sociological method: "It is its representative character, the character which makes it possible of verification by further observation which makes it a scientific fact."[45] Just as natural science is concerned "not with individuals, but with classes, types, species," so, too, social science, based on statistical information, is intent on fixing individuals within group formations in which they "come into possession and become the bearers of their cultural heritage."[46]

The earliest conceptions of "subcultures" emerged out of work that Park and others did on the American city. In his 1925 work, "The City: Suggestions for the Investigation of Human Behavior in the Urban Environment," Park proposed that "civilized man" is just as deserving of study as "primitive peoples" and, importantly, is "more open to observation and study."[47] He decried the current situation where "we are mainly indebted to writers of fiction for our more intimate knowledge of contemporary urban life."[48] He characterized the modern city as a "mosaic of little worlds which touch but do not interpenetrate."[49] Within each self-enclosed neighborhood are isolated "immigrant and racial colonies" where "neighborhood sentiment tends to fuse together with racial antagonisms and class interests," making for an unknown crucible of behavior.[50] The modern city was thus a "laboratory for the investigation of collective behavior" in modernity's "chronic condition of crisis."[51]

We can see that Grierson was influenced by Park in at least two ways: first, in his commitment to empirical research and centrally organized reform; second, by the notion of human ecology, which views the environment, rather than essential nature or politics and economics, as being paramount in the influence on individuals. Chicago School thinkers adopted an instrumental pragmatism – that the world was constantly changing and people were continually adapting themselves. Understanding society's "natural evolution" would provide insight to "guide social development towards the best ends."[52] But perhaps most interesting about this biological approach to the study of society was that it presumed an epistemological universalizability of sociological facts. Historical occurrence was considered to be unique and impossible to repeat exactly, whereas sociology resembled biology in its ability to extract "from specific situations incidents that repeated themselves, and this reduction of unique occurrences to typical events, which were then given a generalized description, was the first stage in the scientific process."[53] Thus, empirical research could be distilled into typification, which led to anticipation and finally to "scientific control." Modern society was a laboratory that government could ill afford to ignore.

While his affiliation with the famous American publisher and democratic theorist Walter Lippmann is a significant part of the Grierson legend,[54] the connection of his ideas to the widely influential Chicago School has never been explored. In a statement that could never have emanated from the Chicago School, Lippmann declared in 1922 that the pursuit of the "ideal, omnicompetent, sovereign citizen" was "useless."[55] "The individual man," he wrote, "does not have opinions on all public affairs. He does not know how to direct public affairs. He does not know what is happening, why it is happening, what ought to happen."[56] In 1925, the year after Grierson arrived in the United States, Lippmann published *The Phantom Public*, in which he went so far as to posit that education was not the answer to the problems of democratic citizenship: "The problems that vex democracy seem to be unmanageable by democratic methods."[57] Lippmann's views differ substantially from those of Merriam and Park, who encouraged the use of education and social science to bring forth a fully functioning democracy. In many instances in his writing, Grierson grappled with Lippmann's pessimism, trying to find a compromise between the difficulties and limitations facing the common citizen and the possibility of using film to educate: "The key to education in the modern complex world no longer lies in what we have known as education but in what we have known as propaganda."[58]

SOCIAL SCIENCE AT THE NATIONAL FILM BOARD

Once Grierson became general manager of the Wartime Information Board (1943), social scientific and polling techniques resisted by the old guard (especially Mackenzie King)[59] were brought into play. "During the first months of his general managership, Grierson's goal," according to one historian, "was to reach apathetic Canadians with specific issues, rather than general patriotism."[60] To this end, Grierson commissioned studies on "voluntary war workers, art and information, exhibitions, newspapers' views of information work, newspapers' use of government publicity material, industrial morale, youth morale and consumer information."[61] Grierson's focus was on using educative methods to promote immigrant support for the war effort. One goal was to "convince ethnic communities that their future lay in Canada and that living in a common Canadian environment had molded them into citizens with a future shared by all citizens of the country."[62]

Public opinion polls played an especially important role in determining social insurance policy in Canada's plan for postdepression, postwar reconstruction, as the Liberals attempted to assuage various constituencies during the long period of their ascendancy, which continued until 1957. Minutes of the thirty-ninth meeting of the National Film Board on 8 June 1943, for example, include the summary of a concerned and confidential report from Grierson, in which "it was pointed out that our information on the Canadian war effort was not penetrating all classes of the population evenly. People in the low-income groups, poorly-educated people, young people and women are poorly informed in comparison with the high income groups, well-educated people, older people and men. Blanket information policy was not entirely adequate, and our chief problem is how to reach the relatively inaccessible groups."[63]

Grierson made use of marketing tactics in his understanding of the public as a series of audiences. In a confidential memo written soon after passage of the 1939 Film Act, Grierson discussed the usefulness of sponsored films for the development of the non-theatrical market. Since companies wanted to reach narrow segments of the population, the non-theatrical or educational markets could be subdivided into "the schools, the business clubs, the women's organizations, the specialized groups interested in scientific films, social films, etc. etc.," he suggested:

That is what we have done in England. Once there is a sign that these groups are being organized or can be organized for film showing, selling sponsored

films is easy. They represent all kinds of audiences which industrial and national groups want. It does mean, however, that they have to produce films
that will meet the needs of these groups; i.e. relate their own interests to the
needs of social, educational, business, and other groups. The trick of selling
sponsored films is to show industrial and national organizations how these
films which are in increasing demand can be related to the purposes of industrial and national propaganda.[64]

Grierson reiterated this point repeatedly: "You know how I keep
hard on the 'each' to 'each' policy: the notion of sending films which
are tailor-made for specific audiences."[65] Grierson's vision for the provision of public information was predicated on the subdivision of the
population: "I have urged the doctrine of the 'moving target': – with
the Information service neither a Ministry nor a Bureau (with entan-
gling alliances, encumbering routine, etc.) but as a simple group of responsible secretaries acting as liaison officers for the P[rime] M[inister]
in the various fields of information ... Thus each field of information
(radio, news, film, women's organizations, labour, foreign born Canadians, as may be decided) will be assigned one secretary who will travel as light as possible, with a chief secretary reporting direct to the P.M.
and keeping the policy of the various liaison officers in line."[66]

Grierson's wartime plan for the National Film Board took up the
themes of both social science and public relations:

Films can serve to:
(1) promote public encouragement and the maintenance of civilian morale;
(2) provide a service of information of such a nature as to increase understanding of the democratic cause and keep Canadian opinion in close
touch with national policy;
(3) provide direct instruction to the public in general, or to specialized
groups, in matters of civilian defence or specific services essential to the
nation;
(4) increase the effectiveness of military training by such devices as slow
motion and moving diagrams; promote the health and comfort of troops
by visual demonstration; stimulate recruiting and other forms of national
service; provide recreation to troops in training camps through the
organization of shows of entertainment films;

(5) keep Canada's effort vividly before Great Britain and the other Dominions for purposes of public encouragement; help in maintaining "good neighbour" relations with the United States.[67]

Grierson's ideas were echoed in parliament. For example, MP Roy Theodore Graham projected in 1944 that the NFB had an important role to play in postwar reconstruction and the encouragement of national unity: "Government, after all, is but the agent chosen by the people to conduct their business, and I am much alarmed as I notice the chasm that separates the people's mind from the activities of government. One of the things we must do is to realize that such agencies as the national film board can interpret government to the people and help them to be fully informed of the details of different regulations and laws that affect them in their daily life."[68] In the next section, I examine a range of films made at the NFB in the 1940s and 1950s that deploy sampling and government information as part of their narrative strategy.

GOVERNMENT INFORMATION AND DOCUMENTARY FILM

Created on the eve of the Second World War, it is perhaps natural that the NFB should be closely associated with wartime propaganda. Yet to think about the NFB in this way obscures the contemporaneous projects of nations such as Canada that were undergoing massive growth and modernization in this period. As we have seen, the rise of the welfare state in the West was inextricably linked to the powerful discourse of eugenics. In the early years of the NFB, films about cultural identity and social security were almost as prevalent as those about the war. With the depression still fresh in everyone's mind, issues of postwar employment and reconstruction were highlighted almost from the outset of the war. During the 1940s, as the blueprint for the Canadian welfare state was being drawn up, public opinion polling and population studies were becoming accepted practice in Canadian government. Robert Park's conclusions, in the early decades of the twentieth century, about subcultures as complications in population management and education had by now become common government practice. "The war placed demands on the Canadian economy and its political structure that made it difficult for the country to allow the continued existence of a large bulk of its population outside the mainstream of Canadian life."[69] In effect, subcultural studies were a key aspect of the design of the welfare state in the 1940s. The documentary film movement's basis in both sociology and marketing made it an obvious tool for envisioning the social world as a congeries of social types.

In this light we can understand why, from the 1940s to the early 1960s, the bulk of NFB films were about health, housing, work, and citizenship. In an unpublished study, Peter Morris discovered that films dealing broadly with "people and places," "leisure," and "people and problems" represented 71 percent of NFB films in circulation in 1948 and had diminished to 63 percent in 1961.[70] It can be seen, then, that at least over the first twenty-five years of the NFB's existence, films about the population represented a healthy majority. In these films, nutrition and emotional stability in the family are held out as the highest national aims. Eugenic concerns of civic engineering, such as the health of the greatest number through the organization of citizen nutrition, housing, and fitness needs, were a common concern.[71]

Let us now look at some representative films on social scientific themes, such as mental hygiene, housing, and ethnic identity, made during the 1940s and 1950s. *Mental Symptoms* was a series of films made in the late 1940s and early 1950s primarily for students of psychiatry. The most common template for these films was the introduction of a type of abnormality by a psychiatrist, after which the film cut to a hospital where a person who typifies the affliction is led out by the doctor and interviewed for the camera. After approximately ten minutes of this case study, the doctor addresses the presumably professional audience once again, decoding what has been seen as a typical case of mental illness: depression, hostility, rejection, and so on. Recalling Merriam's drive for good mental hygiene as a "measure of social efficiency," the stories are framed by the medical steps required to return patients to productive citizenship as labourers and housewives.

Yet people are not fully contained by the medical narratives that enframe them. In both *Depressive States 1* (1951) and *Folie à deux* (1951), the patients being interviewed speak clearly about their hatred of the institution. In the latter film, the articulate "paranoid" woman resists being returned to her ward after the interview, a process she had understood to be linked to having a hearing. "I'm a human being," she says

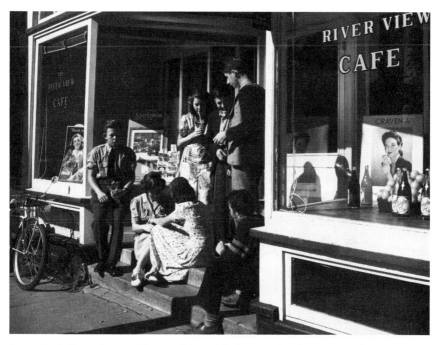

In its depiction of mass leisure, *When All the People Play* (1948) demonstrates eugenic social scientific concepts at work.

dramatically as she and her mother are being led away, "I want freedom." Yet the psychiatrist ignores these clear sentiments in favour of a clinical analysis of her "delusion." The eugenic position of "knowing better" what is in the interest of each individual and of society as a whole comes out clearly in this series.

When All the People Play (1948), sponsored by the Physical Fitness Division of the Department of National Health and Welfare, links health and citizenship directly. A scripted story about a generic town (shot in Annapolis Royal, Nova Scotia), an avuncular male voice-over asks the quintessentially modern question: "How can children be happy in a town built on traditions?" In a series of re-enactments, mothers discuss the problems of their children's pastimes – there is not enough for their kids to do in this sleepy town. What is needed is a properly trained "recreation director" to "lead children and their parents into a new world of fun and accomplishment." Cut to British Columbia, where recreation leaders show kids how to get started in "wholesome, enriching activities," such as crafts, games, sports. Programmatically, the narrator says, "Like health, welfare, and education, people are starting to recognize recreation as an important right ... Working together for the world they wanted gave a new interpretation to citizenship." Thus, national citizenship is linked to health and modern recreational activities.

Community spirit, exemplified by volunteerism, is tied in many early films to the physical health of the community. Sponsored by the National Physical Fitness Division of the Department of National Health and Welfare, *Fit for Tomorrow* (1948) ties the health of the individual to the collective health of the nation. Beginning with images of "sturdy settlers" who saw a "vision of a united Canada," we are told that with its vast resources, its space for harmonious living, and its great cities, there is the opportunity for a healthy, happy way of life in Canada. "But there is another side to the picture," says the narrator ominously. "The needs of our citizens of tomorrow are not always met." Scenes of filth and poverty follow, featuring the synecdoche for urban strife – dirty kids playing on the street. Not only crime but also ill health can result. However, fitness programs can provide an answer: "Fitness makes us look and feel better; we work better; and it's fun." The plan of the World Health Organization for global rights to health is defined, followed by scenes of school inoculations and fields of people doing exercises. "Calm, clear-thinking minds in healthy, vigorous bodies are one of the world's great needs. Only healthy, well-adjusted people can make a lasting contribution to lasting peace." This desire for healthy, well-adjusted citizens dovetails with government objectives of national security and economy.

Housing, often linked to social problems, is one of the key aspects of civic engineering with which governments are involved. Postwar housing issues included the accommodation of a growing population, the development of suburbs, and the emergence, influenced by environmental urban sociology, of so-called housing projects. Films about this topic often highlighted the public interest in the private domicile. For example, *On a Day Off* (1959), sponsored by Central Mortgage and Housing, is a fictionalized story that uses typical working-class families to prove that with the help of the federal agency, even working-class people can one day own their own homes, and with better homes come "better families." Also sponsored by Central Mortgage and Housing,

The Changing City (1963) proclaims that although "a magnet draws us to the city centre, few call it home." A scripted voice-over, attributed to a woman with six children living in a downtown housing project, describes how her new apartment is such an improvement over her former housing: "The kids are better, more proud now that they have a clean environment and more privacy." However, this family alone has not benefited. Exemplifying the eugenic focus on central planning and the good of the greatest number, the narrator proclaims that "every citizen is better off because this was done."

In films about urban planning, social inequalities of city life are addressed more or less directly. Housing and the central planning of human environments are key sites for the confluence of individual and collective government. According to this conception, the way one conducts oneself at home is based in part on the kind of space to which one has access. The message is not only that there is an idea of efficient and appropriate housing for each social and economic group, but also that if each subgroup is served correctly, society as a whole will be better off.

Films about the east-to-west narrative of Canadian colonial settlement constituted a subgenre of positive propaganda about frontier identity in NFB films. There are many examples: *Trans-Canada Express* (1944), *Trans-Canada Journey* (1962), *Introducing Canada* (1956), and *Le Canada: ses cultures* (1974). In each of these films, the regions are encapsulated in a typical family or individual who is involved in a productive economy linked to progress and the common good. An early addition to the *Canada Carries On* series, *Peoples of Canada* (1941),[72] begins with colonial contact and the quest for resources. The narrator discusses the prowess of different "races" in different regions. The motif of an ancient map unscrolling provides the narrative structure for the development of industrial Canada. The film begins with shots of the boomtown of Toronto and then proceeds west, where pioneers "drove back Indians and plowed the prairie." The railroad brings "allcomers" in the wake of the pioneers. Scenes of immigrant farmers arriving by train follow. A discussion of tolerance for other races and creeds is heard while a montage of public works and parliament buildings is shown. The film ends with a scene of children in a classroom: "Canada looks to her young citizens with their rich and varied backgrounds. Each one of them makes a special contribution to the new world." In voice-over, a woman – presumably their teacher – discusses tolerance and liberalism, while children of different races look to the front of the classroom in a series of close-ups. Thus, although Canada is represented by places, markets, and modes of transportation, ultimately it is her future citizens who define her.

Peoples of Canada was released in conjunction with a booklet, *Canadians All*, produced for the director of public information by Watson Kirkconnell. *Canadians All* was the best known of the many government pamphlets "dealing with, or intended for, Canada's foreign-born population."[73] The purpose of the tract was to keep Canadians unified against a common enemy abroad rather than succumbing to European racism at home (no mention is made of anti-Asian racism). It announced: "Intrinsically, a nation like Canada, whose population comprises many races and creeds, is perfect ground for the employment of Nazi underground warfare ... The most important thing about Canada is the Canadian nation itself. It is the people that make any country great ... Canada is the Canadians."[74] The publication provided data on the ethnic extraction of the Canadian population, expressed as percentages, and asserted: "Any flat-headed thug can organize a state based on murder and autocracy, but it takes the highest cultural gifts of tolerant intelligence to harmonize variant traditions in a single democracy." The pamphlet made it clear that the coherence of nation building was based paradoxically on the delineation of internal difference. The upshot of this polemic was a call for a government office to "deal with immigrant ethnic groups."[75]

Canadian Profile (1957) is a good example of the unity in diversity approach to the question of national cohesion. It begins with the following on-screen text: "Canada's people have come from many lands, different in language and tradition. They live, work and think in many different ways. Yet all of them today are facing and, each in his own way, reacting to a common change – the change from primary production to industrialization. Let us look at some of the people of Canada in their time of change." What follows is a dramatized series of stories about typical people in each of Canada's provinces: fishermen in Newfoundland, coal miners in Nova Scotia, a young man studying "the science of society" in Quebec City, an ambitious executive assistant in Toronto, some farmers in Kitchener, a couple of second-generation Ukrainian professionals in Winnipeg, and so on. The male narrator intones, "With industrialization increasing, life continues to change for

Canada's people. A people of different origins and traditions who nevertheless can live and work as one nation. Sharing common benefits, yet respecting each other's separate ways." In its emphasis on cultural difference and unified historical change, *Canadian Profile* is an outstanding example of government realism.

All of these national films attempt to make the situations of individuals intrinsic elements of the country as a whole. For the most part avoiding history, except through vague allusions to "colonization" and "industrialization," their principal strategy is to reduce the meaning of each region to an idea easily encapsulated in a single typical figure. No regions have any relation to one another, except through the omniscient narrator and the eye of the film, which travels across the country, much like a train or plane. In acknowledging the difference between regions, the films are intent on overcoming them, serving ultimately to make the whole more rich and various.

A subset of the national film is the "community" or "region" film, told as a story of typical inhabitants of an atypical group, usually defined by race or religion. In contrast to the urban focus of the cross-Canada films, these films have a rural emphasis. Early films in this category recall the social scientific fascination with frontier life. This category of film is united by the linking of specific attributes to communities rather than to typical individuals. The 1940 film *New Horizons*, made in conjunction with the Saskatchewan Wheat Pool, explores the economy and society of the prairies entirely through the people who inhabit the land. *By Their Own Strength* (n.d.), sponsored by the Saskatchewan Wheat Board, begins with stills of stern founding fathers of the prairie farm community. For its part, *Iceland on the Prairies* (1941) attempts to establish an authentic lineage of people of Icelandic descent on the Canadian prairies. Early "peoples of Canada" films such as these tend to send a dual message found throughout the history of multiculturalism discourse. They emphasize the cultural and racial difference of the ethnic community in question for purposes of appreciation by a non-ethnic Canadian "outsider." Yet in so doing they categorize and reify difference as that which is essentially marginal to an imaginary Canadian middle.

This exploration and containment of cultural/regional difference can be found in many of the films about labour. As may be gleaned from the title, *Gaspé Cod Fishermen* (1944), while concerned with labour, is also specifically about region. Like many films about region, it begins with a map of Canada and then zooms in to a specific spot. Men are shown at sea, fishing for cod. No doubt attempting to overcome sectionalism, the narrator says, "They want to cooperate with all other Canadians who are supplying us with food." The attempt is to tie the distinctive culture of the fisherfolk to the commonweal of the nation. Yet the film serves to reinscribe the fishermen's otherness from the central Canadian narrator.

Also addressed to the imagined central Canadian, *Prairie Profile* (1955) examines the life of Abernethy, Saskatchewan, a typical prairie town. In fact, the first question to a member of the town is "Would you call this an average community?" To which the local man answers, "Perhaps there is no such thing as a typical prairie district, but we *are* representative." The segment, hosted by Fred Davis and made to be broadcast on the CBC, clearly relies on the scripted words of "ordinary" people. It is, therefore, highly likely that the description of the town given by the farmer functions at the same time to justify to the producer/viewer why this particular town is of interest.

In *Men of Lunenburg* (1956), part of the *Peoples of the Maritimes* series, the significance of the present-day community is established by telling their "heritage story." They are descendants of the Protestant Germans who settled the south shore of Nova Scotia in the 1750s. Typically, before the film profiles the present community, a map of the world and a male narrator initiate the story with a short version of how this group first made its way to Britain's colony.

It is significant that so many early films made by the NFB are concerned with exploring regionality. In many ways, this is the principle mandate of the NFB, "to help Canadians in all parts of Canada understand the ways of living and the problems of Canadians in the other parts." This focus on labour and culture related to location corresponds to Robert Park's ideas about the effect of environment on its inhabitants and the hardships of frontier living. Not only were these ideas about Canada's frontier of interest to Americans and Europeans, but they also came to be one of Canada's most imposing myths of self-understanding. The actual experience of the Germans in Nova Scotia or the fishermen in Gaspé or the prairie farmers is of less importance than how these stories may be used for the purpose of multicultural government.

Prairie Profile (1955), self-reflexively depicting
the typical

NFB, CITIZENSHIP, AND WELFARE

Many of the films made in the 1940s and 1950s were about labour, welfare, and citizenship. *A Man and his Job* (1943) was one of the first NFB films to depict the citizen's encounter with the public service, which soon became a recurring trope. An introduction to the newly forged federal system of unemployment insurance, the film is a dramatization of labourers being laid off and their subsequent unsuccessful search for work. The "everyman" labourer, a statistical figure, is helpless in the face of unseen market forces. The film serves to advertise the central administration of the labour market by showing a labourer, Joe Martin, going to an Unemployment Insurance office and being placed in an appropriate job in another part of the country, a job that he most likely would not have found by himself. "We are fitting jobs to men across the country, and not men to jobs," says the narrator. Not only does this new system promise the right of each worker to freedom from fear and want, regardless of the economy, but it justifies laying off workers in deference to a national plan of progress.

In the production file for the film is a letter puzzling through the approach to the subject of dramatizing unemployment insurance: "Unemployment insurance is admittedly only the first step in a properly-planned, well-rounded, nationally-geared system of social security – Beveridge, Marsh, and the others recognize that fact. Well, if such is the case, how much can we, or ought we, to include in our ending visuals?" The author sketches out the scenario: "A guy had some security – and he lost it; and society decided it wasn't right; so, the next time he lost his security, he got it back. He's got a future now; his missus is happy; his daughter has a job and a good prospect. All that adds up to a lot – certainly so far as our picture audience is concerned; and it rings true to them – and it's personal, human, and close to themselves. If that can come away from the picture with that on the credit side, the Department of Labour and Unemployment Insurance are very much farther ahead than they were before the audience saw Joe Martin."[76] The production file also contains a reprint of an article from the *Labour Gazette* of May 1943 entitled "Unemployment Insurance in Canada, Historical Background and Administration of Act, 1940–3," as well as a memorandum from V.C. Phelan, director of information at the Department of Labour, authorizing $7,500 for films about Unemployment Insurance. The connection to government aims is direct: "I wonder if you would be good enough to have your people draw up a rough outline of what they might propose, and submit it to me."[77]

During the Second World War, labour unrest arising from short-staffing and unrealistic demands placed by the wartime economy, as well as a groundswell of support for the Co-operative Commonwealth Federation, forced Mackenzie King's Liberals to establish the ground-

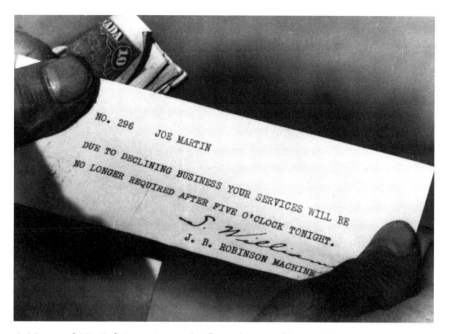

A Man and His Job (1941) was the first of many films to depict citizens in contact with government agencies.

work for collective bargaining and the cultivation of labour-management boards.[78] These developments are reflected in many of the films made about labour in the 1940s and 1950s. Beginning in 1943, industrial circuits inserted film screenings into the interstices of the work day at factories, shipyards, lumber camps, and munitions plants during the breaks and the shift changes. Co-sponsored by the Wartime Prices and Trade Board, Munitions and Supplies, Labour, and National War Services, many films brought to light the industrial aspect of war, making the "labour front" one of the prime aspects of Canada's war effort.[79]

According to labour historian Peter S. McInnes, "The Second World War brought about massive state intervention on a scale thought unimaginable during the years of the Great Depression. Now, Ottawa held the reigns of a 'command economy' and, with it, had considerable leeway for implementing a wide range of programs for social engineering."[80] The aircraft industry in particular experienced massive strikes in the middle of the war. But many industries were plagued by low wages and unrealistic demands, which led to labour unrest during and immediately after the war. Woodworkers, automotive workers, coal miners, steelworkers, textile workers, electrical and rubber industry workers, and meatpackers all aimed to ensure that the era of reconstruction was of some benefit to them.[81] In order to placate industrial workers, the government extended its wartime Labour-Management Production Committee strategies into the 1950s, using newsletters, posters, and NFB films to send its message about worker cooperation. The federal Labour-Management Cooperation Service sponsored the bulletin *Teamwork in Industry*, which featured a cartoon worker, Tommy Teamwork, "enlisted to remind production workers of the importance of cooperation and the commonality of interests they shared with their employers and the state."[82] As late as 1967, the NFB produced a filmstrip for Labour Canada on management-labour cooperation, entitled *Labour-Mangagment in a Changing World*.[83]

In 1944 the film *Democracy at Work* had sent a warning about labour-management conflict in relation to the overall war effort. Overlooking actual labour conflict, the film's narrator spoke of the "common responsibility of management and workers," insisting on the depoliticization of workplaces, which ought to strive for a "cooperative, productive feeling." Silent shots of factory workers are shown before the general manager addresses the camera to discuss the wartime production of his factory. He informs the viewer that his factory considers the workers to be people: factory welfare departments advise on personal problems. Perhaps most importantly, there are labour-management committees to deal with problems that might affect workers' morale.

In the film *Labour Looks Ahead* (1945), stock shots of factory production are shown as a male voice-over celebrates the "new industrial record" that Canada has achieved: "The whole nation has laboured as never before." As labourers are shown marching to the strains of a bagpipe, the narrator encourages cooperation between labour and management. Indeed, he tells us, industrial production cooperation boards have been set up everywhere. Trade union meetings and adult education classes are shown in order to indicate citizens getting involved and becoming more informed. The ultimate message is a "legislated consensus," where labour submits to the greater authority of national governments, assured of the dignity of labour and that workers of all united nations have "a constant share in the rebuilding of the world." As in so many films about labour, the "voice" of the film is that of management.[84]

The information sheet that circulated with *Labour Looks Ahead* stated that the film was concerned with "the role of Canadian workers in the war effort, and their preparations for the post war period."[85] A letter from Stanley Jackson to F.R. Clarke at the Unemployment Insurance Commission discussed the search for an appropriately maimed actor to play the role of the war veteran who was returning to work: "I think our best plan would be to borrow a handicapped person who has already been placed in industry. We could show him being examined and undergoing aptitude tests at the clinic and then move back to the man at his job in the factory. This would give us the whole story in brief. For this purpose we would need a fairly decent looking man, intelligent enough to take direction and with some very obvious though not revolting physical defect. For example a one-armed man doing with skill some job in a war factory would be ideal."[86] The film was presented as a means of exacting consent from workers who were needed for the war effort. "Beyond national boundaries, an international order must be established to guarantee a lasting peace. To be successful this order must have the support of those millions who run the world's factories, mines and transportations systems."[87]

Perhaps *Coal Face Canada* (1944) gives the best indication of how NFB films participated in the information-gathering process so central to the two-way process of social policy formation. In a letter dated 15 October 1941, W.H. Cranston of the Wartime Prices and Trade Board suggested that he might discuss with "Mr. Grierson and colleagues" the possibility of a feature on "the part coal is playing in the war effort."[88] However, it was not until labour unrest in the industry – newspaper clippings of wartime coal strikes are included in the production file – that pre-production began in earnest. In a confidential 1943 report on conditions in the coal mines of Alberta, George Lebeau, western supervisor of the Industrial and Trade Union Circuits, enumerated the causes of the miners' dissatisfaction "with a view to helping change the present situation and unrest that exists throughout the coal mine area of the Province of Alberta."[89]

A confidential report on the coal industry in the Crow's Nest Pass area indicates the degree to which the film was made to appease and cover up labour problems in the industry. The workers were "apparently not pulling their weight in the matter of coal production," said one draft memo on the film, "because they have not been told how important coal production is, nor has any coherent attempt been made on the part of the govt operators to better their conditions."[90] The report continues: "We shall have to show the disabilities under which the miner labours (company towns, dangerous work) – but turn this to a source of pride – occupational hazards and diseases, lack of sympathy on part of company, paucity of entertainment, paucity of housing. We shall also have to admit the govts mistaken policy in regard to certain matters, e.g.: nutrition, the income tax, beer, housing, and posit a future amelioration of these – by implication ... We shall have to sig [sic] the song of the people's war, and link this to the miners pulling thesmselves [sic] up by their bootstraps (admitting that they have more strikes against them than most industries)."[91]

The answer was to link the coal-mining industry to the drama and excitement of war with a "man to man" approach: "The incidental steps in tracing coal to high explosive bombs, and coal to ships and medical supplies, we think will provide material for a very interesting moving picture with plenty of scope for dramatic presentation, both of industry and warfare ... We lay some emphasis on the fact that coal miners are realists. Therefore, the story must carry all the evidence that is necessary to be convincing and take it out of the realm of propaganda."[92] In practical narrative terms, this meant that all references to strikes were deleted from the final script, and the soldier returning to the coal town was changed from a conscript to a volunteer.[93]

Direct government and social scientific involvement in the NFB is indicated by a letter from David Petegorsky suggesting that the NFB consult David Dunton and psychologist J.P. Ketchum of the Wartime Information Board, "both of whom have considerable experience in the preparation and evaluation of [absenteeism] surveys."[94] Petegorsky also suggested that the film be released in conjunction with positive government action: "A statement should be made by the Prime Minister and Mr. Howe, emphasizing the vital importance of coal mining and production in the national effort, the contribution of the coal miners to the war effort, the fact that a miner in the coal pits is performing a duty as vital as a soldier in the line of battle."[95]

In a strategy found throughout wartime films that resembles the social scientific tendency toward typification, the story of coal mining in Canada is told about a fictional place composed of typical elements of existing towns. On the suggested script treatment for the film, the fictional town is described as "a mythical, composite coaltown, in which we find the excellent housing conditions, for example, of Blairmore, with its completely labour Town Council, the Victory Gardens of Nanaimo, the Recreational Institute of Cumberland, etc., etc."[96] To obfuscate the location further, a recommendation was made by Dan Wallace to the army public relations office that "not an actor but a typical soldier" be used: "It is important that this soldier should have a Cape Breton accent ... The location will be Blairmore, Alberta."[97] After the film was made, a good deal of group comment went into its re-editing. Graham McInnes chided Robert Edmonds for taking the film too far from its original intention:

There must be some reference to what management has done, and to the hope of the formation of labour management production committees (to which the Government is committed). I realize that the bosses have done damn little, but if we point the thing up so strongly from the workers' point of view, there will be a terrific kick-back from the sponsor ... I am seriously disturbed by the thought that you have had to get actors. You know it's a sort of standard rule in documentary that if you can find someone on location and make him act, it's much better than having an actor ... This film on the home front is as difficult and tricky to make, politically and filmically, as was *The Gates of Italy*, on the warfront. We cannot risk a political misjudgment. We cannot risk the documentary value of a mining film being lost through a story which doesn't ring true at each and every point.[98]

Reports in the production file indicate that the NFB relied on plant managers and superintendents to record their responses to films before releasing them on the trade union circuits.

This range of examples gives some indication of the ways in which NFB films of the 1940s and 1950s utilized social scientific theories of typicality combined with popular management strategies. Organized around labour, health, and welfare, the ideas of government realism apparent in the films is reinforced by material in the production archives that indicates not only the close cooperation between government departments and NFB filmmakers but also the degree to which strategies for telling statistical stories were front and centre for the creative teams.

CONCLUSION

Conversant with ideas current in marketing, government, and the social sciences, Grierson was clearly influenced by ideas about communication and citizenship in the welfare state. Documentary film at the NFB was poised in a critical position in relation to all three of these discourses. The site of operation was the malleable citizen, increasingly understood in marketing terms as a member of any number of subcultures with competing allegiances. In Grierson's view, propaganda could be used to educate citizens about the objectives of the state and their role within the national project. He seemed little bothered by the contradiction this position posed for democracies. After all, social science was deemed the information technology appropriate for liberal welfare states. An exploration of a range of films made at the National Film Board seems to support this reading of the NFB as a welfare state technology.

Having established a relationship between documentary, social science, and the welfare state apparent in government realism, in the next chapter I shall examine the role of film in theories of education in Canada before, during, and after the war, during the first decade of the cold war. Specifically, I shall draw connections between empire communications before the war and the effect of UNESCO on postwar cultural nationalism. The NFB continued to be an important aspect of state information and education policy, and documentary film continued to be deemed the best way to express this form of information about the population. During the 1950s, filmmakers began to engage with the state mandate more playfully and critically, and out of this emerged some very complex work within the paradigm of government realism.

FOUR

Nationalism and Internationalism at the National Film Board

*One foresees ... a situation in which the press liaison service now main-
tained by the* WIB *will be carried out either by External Affairs or, even
more simply, by a Bureau of Statistics, revised and extended to meet the
increasing demand for basic information about Canada. Those other
educational and cultural information services which are now a matter of
joint operation by the* WIB *and the* NFB *will fall naturally upon the* NFB
*as the only organisation equipped in personnel, skill and experience to
do the complex technical work of production and distribution involved.*
– John Grierson, policy outline[1]

*Evidence continues to mount ... to show that the effect of the operation
of the* NFB *has not been to make "passive subjects" or centralize power
in Ottawa, but to stimulate free voluntary effort of citizens in thousands
of communities.*
– J.R. Kidd, *Pictures with a Purpose*[2]

One of the most famous and best-loved NFB films is Norman McLaren's
cold war parable, *Neighbours* (1952). This stop-motion live animation
short depicts two neighbours senselessly bickering over a flower blooming on the line between their properties. In their short-sighted attempt
to claim ownership over the bloom, they destroy not only the flower but
also their lands, their families, and themselves. Although it was made as
part of the *Freedom Speaks* program initiated by film commissioner
Arthur Irwin as a contribution to anticommunist psychological warfare,

Neighbours is rarely interpreted in the context of the NFB's involvement with international affairs.[3] Yet it is useful to situate the film in relation to the dozens of films the NFB made supporting the aims and objectives of the United Nations and its educational arm, UNESCO. While some films promoted good citizenship at home, others promoted good citizenship in an international community. In many films, the image of Canada as a mini United Nations is made explicit.

In the last two chapters, I traced the connection between the National Film Board and international ideas about government, social science, and publicity before and during the Second World War. In the postwar period, many of these tendencies were intensified as the world divided along the ideological lines of the cold war. Internationalism worked to bolster the centralizing tendencies of nationalism and gave an advantage to the federal government over the provincial governments on the international scene. During the cold war, internationalism became a prime aspect of national cultural life.[4]

Made as part of the *Freedom Speaks* series, *Neighbours* (1952) provides a compelling example of an artist negotiating with a governmental objective.

The Massey Commission that reaffirmed the NFB's mandate in 1951 is commonly linked to the rise of postwar nationalism in Canada.[5] But as with the internationally oriented education movements and educationalists of the National Film Society and National Film Board that I discuss below, everyone involved with the Massey Commission was actively engaged with international affairs.[6] All five commissioners had been active in the Canadian Association for Adult Education and the Canadian Institute of International Affairs.[7] The institute had been founded in 1928 "to promote and encourage in Canada research and discussion in international affairs and to give attention to Canada's position both as a member of the international community of nations and as a member of the British Commonwealth of Nations," and it was a gathering place for Canada's elite.[8] It was at a meeting of the institute in 1934 that Brooke Claxton, who initiated the inquiry that ultimately became the Massey Commission, first met Vincent Massey.[9]

Massey was a supporter of international and imperial connections from his days at Oxford, where he had established a "round table" chapter, an empire-wide association based on the imperialist notions of Cecil Rhodes.[10] In 1922 Massey became president of the National Council of Education, where "it was hoped that it could create a bureau of education on a national basis, non-governmental and unofficial, which could be a clearing house of ideas in this field."[11] Massey vigorously pursued his own brand of commonwealth nationalism from his position as high commissioner in London during the war and in his writing. Massey's internationalism – his support of both the United Nations and the British Commonwealth – is apparent in his book *On Being Canadian*, in which both are compatible with his brand of nationalism.[12]

In this chapter, I examine the relationship between film, education, and internationalism at the outset of the cold war, the period of the NFB's greatest vulnerability, and then during the 1950s. I also discuss the NFB films *Everyman's World* and *Film and You*, made to deal with citizenship, and I consider the activity of the film council movement. In order to contextualize this material, however, I begin with a look at the role of the educational lobbies in bringing about the establishment of the NFB and its the subsequent role in governmental citizenship work in the 1940s.

THE CANADIAN EDUCATION LOBBY

As I suggested in chapter 2, the "film board idea," to use C. Rodney James's term, was not indigenous to Canada.[13] The idea of a film board was a particularly British manifestation of ideas of state support for film production and distribution that was popular in the interwar period. In its vision of a decentred network of empire communications emanating equally from the dominions and travelling to, among other places, the United States, the Imperial Relations Trust aimed to establish filmmaking as well as film cataloguing and distributing institutions around the British Empire. These "clearing houses" of film information would serve educational institutions that were eager to employ modern communication methods, as well as the influential film societies that expressed their desire to have access to non-mainstream film, and they would also provide images of local events for inclusion in newsreels. Because of its proximity to the United States as well as its strong affinity with Britain, Canada was a unique site in which to test the film board idea.[14]

The British government's attempts in the 1920s and 1930s to consolidate an empire composed of a variety of different nationalities resembled the work being done from a different angle by American and Canadian educators and social scientists to understand the pressures of immigrant groups on national sentiment. The problems posed to governing an empire were similar to those posed by a broadly dispersed country composed of racially and linguistically different population groups, new cities teeming with immigrants, and a variety of disparate regions. While Hollywood was used as a means of allegiance building in the United States, non-theatrical documentary film was one of the methods favoured by the British and Canadian governments.

Although Grierson travelled to Australia and New Zealand in 1940 as part of his work for the Imperial Relations Trust, his reception there was not as warm as the one he received in Canada.[15] Nevertheless, both countries ended up establishing film institutions (a unit in New Zealand and a board in Australia). There were significant connections between these outposts of the British documentary film movement in terms of mandate and personnel. The first film commissioner in Australia was Ralph Foster, who had been the Australian representative of the NFB. Foster invited Stanley Hawes, an English filmmaker who had been working at the NFB, to be head of production in Australia. He remained there until his retirement in 1970, when the Australian board became Film Australia.

In Canada, the dedicated participation of a small but powerful and well-organized group of educators was essential in the successful establishment of the National Film Board. The film council movement, with its close ties to adult education and liberal internationalist movements, not only played an integral role in the establishment of the NFB, but was also an essential influence on the early non-theatrical methods used in film distribution. In particular, the rural and educational circuits followed by the industrial and trade union circuits instituted during the war remained faithful to this group's philosophy of film in on-site education. Many of the people involved with the National Film Society (NFS) were later incorporated into the NFB.

From the second decade of the century, especially after the First World War, Canadian social reformers and charities providing social services fixed their attention on adult education as a means of bringing about the Canadianization of immigrants. These groups included the Adult Educator's League and the Canadian Association for Adult Education (CAAE). Other groups involved in the adult education movement were based in the extension programs of Canadian universities. For example, in the 1930s the University of Alberta's extension department ran early experiments in using mobile cinema units to reach immigrants.[16] The president of the University of Alberta, Robert Wallace, was involved in the founding of the NFS, which he saw as an extension of his citizen education work.

U.S. philanthropic organizations were deeply invested in both social science and immigrant education. Like the NFS, the CAAE was established in 1935 with a grant from the Carnegie Corporation. Funding for the CAAE was provided by the Canadian Committee of the Carnegie Corporation, a subcommittee founded in 1933, whose inaugural members included Vincent Massey, Robert Wallace, and Harry McCurry, director of the National Gallery.[17] Both Ross McLean and Vincent Massey, who were responsible for the 1936 report that recommended Grierson as a film consultant to Canada, were members of the NFS (see chapter 2). In 1935 McCurry wrote to Massey: "In order to arouse the attention of all interested bodies in Canada such as Museums, the

Provincial Departments of Education, the Universities and other groups, it seems desirable that a report on the Canadian situation should be prepared. Of course we know largely what such a report will contain, but the preparation of it will chrystallize [sic] opinion behind the new movement. The report would describe the need of a clearing house for educational and cultural films in Canada and show the broad field of usefulness of the educational films which is largely untouched as yet in Canada."[18] It follows, then, that when the Imperial Relations Trust became involved in the Canadian film scene, it was through educational organizations and film societies and not through the Canadian Government Motion Picture Bureau. This is probably because the bureau's films, mainly scenics shown outside Canada to encourage tourism and immigration, were largely outside the education mandate and non-theatrical model of the NFS and related organizations. Its films, by and large, were not concerned with the population and did not display the trademarks of government realism.

The close relationship between documentary film and adult education movements was personified by E.A. (Ned) Corbett, president of CAAE from 1936 to 1950. Corbett was a signatory to Buchanan's *Report on Educational and Cultural Films in Canada*, written in 1936 for the Carnegie Corporation, and an NFS board member. In 1939 the National Film Board, whose civilian representatives included two prominent members of the NFS, W.C. Murray and Charles G. Gowan,[19] offered him the newly minted position of government film commissioner, a position many believed should go to a Canadian; he demurred, recommending that the NFB hire Grierson instead.[20]

Although there was a close link between the National Film Society and the National Film Board, there were significant differences in philosophy. For example, with Grierson's arrival in Canada, the concept of non-theatrical film as it had been used in the early days of the NFS was immediately modified. A very limited notion of British educational and documentary film was established as the mandate of the NFS at the expense of a more expansive early mandate that had included European art films. One need only compare the four original objectives set down by the NFS in 1936 with the three reported in retrospect by a member of the education lobby (see the two following quotations) to see that non-theatrical art film was erased from the mandate:

Broadly, four main groups, using films, would be served directly by the national clearing house. There would be provincial departments of education, the universities, and such private schools and colleges as might become affiliated to it; secondly, there would be adult education groups, such as those which are now affiliated to the Canadian Association for Adult Education; thirdly, there would be technical groups, such as research laboratories, medical associations, and also those various museums which are beginning to find that their biological, geological, and anthropological exhibits can be satisfactorily illustrated by documentary and scientific films; fourthly, *there would be those students of life and letters who are interested in the cultural aspects of the film, and from whom the membership of private film societies is already being recruited.*[21]

The intention was that [the NFS] should provide information and distribution services to: (i) universities, provincial departments of education and schools in general; (ii) the Canadian Association for Adult Education and its member associations, also service clubs and other community groups; (iii) research laboratories, medical associations, scientific groups and museums.[22]

The money requested from the Imperial Relations Trust by the Canadian film committee after meeting with Grierson was for a five-year allotment, to be used for distribution of documentaries, British and empire films, and to encourage the production of Canadian documentaries. In 1938 the Imperial Relations Trust grant was expressly for the establishment of a non-commercial film library of British and dominion educational and documentary films and their promotion and circulation.[23] Documentary had replaced the broader concept of non- theatrical film. As the adult education movement institutionalized the educational vision of non-theatrical film at the expense of all others, the NFS was itself all but subsumed into the CAAE, which in turn became aligned in 1940 with the Canadian Council for Education-in-Citizenship (CCEC). The CCEC acted as a conduit for government money directed to the CAAE.[24]

"More was done to involve ethnics in Canadian life in 1940 and 1941," notes historian N.F. Dreisziger, "than had been done in the nearly three-quarters of a century since Confederation."[25] The upshot of these official efforts at education and assimilation was the development of a notion of Canadianism as the amalgamation of established Canadian values with flavours from immigrants' countries of origin.[26] In many ways this approach to Canadian citizenship formation resembled the efforts to create an affinity to empire through the imperial preference campaign.

In a parliamentary debate concerning the Wartime Information Board in November 1941, J.T. Thorson, head of the Bureau of Public Information, defended the publicity expenses on such matters: "The need for proper public relations between the departments of the government and the people is, I think, of paramount importance; indeed, I believe that a proper sense of public relationship is an essential element of democratic government."[27] These efforts eventually led to the establishment of the Nationalities Branch of the Department of National War Services, the progenitor of the multiculturalism apparatus of the Department of the Secretary of State. One of the most intensive strategies deployed was mobile non-theatrical screenings.

FILM CIRCUITS AND CITIZENSHIP

The film circuit idea for non-theatrical film distribution, adapted from the imperial practice of mobile cinema, corresponded to the Canadian state's work on integrating immigrant communities through public information, which became entrenched in government during the Second World War.

Between 1942 and 1946, the NFB ran citizenship film forums in rural schools, churches, community centres, and at factories and trade union halls. Itinerant projectionists, known as field men, drove film equipment and electric generators on provincial circuits. In January 1942, thirty rural circuits, each consisting of twenty rural immigrant communities, began monthly screenings. Films were used to stimulate and monitor political discussion and to instigate the desire for modernizing projects, such as new agricultural methods and the electrification of farms. Because of the cold climate, most screenings were held indoors, but outdoor screenings were organized where appropriate. Children were often reached at school, with the hope that they would inspire their parents to attend a screening at night. The film programs were composed of a set of short films on agricultural improvement, profiles of various "peoples of Canada," propaganda for the empire, and morality tales.

The CCEC prepared books of lecture notes to accompany every program on the rural circuits, giving the leader of the discussion "hints on how to conduct the meeting."[28] "Almost any film about Canadian activities or about international, political and economic issues," commented one journalist, "can be adapted in the hands of expert leaders to discussions of citizenship."[29] In areas populated by "Canadian citizens of foreign origin," star high school pupils were sent on the rural circuits to "stage a panel discussion for the benefit of the community."[30]

Projectionists sent monthly reports back to the NFB. Through interview and observation, the rural circuits were intended as sites of a two-way flow of information between government and citizen.[31] "Essentially, the field man is a community organizer of adult education services. He acts as a technical adviser to film councils and to the committees responsible for film libraries, depots, and the self-operating circuits. Part of his time is spent as an agent in the sale of films or filmstrips. He is responsible for the promotion of theatrical films of the NFB in his area. He arranges showings for the Federal Government, as well as for provincial and municipal governments and often finds time for special demonstrations to community organizations. Any groups wishing to promote an activity which they feel is in the public interest can rely on his advice, and perhaps on his aid in securing films or equipment."[32]

Midway through 1942, the NFB began trade union circuits, sponsored in part by the Workers' Educational Association and the Canadian Congress of Labour. On these circuits, the films shown were accompanied by short promotional films to spark discussion of issues such as absenteeism at the workplace and the role of the worker in wartime production.[33] These "discussion trailers" were included with all the trade union circuits, spurring one commentator to enthuse that they had "proved a fruitful method for stirring up lively, profitable debates on vital issues among members of union audiences."[34] The trailers were customized for the purpose of engaging viewers with government action, and fifteen of them were made under the series title "Getting the Most Out of a Film." Tailored to each program and social issue with which it dealt, and only a few minutes long, each trailer shows ordinary folk at a film screening discussing with a panel of experts the ideas presented in the relevant films. At the end, the moderator turns to the camera and encourages the audience to continue the discussion after the screening. The discussion trailers were a remarkable attempt to provide audiences with examples of how they could begin to discuss the issues posed by a film.

Starting in 1943, industrial circuits funded by the Wartime Prices and Trade Board, Munitions and Supply, Labour, and National War Services were established to reach people working in munitions plants and other industrial settings. By 1944 they were reaching 385,000 people per month with 3,000 screenings.[35] Statistics for 1944, at the height of the circuits, show that there were thirty-seven full-time NFB operators. Over one-quarter of a million people were reached by 1,574 shows in January of that year alone.[36] Worker screenings were carefully managed to try to offset unrest and to channel it into patriotic productivity. There was surveillance of the screenings, and audience reactions were monitored and reported upon.[37]

POSTWAR FILM COUNCILS

After the war, the circuits were taken over by newly formed local film councils, many of which were connected to the prewar National Film Society. Charles W. Marshall, the NFB's western regional supervisor, described the film council movement in a memorandum to T.V. Adams, the Ottawa-based supervisor of programs:

A film council acts as a coordinating body and promotes the production, distribution and effective use of informational visual material for the general welfare of all peoples, providing direction, advice and information on material sources, and leadership and guidance on improved methods of applying such material ... Because membership in a film council gives them greater access to the most powerful medium of information yet devised to provide vital information on critical problems – international, national and local – political, economic and social – racial, industrial, ideological and spiritual – and to stimulate citizen action ... Problems which are old but which assume a new importance in this atomic age.[38]

Citizens were grouped into those to whom social programs were directed and those who might be made interested in helping guide those in need of welfare programs – primarily the poor and members of immigrant groups. Postwar NFB distribution followed two strategies: to

Movies for Workers (1945, Stanley Hawes), depicts labour-management cooperation and illustrates the factory circuits.

voluntary groups and to targeted welfare groups. Voluntary groups included the Canadian Institute for the Blind, Boy Scouts and Girl Guides, the Sailors' Institute, Salvation Army, Humane Society, Victorian Order of Nurses, and the Catholic Women's League. The "other half" could be reached by giving "special showings to ethnic groups, Unions, and by invitation to welfare clients," as a distribution officer working in Fort William, Manitoba, suggested.[39] Mothers-to-be could be reached on matters of infant health by means of filmstrips strategically located in the waiting rooms of maternity clinics.[40] The films were organized into specialty catalogues, such as *Films for Women* and *Movies for Workers*.[41]

The NFB still provided the option of complete programs of short films, but the possibility of making the programming decisions locally was increasingly facilitated by newly established film libraries and regional depositories.[42] As well as providing film programs and supplying film libraries, the NFB continued to be involved in the circuits by sending representatives to screen new films at the annual meeting of the Canadian Education Association. In 1949 a formal link was made between the association and the NFB. The information sheets and discussion guides that the NFB began to supply with their films were the fruit of this convergence and were "designed specifically for teaching purposes."[43]

According to some experts of the day, film screenings had the potential to be more effective than television because of the "flexibility of presentations" and the "permanency of the recordings."[44] The preferred stories were about "normal, ordinary folks" with whom audiences could become emotionally involved so that they would want to discuss their particular problems after the film's preferably open-ended resolution.[45]

In late 1952 a draft report about community screenings, "Getting the Most Out of Your Film Screening," suggested that introductions and postscreening discussions would help maximize the effect of the film:

Sure, they will talk about it after the meeting, outside, or over a cup of coffee or perhaps when they go home but, why won't they talk about it when they are all sitting together and the film is just finished? There must be something wrong with the way the showing is run. We know that the films shown are generally of interest to the people but after a showing no one seems to want to talk about what they have seen. The best meetings are those where people are at ease and interested enough to talk. When people discuss a film they share their feelings and ideas and really come to feel that they have a lot in common with one another. Discussion also helps people to make up their minds what they really think about a film. This last point is important when a particular film is shown to a group interested in that subject. You will only get people to do something about a problem if they have discussed it and convinced themselves what needs to be done, and feel they have made the decision themselves.[46]

In anticipation of the Canadian Citizenship Act of 1947, the NFB produced a film called *Everyman's World* that was used extensively for citizenship work. Produced for the Farm Improvement Loans Branch of the Department of Finance in 1946, the film features Canadian politicians involved with the United Nations, as well as immigrants arriving in Canada and attending naturalization ceremonies. According to a 1948 description, "Men of different colour, creed, and background are portrayed in various occupations such as farming, mining, manufacturing – all the elements which go to make up a nation." The emphasis is on Canada as a microcosm of the world: "The face of Canada reflects in many respects the face of the world. The people of Canada are as diverse as the peoples of the world themselves. Within her borders are members or their descendents of almost every nation, every race and every religious concept." The press release for the film describes a film that attempts to help Canadians visualize Canada's international role while highlighting ordinary Canadians' roles in government at home and abroad. *Everyman's World* was used as part of a citizenship campaign underwritten by the Department of the Secretary of State.

The NFB distribution officer M.C. Roberts described the use of the film for citizenship education in British Columbia: "On December 6th, I attended an executive meeting of the newly formed Citizenship Group in Vancouver which was also attended by the Solicitor General of Canada, and Dr. King, Speaker of the Senate. The main body of the meeting was made up of representatives of service clubs, churches and miscellaneous organizations. I told the group about the film, *Every Man's World* [sic], and how it was specially designed to fit in with Citizenship Week. I let them know that voluntary projection services would be available from the Vancouver office and that sufficient prints would be on hand for special requests."[47]

The ideology of the National Film Society and adult education groups can also be seen in *Film and You* (1948), an NFB movie about film societies that epitomizes the ethos of the film educators. The *Film and You* file at the NFB Archives contains many indicators of the degree to which this film was steeped in philosophies of film use in adult education and grassroots community modernization. The film's official information sheet proclaims that "*Film and You* answers the public's questions as to how documentary films can be obtained and how they can be made a permanent part of community life ... This film is intended primarily to show the advantages and possibilities of the film council to those unfamiliar with the idea. It will also be of interest to established film councils."[48] The accompanying film discussion guide reads:

This is a film about films – and you. It is concerned with those films we call "documentaries" because they are like pages from the story of the way we live; and the people, you and I and thousands of other Canadians who have found a way of using films ... In the first part of it, we see an audience which might include you and I. It is made up of all kinds of people – men and women, young people and adults. On the screen, they see short pieces from a number of films. As we watch, we see how each film affects them. We see one man nodding over a film obviously intended for someone else, a woman who disapproves of a film which pleases the man, and then when we have studied how people respond to films, the lights go on and hear someone ask: "Why couldn't we have a film library?" ... From this story of the Canadian documentary film movement, we see that there are films which bring us to grips with life without losing the dramatic interest we find in other kinds of films.[49]

The didactic aspect of *Film and You* was discussed in the NFB submission to the Massey Commission, in which Ross McLean wrote that *Film and You* had been "widely used by NFB representatives to promote the organization of new film councils, and to give existing councils a broader picture of the service they can contribute to the community."[50] As with all international uses of film, thoughts about the potential for good publicity for Canada were never far from the surface. After a three-week survey of community use and distribution of film in Ontario, Don Fraser reported to Ross McLean that *Film and You* could be used for many purposes: for showing to general audiences in Canada; for use by "NFB field men in their promotional work"; "to show the world how Canada is using film"; "as a prestige film for the NFB"; and "as a focal point leading to closer relations between NFB production staff, field staff and our audience."[51]

Film society members saw themselves as community activists, improving themselves and those around them. The question of volunteerism as a governmental mode of democratic participation was especially pertinent to women, the largest sector of volunteers and a likely target for non-theatrical screenings. *V for Volunteers* (1951) draws on the wartime implications of "V for Victory" for a cold war army of civilian volunteers. Sponsored by the Canadian Welfare Council of the Department of National Health and Welfare and the Association of the Junior Leagues of America, the film tells a fictionalized story of an exemplary volunteer, "Janet Miller." Janet introduces herself in voice-over as a woman is seen entering a middle-class kitchen with a laundry basket. "I live in a suburb called Glendale, which is about as pleasant and average as it sounds." She is shown spending her day as a housewife, tidying and cooking.

Film and You (1948, Jean Palardy and Donald Peters) was an information film for members of film councils and film societies.

Film and You highlighted the connection between film and other government services, such as health, welfare, and recreation.

"Carol, my neighbour, thinks I should be more involved in civic affairs," says Janet, but she is clearly content with her little corner of the world. However, in attending a lecture series, "The Community and You," Janet begins to feel attracted by the concept of community involvement. The lecturer speaks directly to the camera, addressing not only Janet but also the middle-class female audience, the women who are potential volunteers. When the lecturer uses the personal form of address, saying, "Your right to be useful is a symbol of your personal dignity and worth," it serves to include both the likable fictional character and the women watching the film.

The idea to make a film about "volunteer social workers" came from the Canadian Welfare Council.[52] In a common strategy of typification, in 1949 filmmaker James Beveridge suggested, "You could make your entire film in one town, strictly anonymous, or you could pick out five or six cities that have five or six outstanding features and represent that all of these were one composite city, but that naturally would increase costs."[53] In the event, Mert McKinnon of Ottawa's Recreation Centre was cast, along with "actual hospital nurses and patients in the hospital scenes, actual volunteer workers in other scenes, an actual polio case for the role of a little boy, an actual square dance caller for the part of Mrs. Shadbolt, actual members of the Boys' Club for the scenes in that club." When Leslie McFarlane was questioned by Commissioner Arthur Irwin about the use of McKinnon in particular, McFarlane responded with a philosophical position on documentary film: "In the making of a documentary film one uses material to create the illusion of truth ... I might suggest that if all stories are to be scrutinized for removal of any situations which may parallel, even remotely, real-life situations, the making of documentary films would become impossible."[54]

The pamphlet that was released with the film gives an idea of how the film's non-theatrical release was planned: "How *V for Volunteers* may be used: by Junior Leagues, the Community Chest, the Kiwanis, Rotary, Chamber of Commerce, Junior Chamber of Commerce, Museums, Veterans' Organizations, Settlements, YMCA's, Hospitals, the Red Cross, and all organizations and institutions interested in enlisting volunteers for social, cultural and welfare work."[55] The film was originally screened privately for "government and Ottawa officials" at the Elgin Theatre in Ottawa, and photographs were taken for the Canadian Welfare Council's publication, *Welfare*.[56]

V for Volunteers (1951, Leslie McFarlane) was co-sponsored by the Canadian Welfare Council.

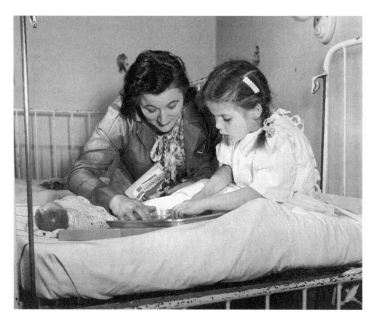

V for Volunteers staged reenactments of daily life in an ordinary family.

As this discussion of the connection between the National Film Society, the Canadian Council for Education-in-Citizenship, and the National Film Board indicates, the establishment of the NFB may be seen as a result of the combination of the push by the Imperial Relations Trust to encourage and support more production in the dominions and the conditions of reception in Canada. Built with support from the powerful education lobbies and the National Film Society, the NFB also fulfilled the empire mandate for a broad-based publicity strategy using positive propaganda to build up Canada's status on national and international screens. This was seen to have the effect of improving Canadian citizenship and having a beneficial effect as a panacea against American cultural and economic domination. Thus, although the NFB was put under harsh scrutiny in the latter half of the 1940s, the integration of documentary film into theories of government and education was most probably too fundamental by this point to have caused the demise of the NFB. However, it does help explain why the gambit of NFB films were so narrowly focused on citizenship during this period.

THE NATIONAL FILM BOARD, THE COLD WAR, AND THE MASSEY COMMISSION

In 1945 the Soviet cipher clerk Igor Gouzenko went to the Canadian police with evidence of spying in Ottawa. The allegations centred on the Soviet military attaché, Colonel N. Zabotin, and his alleged coordination of agents to obtain confidential information about radar equipment developed at the National Research Council, about munitions stored in Valcartier, Quebec, and about a nuclear project at Chalk River, Ontario.[57] Among the papers examined by the investigators was the cryptic message, "Freda to the Professor through Grierson." The Professor was thought to be Dr Raymond Boyer, chair of the Canadian Association of Scientific Workers (CAScW): Grierson was assumed to be the national film commissioner John Grierson: and Freda was the name of a secretary at the NFB. Prime Minister Mackenzie King declared the War Measures Act and appointed a royal commission, headed by Supreme Court Justices R.L. Kellock and Robert Taschereau, to investigate the many people accused of being communist agents or sympathizers.[58] Raymond Boyer was detained, and the commission's report in July 1946 "accused the CAScW of being a 'front' for the Communist Party's prop-

aganda, and of being susceptible to its recruiting techniques for new espionage agents."[59] With its credibility destroyed, the Canadian Association of Scientific Workers folded in the mid-1950s.

As for the NFB, its supposed access to sensitive government information rendered it a "vulnerable agency," along with the Prime Minister's
Office, the Privy Council Office, External Affairs, Defence, and the
RCMP, and every employee was required to pass security clearance.[60]
Grierson's contract was not renewed, and over the next few years, until
the official RCMP investigation began, untold numbers of NFB employees, most on temporary three-month contracts, were quietly let go.
Personal gatherings were infiltrated and monitored, and some NFB
employees were placed under constant surveillance: "Mounties in con-
cealed locations carefully noted the time and place of private conversa-
tions between suspects."[61]

Aside from Grierson, the known victims of the chill and purge included filmmakers Evelyn [Spice] Cherry and Lawrence Cherry and
activist Stan Rands, who was attempting to unionize NFB employees.
Most of the victims never came forward with their stories.[62] This communist "witch hunt" did not exhaust itself until Grierson's successor,
Ross McLean, was unceremoniously replaced by *Maclean's* editor
Arthur Irwin in 1950 and the NFB was subjected to a management review by the consulting firm Woods-Gordon and then thoroughly in-
vestigated and exonerated by a multiparty parliamentary committee in
1952.[63] This process was so successful that, at the end of it, Conservative Leader George Drew could say, "Films which illustrate in pictorial
form certain types of our system of national, provincial and educational government, certain types of our own characteristic Canadian way
of doing things in different parts of the country, would all be very
helpful."[64]

This political intrigue coincided with the striking of the Royal Commission on National Development in the Arts, Letters, and Sciences
(Massey Commission) in 1949 and its two years of hearings. Many
thought that this would sound the death knell for the NFB, but even before the commission reported, a revised film act was passed. The major
modification of the National Film Act of 1950 was to add an international reference. The NFB was now mandated to produce and distribute
films "designed to interpret Canada to Canadians and to other nations."[65] Part of the reason for the survival of the NFB during this

fraught period can be attributed to the education lobby, which had made strong arguments for film as a tool of education. The Canadian Association of Adult Education (CAAE) played a particularly important role in coordinating briefs submitted by voluntary associations to the Massey Commission.[66] Closely aligned with the CAAE, the film councils and the National Film Society (NFS) also proved to be important influences on the commission's report.

As discussed above, with the rural, school, industrial, and trade union circuits of the war period, the NFB had centralized and institutionalized the concept of non-theatrical film screenings. At the end of the war, as film circuit funding dried up, local film councils were established across Canada with the sponsorship and participation of the NFB; the bulk of their showings were of NFB films. Many local councils were brought together with members from voluntary associations such as "service clubs [and] fraternal societies."[67] In 1946 the NFS and the CAAE, along with other groups interested in education and communications, such as the Canadian Education Association, the Canadian Welfare Council, the Canadian Congress of Labour, and the Citizenship Branch of the Department of Citizenship and Education combined to form the Joint Planning Committee of the CAAE.[68] Not only did the Joint Planning Committee inaugurate and finance the Canada Film Awards,[69] but it also began to strategize about how best to mobilize resources for submissions to the Massey Commission.

Donald Buchanan, author of the 1936 report on the NFS, submitted a fifty-one-page history of the film society movement to the Massey Commission entitled "Documentary and Educational Films in Canada, 1935–1950." The crafting of the report was a strategy between Massey and Buchanan, its objective being to obtain continued funding for cultural films in Canada. Privately, Buchanan wrote to Massey, "Whether the recommendations contained therein will ever be carried out remains a question of finance. We shall eventually have to have grants from educational institutions and provincial departments of education ... The Carnegie Foundation may be prepared to give us a further sum of money."[70] The Massey Report ultimately supported the NFB over the NFS (renamed the Canadian Film Institute in 1950). However, by this time, the NFB had institutionally entrenched the goals of the NFS, minus the promotion of alternative forms of narrative or experimental cinema.

THE NATIONAL FILM BOARD AND UNESCO

Another, related reason for the renewed support of the NFB had to do with UNESCO. The Massey Commission was mandated to examine "methods by which the relations of Canada with the United Nations Educational, Scientific and Cultural Organization ... should be conducted." Of the four issues stipulated in the order-in-council that created the royal commission, the third – following the pressing issue of broadcasting policy and the "operation and future development" of federal arts agencies and preceding the relations of the government with voluntary bodies and the preservation of historical monuments – was explicitly concerned with UNESCO and "similar international bodies." As the Massey Report documents, seventy briefs from voluntary organizations expressed some concern about Canada's relations with UNESCO,[71] and many of the submissions urged the formation of a national commission dedicated to matters of international cultural concern like those established by this time in thirty other countries.[72] The order-in-council begins with the assertion, "It is desirable that the Canadian people should know as much as possible about their country, its history and traditions; and about their national life and common achievements ... It is in the national interest to give encouragement to institutions which express national feeling, promote common understanding and add to the variety and richness of Canadian life, rural as well as urban." The NFB is listed as one of the federal agencies already contributing to these ends.

Upon its foundation in 1945, UNESCO expressed overwhelming support for film both as a method of transmitting "fundamental education" at home and as a cultural missionary abroad. As a UNESCO report from the late 1940s put it, "Educational films not only provide a means for communicating important ideas to illiterate people but they also provide an excellent method for eliminating illiteracy itself ... It is the sub-commission's conviction that entertainment films have a cultural mission especially in bringing about mutual understanding between peoples. The production and distribution of entertainment films raises many problems in the international field which are not normally recognized in national production circles."[73]

NFB initiatives in film and citizenship melded well with the postwar institutionalization of interwar international liberal philosophy of education in UNESCO. UNESCO ideology was directed at the ends of mass education and economic development. "Experience has shown," said one early UNESCO study on film, "that any useful attempt to discuss concepts and definitions at an international level must await the arousal of at least a minimum of interest at national levels."[74] The preamble to the UNESCO convention (written by American poet Archibald Mac-Leish, who was the librarian of congress) describes the modern mind as a battlefield: "Since wars begin in the minds of men, it is in the minds of men that the defences of peace must be constructed."[75] Inspired by the use of the phrase by Britain's deputy prime minister, Clement Attlee, at the Conference of Allied Ministers of Education in 1942, it also clearly recalled the title of one of the NFB's most famous wartime films, *The War for Men's Minds* (1943).

Film was given exemplary status in UNESCO discussions, for it functioned in many ways. It had educational applications that extended from demonstrations of practical skills to the circulation of information about national ways of life and the documentation of national cultural production. Film was also the leading form of amusement and entertainment, a situation that continued in the Third World long after television had displaced film in the domestic North American market: "The commercial cinema remains of sufficient interest to any student of education and culture, as the only mass communications medium which effectively crosses frontiers and perhaps the most potent force by which one modern culture influences another."[76] Finally, film was a burgeoning humanist art form, which was seen to be able to express and transmit the soul of a people, the essence of a culture.

After the war there was a groundswell of support in Canada for the United Nations and its specialized agencies. "After 1945," writes Maria Tippett, "Western governments particularly developed a strong attachment to the idea that they could be used in the fostering of the habits, outlook, and life-patterns those governments preferred. UNESCO was created partly in the service of this idea, and, in time, individual nations introduced their own programs ... to aid the attainment of this goal."[77] In July 1947 the advisory committee of the U.N. Association in Canada held a meeting of fifty interested groups at the University of Toronto.[78] "Immediately after the meeting of October 23, 1947, the film 'Hungry Minds' ... was produced at the National Film Board in Ottawa in the remarkably short time of six weeks ... This film was given the most ex-

Hungry Minds (1947, Tom Daly) was made to support the educational aims of UNESCO.

tensive distribution ever reached by one film in Canada, and it is esti-mated that nearly 5,000,000 people saw it during the campaign."[79] *Hungry Minds* publicity material reflected the UNESCO outlook, stating, "War begins in the minds of men – and the minds of children too, whose young bodies grow hungry for food and whose young minds grow warped for lack of education."[80]

After being fired from the NFB in 1945, Grierson decamped for Paris, where he became UNESCO's director of mass communications and public information.[81] At the first UNESCO meeting on mass media and international culture, Grierson gave an address in which he linked strong mass media infrastructure to national reconstruction and devel-opment.[82] Echoing the strategy of empire communications for non-com-mercial and non-theatrical film, the film subcommission recommended that UNESCO act as an international clearing house of information but warned that its success depended entirely on individual national ef-forts: "UNESCO could only act efficiently as an International Clearing

House if each country has a national film information center or national film committee."[83] Grierson and Basil Wright drafted a plan for the production of a series of films on UNESCO subjects by "national film-producing groups" for international distribution.[84] True to the ideas about representative typicality that dominated Grierson's view of documentary, the proposal included a list of films to be "produced by member countries about their own 'specialities'; e.g. French cooking, English landscape painting."[85]

The Canadian delegation to the meeting to draw up a constitution for UNESCO, which took place in London on 1 November 1945, consisted of Robert Wallace, an adult educator and NFS stalwart; Edmond Turcotte, editor of *Le Canada*, a former member of the NFB and later a member of the Fowler Commission; and Vincent Massey, who was finishing up his term as Canada's high commissioner to Britain.[86] The Canadian team was already well aware of the uses of new media such as film and radio for adult education. There could be no objection from this group to the UNESCO principles of advancing "mutual knowledge and understanding of peoples, through all means of mass communication ... to give fresh impulse to popular education and to the spread of culture, [and to] maintain, increase and diffuse knowledge."[87]

Regarding the relations of the Canadian government agencies with UNESCO, McLean wrote in the NFB submission to the Massey Commission:

After the war, NFB was among the first of the documentary film producers to apply an international approach to peacetime themes. A number of pictures produced in the first two post-war years supported the United Nations Organization and particular agencies of the U.N. In some cases, film productions have been commissioned directly by the United Nations Public Information Office, or by specialized U.N. agencies. These films were designed both for Canadian and International distribution ... Films and filmstrips have been produced and distributed dealing with UNESCO, UNRRA, FAO, ILO, ITO, and U.N. as a whole; personnel has on occasion assisted special United Nations projects, and opportunities for workshop study have been offered to fellowship holders, students and visitors from other countries. It is submitted that any body which may be established by the Canadian government as an official liaison channel to UNESCO, should include senior representation from NFB.[88]

The Massey Commission's final report contains the assertion that "the exchange of information and cultural goods with other countries has become an essential activity of the modern state. In the case of Canada it is important for trade reasons, but there are also less tangible results in terms of improved understanding which must also be earnestly sought."[89] And the usefulness of the NFB for adult education is corroborated: "In a democratic state, national effort in war and national unity in peace are maintained only by the informed conviction of its citizens. No democratic government can afford to neglect at any time a means of public information so far-reaching and so persuasive as film. The provision and distribution of films by the national government is as little open to question as the issue of the white paper or the blue book."[90] Although McLean was let go soon after, his replacement, Arthur Irwin, editor of *Maclean's* magazine, was also involved with UNESCO, having represented Canada at the U.N. Conference on Freedom of Information and of the Press at Geneva in 1948.[91]

The recommendation for the establishment of the Canada Council, in many ways the culmination of the Massey Report and widely considered the commission's only substantive recommendation, was originally a call for a council for arts, letters, humanities, and social sciences to serve as a catch-all for the problems set out for the commission to solve, including relations with UNESCO. "We ... recommend," stated the report, "that a body be created ... to stimulate and help voluntary organizations within these fields, to foster Canada's cultural relations abroad, to perform the functions of a national commission for UNESCO, and to devise and administer a system of scholarships."[92] The Canada Council was also mandated to call an annual national UNESCO affairs conference and "take appropriate measures to extend the knowledge in Canada of UNESCO's purposes and programmes" as well as bringing Canadian needs to the attention of UNESCO by way of External Affairs.[93]

External Affairs was strongly behind the use of educational film for such ends, as long as its department took the lead.[94] During his stint at External Affairs, Lester Pearson suggested to Ross McLean that a film be made on Canada and the United Nations as part of a larger media campaign to "make Canada's role in international relations better known, both at home and abroad." He explained, "I think there can be little doubt that it is very much in the national interest to use all forms of information available to assist Canadians to become better acquainted with

their country's part in world affairs. This view was very strongly emphasized at the recent Conference of the Canadian Association for Adult
Education."[95]

In Canada, a series of films was produced over the next few years, including French and English versions of *Introducing Canada* (1956), to
fulfill this international communications objective. Other Canadian-
made films associated with the United Nations and the British Commonwealth during this period include UNRRA: *In the Wake of Armies*
(1944); *Now – the Peace* (about the U.N., 1945); *Guilty Men* (International Courts of Justice, 1945); *Suffer Little Children* (1945); *The
Peace Builders* (1945); *Canada, World Trader* (1946); *Out of the Ruins*
(UNRRA, 1946); *Everyman's World* (1946); *The People Between* (1947);
Common Concern (FAO, 1947); *I.L.O.* (International Labor Organization, 1947); *Stuff for Stuff* (multilateral trade, 1948); *Maps We Live By*
(1948); *The Road to World Peace* (1950); *Thunder in the East* (1950);
The New South Asia (1953); *Sight and Sound* (1954); *The Common-
wealth of Nations: A Study in Thirteen Parts* (1957); *Overture* (1958);
On Guard with UNEF (1959); *U.N. in the Classroom* (1959); *New Voices* (1961); *Tomorrow Begins Today* (1962); *You Are Welcome Sirs, to
Cyprus* (1964); and *Postmark* UNEF (1965). Films made by the U.N.
film service itself, such as *The General Assembly* (about the United Nations, 1962), *The Trusteeship Council and System* (1962), *The Security
Council* (about the United Nations, 1963), and *International Court of
Justice* (1964), remain in the NFB catalogue to this day.

In 1950 Stanley Jackson directed a film called *Our Town Is the World*,
which used the allegory of children fighting to make broader conclusions about the tolerance for difference and the need to respect the Universal Declaration of Human Rights as laid down by the United Nations.
The film originally used boys of French and English descent and portrayed the conflict as linguistic and cultural. This script was quashed by
the NFB for fear it would portray Canada to an international community as a country unable to reconcile its ethnic groups. The story was duly
changed to a conflict between children from two sides of a river. "Our
town is the world now," concludes the narrator, "and if we are to live,
we must live in peace." This image well sums up the vision of Canada
promoted by government realism: typical yet anonymous people and
places crafted into allegories of citizen and nation building. In the cold
war this function took on new importance, despite the increasing dominance of national broadcasting over film.

Introducing Canada (1956, Tom Daly) was made as a national profile requested of all U.N. member countries.

The avuncular newspaper editor of *Our Town Is the World* (1950, Stanley Jackson) advises two warring groups of boys about the substance of the U.N. Charter, which he keeps handy on the wall of his office.

CONCLUSION

In his article "The Cultural Industries Policy Apparatus," Kevin Dowler argues that the rationale for state-funded Canadian culture in the 1950s was national security.[96] Following Maurice Charland, he posits that the cultural agencies of the 1950s constituted a "simulated civil society."[97] While it appears to be true that the NFB of the 1950s was bound up in security discourses of the cold war, I think that its simulation of a civil society may be seen as productive rather than empty. What this period appears to have produced, in fact, was an engaging dialogue between official needs for NFB films and films that Canadians could imagine making and watching. *Neighbours* is a good example of how a filmmaker can use the confines of an official mandate to make evocative art. More generally, the philosophy of film and citizenship was closely linked to spaces for discussion and education. Rather than bemoan the absence of an ideal civil society or a disinterested public sphere, it seems more instructive to think about how and why real, perhaps compromised, spaces were actually planned and brought into being.

In both content and nation-building philosophy, the NFB supported the aims of UNESCO and the Massey Commission. This was consistent with the philosophy of the interwar and wartime use of media for education and nation building. These connections help explain the endurance of the NFB after the scandals of the cold war. But the connection between the NFB and UNESCO was not limited to film on international subjects. Canada had its own international problems at home in the shape of immigrants and First Nations people. It is to this citizenship work that I turn next.

FIVE

Pages from the Story of the Way We Live: Film and Citizenship in the 1950s and Early 1960s

This institution does and must, I feel, play a vital part in making Canadians conscious of their country and what is going on in it. Canada is vast and complex. Few of us have the chance to see more than a small part of it, but through the eyes of your cameras we can get to know every nook and cranny. Your imagination and skill can link our people more closely together and give us an awareness of our country and our own identity.
– Vincent Massey, at the official opening of the National Film Board in Montreal, 27 January 1956[1]

If what I have been calling government realism was concerned with a particular way of seeing the population as material to be managed, citizenship has been one of the most important discourses and outcomes of this approach. In 1952, after the reprieve of the Massey Commission, responsibility for the National Film Board was transferred from the Ministry of Reconstruction and Supply (1945–48) and Resources and Development (1949–51), where it went after the war, to the newly minted Ministry of Citizenship and Immigration, where it stayed for the next decade. In governmentality theory, citizenship is seen to be concerned with a self-disciplining subject for whom cultural policy and education play crucial roles. From this perspective it is instructive that postwar NFB practice was based not only on stories about typical ordinary Canadians but also on non-theatrical screenings supposed to spur discussion of citizenship issues. In this chapter, I try to show connections between the Canadian state's information and communication policy in the postwar period and theories of citizenship. One of the key issues in the historical record of this period is that of cultural difference, and this theme was made very clear in NFB films. Along with francophone filmmaking, which picked up steam during these decades, films about cultural minorities were often made by people from the same – or similar – cultural backgrounds as their subjects. (The shift to identity-based filmmaking did not occur until much later, in the 1980s and 1990s.) Nevertheless, whoever they were made by, NFB films about citizenship reinforce a view of government realism: citizens face typical problems and their lives stand in by implication for those of many others. The postwar phenomenon of the teenager was a target for citizenship training, and the films of the era reflect this demographic challenge.

FIRST NATIONS AND IMMIGRATION:
CITIZENSHIP AND LABOUR IN THE COLD WAR

Given that the postwar NFB, in conjunction with film societies, took two approaches to non-theatrical screenings – one for the middle class and another for those who were creating problems for the state – I turn now to examine representations of two "difficult" groups: First Nations and immigrants. Attention was paid to "ethnics" and workers precisely because they were problematic categories of citizenship; films were made to address their place in Canadian society.

First Nations
The production of films about First Nations followed federal Indian policy closely. Since the establishment of the Indian Act in 1884, many native practices had been criminalized and native children were taken from their homes and placed in residential schools in an attempt to assimilate them forcibly. From the outset, NFB films romanticized native customs as vanishing folkways. Director Laura Boulton alone made more than a dozen films for the NFB in the early 1940s, primarily on folkloric or ethnographic subjects.[2] Boulton was particularly interested in "primitive" artifacts and rituals, and both of these figure prominently in her films. One example of her work about aboriginal culture (she also made

films about Quebec and Prairie lives) is *Totems* (1944), which like many NFB films from this period begins with a map. Aboriginal art figures prominently on it, presumably locating different tribes, and an anglophone male voice-over adopts the outsider's perspective as he describes the sophistication of the kind of metaphoric language totem poles use, calling them "great art." Awkward shots pan up the poles, followed by a series of nature scenes, such as ants swarming and flowers blooming.

Another Boulton film, *Eskimo Arts and Crafts* (1944), enlisted as a consultant the famous ethnographer of *Nanook*, Robert Flaherty. The film begins with a map of Canada. It then zooms in on the Eastern Arctic. A male voice-over speaks about the resourcefulness of the "Eskimo" in this seemingly barren land. Scenes of kayaking and boat building are shown. Women make mukluks and kayak covers. On the soundtrack, women are heard speaking, but there is no translation. Men are shown carving ivory to the accompaniment of a man singing on the soundtrack. In a drum-making episode, the narrator rhapsodizes about the long winters and the need for forgetfulness that dancing can provide. Wrestling is shown and characterized as "primitive" and "Oriental." "It came with the Eskimo when they came from Siberia," the narrator says.

As in many of Boulton's films, there is very little structure to *Eskimo Arts and Crafts*. Scenes are strung together without logic, and the soundtrack is often unrelated to the image. Both of these films send a conflicted message about Canada's aboriginal peoples. We are informed that they are immigrants ("they came from Siberia"), which places them in the general category of Canadian. However, their preindustrial lives seem entirely other to the national project of well-managed modernization seen in so many representations of Canada from the period. Aboriginal people are depicted as being as close to nature as flowers and insects. Nevertheless the films, for all their problematic intentions and results, do succeed in conveying something of the untranslated and untranslatable lives of the subjects. What little there is of the sporadic narration is hardly able to contain the sounds and images, and unlike Flaherty in his *Nanook of the North* (1922), the filmmaker does not attempt to root the presentation of ethnography in the story of a heroic individual. Nevertheless, it would be a misrepresentation of Boulton's work to impute cultural sensitivity. She was clearly fascinated with recording the picturesque and folkloric aspects of native culture before it inevitably made way for modern life.

The integration of aboriginal people into modern life is the thrust of *Peoples of the Skeena* (1949). An anglophone male voice-over explains that modern aboriginal children are like any other Canadians. There is an imperative that the "Indian must understand the white man's world and live in it." A wedding, which uses Christian costumes and customs, is shown as evidence of the aboriginal peoples' will to assimilate: "All along the Skeena you can see changes in the lives of its Indian peoples. They're making their own way; they're taking a full part in the life of this country from the Rocky Mountains to the coast of the Pacific." Although made only five years after *Totems*, this film locates aboriginal people as "modern" citizens. However, the price for citizenship is the renouncing of the traditions and customs of their culture.

Emerging out of the wartime Canadian Council for Education-in-Citizenship and amalgamating the departments of citizenship, immigration, and Indian affairs, the Department of Citizenship and Immigration came into force at the beginning of 1950 with the objective of making Canadian citizens out of immigrants and aboriginal people. A new Indian Act followed in 1951.[3] A 1955 background paper put it as follows:

I believe it is the policy of all members of the House to attempt to have the Indian Affairs Branch administered in such a way as to bring the original inhabitants of Canadian territory to citizenship as quickly as that can reasonably be accomplished. It was felt that it would have some psychological effect to say that these three activities dealing with human beings, and designed to bring these human beings to the status of full citizenship as rapidly as possible, were under the one head ... Having Citizenship, Immigration, and Indian Affairs in one Department would indicate that the purpose of the activities of that Department was to make Canadian citizens of those who were born here of the original inhabitants of the territory, or those who migrated to this country.[4]

As responsibility for administering the Indian Act was moved to the Department of Citizenship and Immigration in the 1950s, new representations of the relationship between the First Nations and the state were required. "The branch became more involved with Native Indians and Métis as more of them began to leave reserves for urban areas. The branch could quite easily accommodate this new responsibility by conceiving of it as simply a matter of 'internal migration,' an analogue of

Peoples of the Skeena (1949, James Beveridge) looked at aboriginal Canadians becoming "modern" citizens. This image depicts the lingering practices of self-sufficiency.

overseas migration."[5] In 1954, on an initiative of the Department of Indian Affairs, work began on a film that became *No Longer Vanishing* (1955). Colonel H.M. Jones, director of Indian Affairs Information Division, sent out a call to government workers across Canada to inform him of "successful initiatives," noting, "We will not, of course, be able to use all this material in one short film! It will have to be carefully studied and a selection made of those items that give representation to the greatest variety of activities and to as many areas of Canada as possible." Using the strategy of typicality, the department aimed to make a film that would be of use to aboriginals and non-aboriginals alike: "This film will be designed primarily to show the non-Indian population of Canada the extent to which Indians have adapted themselves to the modern Canadian economy, becoming self-supporting and useful members of the

No Longer Vanishing (1955, Grant McLean) was made in conjunction with
Indian Affairs to correspond with government assimilation policy.

Canadian society. At the same time it is hoped that such a film will be
useful among the Indians themselves, to promote pride in their own
achievements, and to encourage some of the less progressive to make
greater efforts toward self-advancement."[6]

The writer, Norman Klenman, offered the NFB two possible scenarios: the survey documentary, which would convey a range of facts, or
the story, which would appeal to the emotions. The dichotomy gets to
the heart of narrative strategies of government documentary:

It may be the Department's view that what is missing from the Canadian view
of Indians is not facts but interest; that facts themselves are just facts, competing in the minds of Canadians for attention with masses of other facts,
poured out by newspapers and magazines and quiz shows and television and
movies and speeches. It may be that the Department's aim in this film is to

interest the people of Canada in the Indian and his problem, make under-standing of the Indian and his problem easier, and show – as a by-product of the film – the Indian himself how his brother has met his problem and solved it and made his own life better. If this general approach is more descriptive of the Department's aims then the survey-documentary is in my view not the most useful form to use. Another form to consider is the story film, short or long. This kind of film deals with a more limited scope, but it deals with it in depth. It cannot deal with every situation or problem affecting, for example, the Indians (neither can the survey-documentary – the difference is of num-ber), but it can deal most effectively with a few representative situations. The facts themselves emerge between the lines; the problems emerge naturally from the characters and the situations. No problems are solved easily in the last reel but – as in life – only with pain and trouble and time. The effect on the audience in electrically different to that of the by-now-hackneyed survey-documentary. Not a mild dose of facts, but people and their troubles, rouse an audience to its highest pitch of interest and sympathy. Facts are abstract; delightful, of course, to the curious; mildly satisfying to the great mass of us. But the honest, sympathetic presentation of people – sad, happy, alive, mis-erable, troubled, smug, delightful – awake and move us.[7]

In the event, Grant McLean wrote the script and directed the film, though the Department of Indian Affairs had the final say: "Some of the ideas expressed by Mr. McLean may not be in accord with the policies of the Branch; that is something that can be discussed with the Board representatives at the proposed meeting. On the other hand, we should not worry at this stage if Mr. McLean has used terms and expressions which are not completely acceptable to the Branch. There will be ample opportunity to go over the final commentary word by word before any-thing is recorded on film. What we must consider at the moment is whether this treatment, and the visuals suggested by Mr. McLean, will be a satisfactory vehicle to convey the information and the ideas that the Branch wishes to establish."[8]

In the final government-approved version, an anglophone male voice-over says, "This is a story of the original Canadians who preceded the white man." Originally, we are told, reserves were designed to shelter natives while they learned the white man's ways; instead they stayed there. However, well-intentioned mistakes of the past can be rectified by goodwill today; the full value of aboriginal arts and culture is coming to be respected. Scenes of the reserve are acted out, highlighting poverty and filth: "Isolation, paternalism have hurt them, made them dependent." In voice-over, a First Nations man who has been away from the reserve describes his return visit. The "bitter Indians" refuse to believe that he does not experience discrimination in the city. A First Nations woman who has become a city nurse is interviewed. While she watches buffalo being fed at the zoo, she says in voice-over, "They've stopped dying out and are coming back, like our own people." According to the narrator, education in mixed schools is one of the best ways to help aboriginal people make the transition: "Old prejudices are falling away in mixed classes." As in films about immigrant groups, exceptional, assimilated First Nations people, such as doctors and judges, are introduced to the non-aboriginal viewer with a series of photographic portraits. After the film was seen by children at Wetmore School in Regina, the letters they sent the NFB were testament to the patronizing message of the film. One student wrote, "I enjoyed the film on Indians. I learned that the Indians are the same as we are except their skin is different! At our church they were packing clothes for the Indian Reserve. Now I know what it looks like. Thank you very much."[9]

Drawing an image from the contemporary public discussion about aboriginal Canadians, The Transition (1964), sponsored by the Indian Affairs branch of Citizenship and Immigration, is the story of a young First Nations man who moves away from the reserve to the wider Canadian society. Framed by his visit home after ten months in the city, this fictionalized story is told from the point of view of this aboriginal man, Jimmy. As he returns to the reserve, a white male voice-over tells us that Jimmy is a "bright light" in his aboriginal community and that he is returning to the reserve where there is nothing to do. Jimmy is torn between wanting to live in the world he knows and wanting to be a more fully contributing member of Canadian society. When he arrived in the city ten months ago, "he didn't keep a diary, of course," the narrator says, "but if he had, it would have sounded something like this." The film is thus explicitly structured around the fictionalized reflections of the "typical" man in question. From his fictive "diary," Jimmy speaks in voice-over of missing his family and feeling lonely. He attends a dance at a First Nations social club. As they dance, the camera freeze-frames on each young person so that the narrator can explain who they all are and how they "made the transition" to life in a wider society. "'Things are bad in the city because you're an Indian,' Jimmy says. He doesn't admit that he's made mistakes, too," the narrator tells us. Although there is a dominant message of assimilation, in the interplay between the various voice-overs, the film allows for different ways of thinking about aboriginal-state relations.

A final example is the Don Owen film *High Steel* (1965) about Mohawks from Gananoque, Quebec, working on steel construction in New York City. The film combines myths of both cowboys and Indians in the frontier-building image of the skyscrapers of New York's modern skyline. In presenting such sensational working conditions, the film takes a twist on typical occupations of typical Canadians. Nevertheless, the voice-over narrator gives a name and identifies himself as a "Mohawk Indian born in Gananoque, outside Montreal." Ask anyone in New York City, he challenges, and they'll tell you "those Indians are damn good iron workers." The film's soundtrack is composed largely of a country and western song sung by Bruce Mackay, "Mountains of Iron and Steel," which clearly combines the images of nature (mountains) and industry. The Gananoque aboriginals of the film are presented as curious subjects of modernity, both oppressed by it and excelling at its most extreme tasks. During a sequence of shots of the reserve, the narrator speaks about how important it is for him that his children get in touch with their roots on the reserve. Evoking a pastoral image, he remembers going hunting with his grandfather. But before this becomes a modernization/antimodernization dichotomy, he tells us that his grandfather was an ironworker too. The final section of the film is about the danger and death of this kind of work and, by extension, the limited opportunities of modernization for First Nations people. The story of a Quebec bridge on which dozens of Mohawks were killed when it collapsed as they were working on it is intercut with images of the graveyard on the reserve. Yet out of this disaster came the Mohawk tradition of steelworking. In the final scene, as workers are shown constructing a building in New York, there is a succession of rapid intercuts with sunny images of the reserve, including flowers and women and children. The home of a steelworker, it implies with irony, is both on the reserve and on top of the biggest building in New York.

Of the many films about aboriginal Canadians made by the NFB in the first two decades following the Second World War, *High Steel* demonstrates as well as any the attempt to understand a population in relation

Gananoque Mohawks work on mountains of iron
and steel in New York City in *High Steel* (1965,
Don Owen).

to the Canadian state as a whole. However, all the films I have discussed
demonstrate an active attempt to depict the indigenous population as a
part of the Canadian state plan, although that plan changed continually. What remains is the governmental rationality – and the government
realism – of providing a visual representation of this group for the wider
society to understand its relationship to them.

Immigrants

After 1901–11, the period 1951–61 was the decade of greatest immigration in Canadian history, the vast majority of people coming from Eastern Europe.[10] Refugees from cold war conflicts with communist states such as Hungary and Czechoslovakia were welcomed.[11] In this section, I shall examine how the discourses of cold war internationalism and the acculturation of European immigrants manifested themselves in NFB productions after the Massey Commission's reaffirmation of the NFB's mandate.

In 1953 a new immigration act came into effect, which categorized immigrants' desirability according to criteria such as race. Mackenzie King had made clear the state's position when the Citizenship Act was introduced in 1947: " With regard to the selection of immigrants, much has been said about discrimination. I wish to make it quite clear that Canada is perfectly within her rights in selecting the persons whom we regard as desirable future citizens ... There will, I am sure, be general agreement with the view that the people of Canada do not wish, as a result of mass immigration, to make a fundamental alteration in the character of our population." Accordingly, British subjects as well as French and American citizens were admissible upon application without sponsorship on being in "good health and of good character."[12] For others, sponsorship was often the price of admission – but not those from Asia. "Suitable" and "desirable" were often racially loaded euphemisms. Quotas kept the number of immigrants accepted from India, for example, to a meagre 150 per year; from Pakistan, only 100 were admitted annually.

In the aftermath of the pressures exerted by External Affairs after the war, the NFB attempted to bring its production into line with state objectives. Meeting with External Affairs officers in 1952, representatives of the NFB requested policy guidance on film distribution and selection of films for foreign versions: "1. Should there be a particular emphasis on certain areas? 2. What themes should be emphasized or avoided in various areas? 3. What subjects are of particular importance for foreign language versions?" The NFB was encouraged to follow the Department of Immigration's emphasis on the United Kingdom, Western Germany, and Scandinavia, avoiding Italy, Japan, and Southeast Asia. Indeed, films "emphasizing our high standard of living" were not to be shown in Japan for fear of attracting unwanted immigrants. While the Department of Trade and Commerce was concentrating its attention on Latin

America, it was thought that "from the political point of view, the greatest information emphasis should be on Germany."[13] The liaison with the Department of National Defence suggested that films giving a general knowledge of Canada should be shown in countries where Canadian forces were stationed, such as Germany, Japan, France and all NATO countries, including Turkey and Greece.

Film production was linked directly to the cold war foreign policy of both the United States and Canada. Films emphasizing the "benefits of democratic processes of Government and democratic institutions" were seen to be a preferable alternative to "direct propaganda." To that end, NFB films about the administered and organized state were expanded and extended in the cold war context. Where the United States government spent millions of dollars in the 1950s on filmmaking, Canada's National Film Board was already in place to fulfill this aspect of the country's postwar propaganda work. In the fall of 1950, the under-secretary of state for external affairs suggested to Arthur Irwin that as the U.S. State Department had been given a budget of some $12 million to produce pro-democracy films for use in countries facing "communist pressure," "you may wish to consider the advisability for Canada of making a similar effort, on a reduced scale, in order that our film activities abroad may support more efficiently the political, economic and military aspects of our external policy."[14] The outcome of this initiative was the *Freedom Speaks* series.[15]

Films produced at the NFB were to be weapons used both in Canada and abroad to fight communism. Not only were films about immigrants circulated for domestic purposes, but films and filmstrips about Canada were used in Europe to attract displaced persons living in refugee camps. Particular films were *Canada from Sea to Sea* (1956), *Peoples of Canada* (1941), *Building for Tomorrow* (1947), and *Trans-Canada Express* (1944),[16] which was later withdrawn on the advice of the International Refugee Organization that it was "unsuitable."[17] The content of *Canada from Sea to Sea* was partly determined on the basis of questionnaires sent to Canadian foreign posts asking, "(a) What aspects of the Canadian scene are of greatest interest to your audience? (b) Upon what particular aspects of the Canadian scene do you wish your audience to become informed?"[18] Filmstrips included *The Canadian People, A Loaf of Bread, This Is the Milk That we Drink*, and *Internal Triangle*.[19]

Films on child health and welfare were distributed to the World Health Organization.[20]

The films were linked directly to immigration policy in terms both of content and of distribution. A 1952 note on the subject of NFB film distribution in Europe drew attention to the general lack of history in favour of geography:

> I wonder ... if too much emphasis has not perhaps been laid on Canadian geography and not any on Canada's historical development. If Canada's constitutional position is occasionally misunderstood at the Council of Europe, such misconceptions must be fairly widespread among the European "masses." A film on this subject and on Canada's international position (e.g. our role in the Colombo Plan, the extent of our NATO effort, our traditional concern for world affairs as witnessed by our participation in the two world wars) are examples of what might be desirable from a general prop[aganda] point of view. Ignorance concerning Canada relates not so much to its geographic vastness but rather to its economic and political importance, yet I think it is probably true to say that the Film Board has tended to emphasize "geography" in their productions.[21]

Good immigrants are the subject of many films highlighting Canada's tolerance of difference in the postwar world. In 1949, for example, *Canada Carries On* presented *Passport to Canada* (1949), a film with a vision of Canada as a multicultural utopia. Beginning with the usual platitudes about Canada as a land of immigrants, the film proceeds to discuss the current influx of so-called displaced persons emigrating to Canada in great numbers from Europe: "They come to live a new life.

In *Passport to Canada* (1949, Roger Blais), enthusiastic immigrants from Eastern Europe are shown learning about Canada in an adult education classroom.

They come here for peace, freedom and a bit of permanence." Immigrants are shown in the customs office and speeding to their destination on trains. Voice-overs by people with different accents express hope and excitement. An anglophone male voice-over explains the use of adult education for language and the Canadian way of life. Like *Peoples of Canada*, the film ends with a scene of a teacher addressing her class about the similarity of all peoples around the world, regardless of superficial differences, as close-ups show students looking on hopefully.

Sponsored by the Department of Citizenship and Immigration, *The Newcomers* (1953) reiterates the message of most 1950s films about immigrants: white European immigrants bring both willingness to start again (a desirable feature in an immigrant) and a knowledge of European culture (a desirable feature in a Canadian). The film offers a possible narrative of integration for immigrants. However, it is also geared to the general population. The information sheet issued with the film suggests the film's appropriateness for the following possible audiences: "any adult audience, for secondary school students, and especially those groups concerned in any way with immigration or the contributions of new Canadians."²² The film was released on rural circuits in English and French in the winter of 1953–54 and was circulated to film councils and to clubs such as the Lions and the Imperial Order Daughters of the Empire. All told, it was screened 1,890 times, including being broadcast on CKCK Regina in August 1954, and reportedly it had been seen by 129,600 people by September 1954. It was also shown to immigration officials, who "approved of the showings of actual individuals who are making good."²³

As in such films as *Women at Work* (1958) and *Why Canada?* (1965), the economic benefits of immigrants were emphasized in *The Newcomers*: "Canada is less dependent upon external sources for trade; immigrants are a vast new market." As was emphasized by citizenship education lobby groups such as the Canadian Council for Education-in-Citizenship, rural schools were depicted as important links in enculturation, teaching immigrant children Canadian ways. The film both provides citizenship education and demonstrates the apparatus of such pedagogy. Films such as this demystify the work of the government and its institutions in the daily life of the population. The film ends with the refrain that Canada is a nation of immigrants: "All Canadian families come from across the sea." This statement, commonly echoed in multiculturalist education, tends to confuse, even while pretending to clarify, the politics and the history of the Canadian "mosaic."

As D.B. Jones puts it, the sponsored films were the unwanted films, but most of the famous Unit B films of the 1950s were sponsored.[24] *Corral* (1954) and *Paul Tomkowicz: Street Railway Switchman* (1954) are described as the first NFB classics.[25] Both were made as part of the *Faces of Canada* series that is linked to the *Freedom Speaks* series. Both films provide portraits of men who are in some way typical of both their occupations and their regions. Although radically different from one another, they are related as part of a series that makes a statistical gesture toward covering different regions and types.

Paul Tomkowicz, directed by Roman Kroitor, is an example of pairing an immigrant with a typical occupation. Kroitor, of Slavic descent, was sent back to his hometown, Winnipeg, to make a film about an Eastern European immigrant. The film creates an opposition between the people riding the streetcar and the dark, snowy, and slightly dangerous space on the roads where Paul Tomkowicz works. Tomkowicz's alterity is emphasized by the fact that no one looks at or speaks to him for most of the film. He is an outsider. In voice-over he speaks about his past in Poland, the loss of his family. The light tone with which he discusses these topics is much the same as when he discusses the decline of the streetcar in favour of the new buses. This idea is emphasized visually by shots such as the one where he arrives at his breakfast diner by streetcar. As he gets off the streetcar after a long night of work, everyone else is pressing to get on it to go to work. Working all night is a visual metaphor for the inverse relationship that Tomkowicz has to the rest of Canadian life. In the final scene he eats his large breakfast and

A Polish immigrant in Winnipeg is shown to be a perpetual outsider in *Paul Tomkowicz: Street Railway Switchman* (1954, Roman Kroitor).

talks about his plans for retirement in voice-over. His plans to go "next year" seem undermined by the vague way in which he talks about his future. The title "The End" appears to deflate his possible future further. Throughout the film Tomkowicz is presented as someone from the past whose way of life is dying.

Often referred to because of its lyrical visual qualities, the film contains an interesting contradiction that is rarely mentioned. The subject of the film is shown working a night shift on the streets of Winnipeg while his thoughts are conveyed in voice-over. Paul Tomkowicz was indeed interviewed by Roman Kroitor, but because of sound problems with the original tape, the voice-over one hears was actually read by an uncredited actor.[26] This substitution is significant in that the actor's voice, directed by Kroitor, produces another delivery, another text, out of Tomkowicz's words. In that the immigrant represented is made into the imaginary immigrant by the government film institution, this film becomes a document of a mode of typification.

Colin Low's film *Corral* (1954) is another celebrated film in Canadian cinema that negotiates its relationship to government realism. In *Corral*, a single event, the breaking of a horse by a lone cowboy on the rolling plains of southern Alberta, stands in as a metonym for a way of life, a philosophy, and an attitude to the land. Organized around the first perilous ride of an unbroken horse, accompanied only by the sound of solo guitar music written by Eldon Rathburn, the film explains nothing about why and says simply, and in some timeless way, "This is." Partly this is because the cowboy simply appears at the beginning, corrals wild horses, breaks one and lets the others go, and then rides off into the horizon.

The region and culture film found many forms. *Frontier College* (1954) is a good example of the demonstration of the role that the conscientious Canadian can play in educating adult immigrants. The story concerns a typical college student who is awakened to his larger civic duties by becoming a continuing education instructor on a railway construction site for the summer. The railway camp is divided between men of Canadian origin and immigrants from Italy and Germany who are in conflict at the camp. As the two groups grow to trust their teacher, he is able to help them overcome their conflicts through learning about Canadian ways. This development is expressed metaphorically by the immi-

Corral (1954, Colin Low) is both a piece of lyrical abstraction and a film about region and occupation.

grants replacing their home-country songs – discordant when sung simultaneously – with an indigenous railway song learned in class: "I've Been Working on the Railroad." *Frontier College* emphasizes the link between citizenship and education and stresses the importance of overcoming ethnic and sectional differences. Culture is depicted in both an anthropological sense, as that which differentiates the immigrants from the Canadian narrator, and as something ennobling and universal, which may be taught through art appreciation and the learning of Canadian ways. The two senses of the word meet in the schoolroom, where Italian immigrants are invited to share the appreciation of Italian high art forms, such as opera, with the class. In effect, the protagonist-narrator serves to sort out which elements of the workers' home "cultures" may be successfully maintained in Canada. Perhaps most importantly, loyal citizenship, or the forging of national allegiance, in Charles Merriam's terms, is seen to be a site of national stability and even defence.

Eastern European immigrants are introduced to Canadian ways at their children's school in *Threshold: The Immigrant Meets the School* (1959, George Bloomfield).

In the "making of citizens" rhetoric of the social sciences, children are the key to integration. This story is shown in many NFB films. *Threshold: The Immigrant Meets the School* (1959) – a film sponsored by the Ministry of Citizenship and Immigration from an idea originally provided by the chairman of the Federation of Home and School Associations[27] – shows immigrants adapting to life in Canada. Indeed, an internal communication about the film suggests that it is geared at the "immigrant parent": "The purpose of the film is to invite the immigrant parent to revise his traditional attitude and to work towards a more objective appreciation of things. This should be the film's implied message."[28] The sympathetic anglophone narrator observes, "The children are adapting faster than the parents can or will." The family goes through "the period of tension" that afflicts many immigrants. Mrs Martin, a fictional member of the home and school association, a voluntary civic group, invites the parents to participate in improving report cards. The immigrant mother decides to get involved.

The script was shown to Elisabeth Czeija of the Canadian Association for Adult Education and to Jean Boucher of the Citizenship Branch of the Department of Citizenship and Immigration. Boucher expressed doubt that the "average immigrant will recognize himself in the Maggs," the film's typical family. Boucher also suggested that the film should make clear that "acculturation in Canada is not solely a newcomer's problem but a more or less permanent characteristic of our very national life."[29] As was usual procedure with sponsored films, the film was approved by the minister of the department concerned before it was released.[30] Upon release, the film was shown in Vancouver to members of the Parent-Teacher Association, to the audiovisual director at the University of British Columbia, United Nations Association, the Citizenship Branch of the Vancouver Public Library, and the YWCA.[31] Comments included the following:

- "Realistic in presenting problems of new Canadians. Particularly liked presentation of young people's quick adaptation to new ways and parents reluctance to part with old. Excellent solution (wish it were a typical one)."
- "For our organization [YWCA], it could be used in several ways. (1) In the orientation course to our volunteers who work with newcomers. (2) With the newcomers themselves. I think it could be the basis for a good discussion group of our more advanced students. (3) With our 'Canadian groups' as we work toward better understanding of the newcomers in our Association and community."
- "PTA, Church Groups, Women's Institutes, Women's Organizations, Teachers' groups, Ethnic Groups. I am sure the film would create lively discussions amongst immigrant groups and it would be a good proof that Canadians do care."[32]

Many films about labour in the 1950s also have an immigration angle. In the early 1950s a series of films about newly legitimate labour unions were made in conjunction with the Trades and Labor Congress of Canada for presentation in the industrial film circuits.[33] Chris Whynot has noted that both the Canadian Congress of Labour and the Trades and Labor Congress had adopted a strictly anticommunist policy by 1950, which helps explain both the films and their tone.[34] The *Labour in Canada* series indicates the prototypical model of welfare state cooperation.

The Clerk (1958, Morten Parker), one of the *Nature of Work* series exploring the anxieties of work

The labour films made by the NFB "absorbed the unions into the new vision of the liberal social order."[35] *Dues and the Union* (1953) – made with the help of Local 46 of the Journeymen and Plumbers and Steamfitters of United States and Canada – is a social drama in which a young worker learns the value of his union by taking it for granted and almost losing it. Although the message ultimately serves to promote the "middle way," the film does succeed in expressing the social solidarity of the union members. Another instalment in the series, *The Grievance* (1954), was sponsored by the Canadian Congress of Labour, the Department of Labour, and General Motors, and takes place in a GM assembly plant. Directed at an audience of manual labourers, a colloquial male voice-over asks series of hypothetical questions: What if one of your co-workers says this or that? Is that a grievance? Although the films in this series support membership in a trade union, their central message is that labour should cooperate with management.

Each film in the six-part *Nature of Work* series (1958) – *The Man on the Assembly Line, The Clerk, The Skilled Worker*, and others – profiles a typical worker, focusing on the stresses particular to his job. Following each dramatized story, H.D. Woods, a professor of industrial relations, and one of the authors of the 1950 report on the administrative structure of the NFB,[36] gives a short, expert commentary addressed to students of "industrial relations" on how to keep employees happy and business thriving. Despite the explicit framing by a management perspective, many of these stories are nevertheless committed to showing the human face of a dehumanized work environment. The skilled worker, for example, is an immigrant from Eastern Europe who is devastated to find that his skills have been superseded by the imperatives of industrial manufacturing. All of the films about labourers confronting the difficulties of both the fact of labour and the shifting labour market express the contradictions inherent in the welfare state, where the much-vaunted free agency of liberal democracy is sacrificed to the market system and the stopgap measures of the welfare state.

THE TEENAGER

As Brian Low has outlined in his study NFB *Kids: Portrayals of Children by the National Film Board of Canada, 1939–1989*, the mental hygiene movement of the early part of the twentieth century had a huge impact on theories of education and child rearing. Much of this social scientific knowledge was an attempt to modernize, and thereby delegitimize, traditional ways of raising children. To that end, the discourses of developmental psychology, education, psychiatry, nutrition, leisure, and recreation can be found in many postwar NFB films in which children feature.[37] The teenager is showcased in many films of the late 1940s and 1950s, often in semi-fictional scenarios. In *V is for Volunteers*, for example, one of the strong reasons given for volunteering is keeping open a neighbourhood community centre that caters to youth.

Many films run over the normal stages attendant on growing up. *Ages and Stages*, made by Crawley Films for the NFB in the late 1940s, lets parents know directly that although they may love their children, they probably don't understand them. A series of dramas are acted out by children representing the ages one, two, four, ten, and fifteen. In voice-over, the parents ask anxious questions about whether their children are behaving normally. The narrator responds by reassuringly recommending social science books and films to which parents can turn for advice. "Research shows they go through definite stages: Children act their age," he says.

The series continued with *The Teens* (1957) and *Sixteen to Twenty-Six* (Crawley/NFB), sponsored by the Mental Health Division of the Department of National Health and Welfare and the Division of Venereal Disease Control of the Department of National Health and Welfare, respectively. In *The Teens*, the voices of narrator, mother and children are contrasted against one another. Mrs O'Conner is annoyed on return from her hospital volunteer work to find her thirteen-year-old son Timmy eating the pie she has made for dinner. The narrator explains that teenagers are by nature exceptionally hungry. Timmy's older sister Joan is bookish, much to her mother's disapproval. Dad is less worried about the kids. Barry, Joan's twin, is "a chip off the old block" – athletic and a bit pig-headed. Both older teens are shown in various scenarios of dating and exploring their sexuality, to the approval of the narrator, who argues that teens need freedom and guidance. The film ends with the happy modern family gathered around the television.

Sixteen to Twenty-Six gets closer to the subject of sex, through the eugenic language of public health and fear about venereal disease. A serious-looking older man sits behind a desk lecturing about gonorrhea and syphilis, one of the oldest "scourges of mankind." Modern young women need healthy bodies, he explains. A period of their lives when they work in factories, offices, and shops should not ruin their future health and happiness as married women: "When she is married one day, she will need to be healthy to raise a family." Animated damage is shown being done to ovaries by gonorrhea. "A couple planning marriage should always have a blood test so they may be confident of each other's health." Without once addressing sexual pleasure, the film manages to convey the dangers of young adulthood and to harness the economic freedom of young women to the anxieties about settling down with the right man.

Other films consider teenagers' seeming resistance to the demands of adult life. Many films were left open-ended, like the 1940s discussion

Joe and Roxy (1957, Don Haldane): teenagers as civic bellwethers

trailers, expressly to stimulate discussion about sensitive topics after the screening was over. *Joe and Roxy* (1957), directed by Don Haldane, is a drama that illustrates the issues of teenage love and gives teenage viewers a chance to debate how much intimacy is appropriate for seventeen year olds. The film is divided into a series of episodes showing the relationship between two teens, while the male voice-over muses about what is shown and offers avuncular advice on life, such as "Moods change swiftly at seventeen." The film presents Joe and Roxy in their respective family contexts and shows them making decisions about career and marriage. Roxy has a single, working mother who dissuades her from becoming serious about anyone. Joe's dad lectures him on college and career choices. The voice-over in the script, written by Gordon Burwash, makes wry comments on society, noting, for example, that ideas are rarely profitable in our world. In a scene depicting cheerleaders chanting, the narrator bemoans the superficiality of education. In the end, the narrator concludes that although Joe and Roxy's fates are unknown, what is certain is that education reflects society and that teens imitate the adults around them.

As Canada's baby boomers came of age in the 1950s, many films featured youth as potentially shiftless and in need of direction. The films often took an understanding attitude to the hormonally chaotic life of young people. But clear biological and social threats were made for those who transgressed. Nevertheless, the films reflected a certain amount of understanding that temptations and problems existed in the lives of young people, and despite the conservative message of most of them, images of single mothers and immigrant families showed that there was a range of experiences of growing up Canadian. In all these documentary dramas, single stories stood in for typical cases and statistical norms, and voice-over narrators helped to anchor the ambivalence of the stories in dominant readings.

CONCLUSION

Liberal internationalism permeated government cultural policy in the 1940s and 1950s. What had started off in the mid-1930s as a movement to use film to educate immigrants about Canadian citizenship had become, by the late 1940s and the 1950s, a cold war apparatus to demonstrate Canada's position in an ideologically polarized world. In this regard, immigrant selection and education had taken on new political importance. The ideas about culture prevalent in interwar internationalism had shifted to functionalist notions of nationalism and fundamental education in the postwar period.

Archival sources show what often seems to be a disproportionate amount of secrecy about NFB films, which appeared to be concerned with innocuous topics about the smooth functioning of everyday life. Appeal to the historical record shows that it was the conscious participation of the NFB in the administration of social life that led to the protection of the origin of its ideas. So, regardless of whether the film concerned agricultural method, the Inuit way of life, the building of social housing, or the functioning of a trade union, the close connection of the sponsored films to government social policy made them sensitive documents by association.

Mired in cold war international and domestic policy, the 1950s films perhaps show most clearly government realism as a site of negotiation with official culture. Although positivist social science was in its golden era in terms of epistemological dominance and government support, there was also a sense of irony and despair in the vision of society being depicted. This may help contextualize the celebrated Unit B films, considered the first NFB classics. Although they engage with typification and observational social science, they also display a lyrical ambiguity. As I have tried to show, this makes the NFB films, both celebrated and prosaic, acts in the establishment of meaning around Canadian life as filtered through the grid of governmental reason.

Up to this point in the study, the NFB has worked in a symbiotic relationship with local, national, and international modernizing projects. In the next chapter, I examine the relationship of NFB films to the "new social policies" of the 1960s and 1970s. The governmental secrecy continued in new guises in the 1960s and beyond as the National Film Board was remade to reflect a new emphasis of the state on participatory citizenship and new social movements. In the final chapter, I shall consider the legacy of film and citizenship at the NFB in the new documentary of the 1980s and 1990s and in a reconfigured climate of cultural policy.

SIX

New Media and New Forms of Citizenship: The NFB in the 1960s and 1970s

While many community audiences still gather in Canada and a hundred other countries simply to be entertained and generally informed by NFB films, our community audiences are becoming increasingly sophisticated, knowledgeable and organized into groups interested in the intensive study of specific subjects, rather than in general information. These audiences want films that challenge and stimulate rather than didactically inform; they are far more inclined to use films to provoke discussion and investigation than to passively accept informative film essays.
–National Film Board, *Annual Report*, 1965–66

By the early 1960s, the National Film Board's mandate had become uncertain. Since the decline of the rural circuits, mediated nation building was increasingly being handled by broadcasting. Not only had the CBC become well established, but CTV, a private national network, had also begun operation. Talk in policy circles was turning to the lack of Canadian feature films, and by the end of the decade the Canadian Film Development Corporation had been established;[1] the concept of a national educational film producer was finding less support. A shift in government policy over the course of the 1960s rescued the NFB from its uncertain position and gave it a new lease on life. The new mandate reflected the shift in politics from the earlier period of Canadian citizenship discourse, which had been organized around eugenics, white settler nation building, and immigrant assimilation, to one built around the emergence of identity politics and the New Left. Quebec politics, First Nations politics, women's politics, student politics, and new immigration policies brought about a new array of social policies through which the state increased its governmental reach, administering and representing citizens with renewed vigour.

For the NFB, the most important policy shift in the 1960s was organized under the banner of *Challenge for Change* and *Société nouvelle*. The new program, which was developed in tandem with the new social policies, was based on the argument that participation in media projects could empower disenfranchised groups and that media representation might effectively bring about improved political representation. In 1967 the NFB submitted a proposal for "a program of film activities in the area of poverty and change." The proposal made special claims for film as a part of government policy: "In the course of its own work and its work for government departments and agencies, the National Film Board has come to believe that programs intended to eliminate causes of poverty in Canada could be greatly strengthened by a coordinated program of film activities. The eradication of poverty demands unorthodox ideas. Support for these ideas and, for radical measures based on them, demands new concepts of communication. For this purpose, film – used imaginatively and unequivocally – is the best medium of communication."[2]

Over the next decade and a half, the program sponsored a range of film activities with marginal communities: the poor, First Nations, and women. By the time the program was disbanded in 1980, eighty-three films had been made under its rubric.[3] The program incorporated the dissatisfaction of many of the young filmmakers associated with the NFB's sponsored films and also highlighted the role of filmmaker as social animator or social worker. Films and videos made on new portable equipment were introduced as part of the process of decision making, consciousness raising, and consensus building in communities across the country. The programs dovetailed with Prime Minister Pierre Trudeau's regionalization objectives, and new production and distribution facilities were opened in urban centres across the country.[4]

The new program emphasized social and generational change. With these shifts came related changes in film style. As stated in the 1968–69 annual report, the "current trend" in documentary film was "toward participation and dialogue." In this way, the *Challenge for Change* program was conceived to stimulate awareness, explore possible solutions, and "promote closer understanding between citizens and their elected representatives."[5] *Challenge for Change* was repeatedly justified as a new mode of democratic communication, allowing channels of access from citizen to government. In the 1960s, changes in techniques of government and shifts in social science were embodied in new documentary practices. But the statistical point of view of government realism was still readily apparent.

CONTINUITIES WITH THE NFB'S EARLIER MANDATE

The internal NFB communication about *Challenge for Change* emphasized the continuity with past mandates and ideas. Recalling the emphasis on discussion of films shown in industrial and rural circuits and in local film societies, *Challenge for Change* emphasized the role of media to catalyze discussion, as a possible "beginning in modifying attitudes."[6] Like earlier justifications of film as a tool of education, *Challenge for Change* highlighted film's ability to use emotion to express unorthodox ideas and to reach people with limited literacy. The organizers also emphasized the use of film to generate participation at the local level, thereby affecting community action. An early proposal suggested that a coordinated effort was necessary because "many aspects of national interest are involved – manpower, health, labour, rural redevelopment, housing, fisheries, agriculture, industry etc." Indeed, in a rhetorical manoeuvre that would have made Grierson proud, the authors made the argument of centralization and efficiency, suggesting that the program could help clarify "information objectives" for departments and thereby avoid wasteful duplication of film activities.

Following from its social science and policy genesis, the report divided potential film audiences into three distinct groups redolent of earlier NFB targeting for non-theatrical audiences: the "general public," "those involved in the poverty field," and "the poor." In each case, the objective was to acclimatize different groups to government intervention. "Films for the general public could develop understanding of and concern for poverty problems, prepare public opinion for unorthodox attacks on poverty, and generate support for government involvement in poverty programs ... But relatively few Category I films should be made. Mass audience films are unlikely to generate action (the prime need) and a surfeit of them could backfire (an affluent society does not like to be reminded of its sores)."[7] Even possible criticism of the state was anticipated. Films for those working with the poor were to "question conventional approaches to social problems and the 'establishment attitudes'" developed to deal with them: "This probing should be thorough and irreverent but also sympathetic. The chief aim should be to impel people to look at what they are doing in entirely new ways."

The end result was to be the elevation of the poor from their condition: "Public understanding, wise planning and dedicated field work will have few lasting effects unless the poor want to educate themselves, train themselves, move to other communities, organize themselves, insist on their rights, change their ways of living and working etc. We believe that film activities, radically conceived and imaginatively carried out, could be powerful stimuli for social change in the hands of the poor." Yet when the report turned to actual strategies, the way was not so clear: "What film activities genuinely would stimulate such action? How can we get films to the poor? How can we help them organize film activities? To what extent must useful films be specifically regional? With whom should we co-operate in regional film activities?" Despite the uncertainties, the report relied a great deal on the possibilities of media to bring about education and social change. "Failures in programs intended to eradicate poverty seem frequently to stem from problems of informing and involving those affected – especially the poor. Film, probably better than any other medium, can provide that information and provoke that involvement."[8] The framework was successful enough to raise $385,000 from the interdepartmental committee and the NFB for the program's first annual operating budget.[9]

In many ways *Challenge for Change* was a continuation of the philosophy of adult education and film modernization introduced by earlier film initiatives, albeit in a form fitted to contemporary sensibilities. Where early documentary film had been influenced by ideas from the social science of the day, 1960s documentary filmmaking was influenced by contemporary thinking in anthropology about the participant observer sharing the means of production with the subjects of study and including them in the process of filmmaking. Just as new fieldwork promised to include the subject of research in the study, new port-a-pack video technology (introduced by Sony in 1968) provided the means to include the viewer on television. Despite the wide reporting of Grierson's unhappiness with the *Challenge for Change* program, in many ways the new mandate was consistent with Grierson's ethic, as was frequently noted.[10] C. Rodney James, for example, asserts that "*Challenge for Change* is a reaffirmation of the principles set down by John Grierson in 1938."[11] D.B. Jones concurs: "The Film Act's command that the Film Board 'interpret Canada to Canadians' allowed such films, for the filmmakers were, after all, Canadians, and their films were the interpretations of themselves and their own Canadian worlds to the rest of Canada. The Board's happily ambiguous mandate allowed these filmmakers to pursue a course of action inconceivable to any other government filmmaking organization."[12] Film historian Rick Moore observes that the division of the audience into the general public, social workers and the poor, "While perhaps making awareness of audience more explicit than traditionally was done at the NFB," was still a familiar strategy.[13]

From early on, *Challenge for Change* had its critics. In 1972 Marie Kurchak highlighted the political nature of the topics chosen, as well as those rejected, noting that a proposed film about radical militants in the Quebec union movement was seen to be too challenging.[14] Kurchak astutely observed, "The problem with a new technique is that it can be seized as a panacea for all kinds of problems, as if the answer lay inside the Arri or the Sony."[15] More recently, Janine Marchessault had provided an important assessment of the program's "highly instrumental view of cultural development [which] paralleled the Liberal interpretation of cultural development (i.e., 'help them help themselves') and would play an essential role in the state promotion of community culture in Canada."[16] As Marchessault notes, "The interactivity and participation that video delivered instituted access without agency. It instituted a particular form of self-surveillance rather than transforming the actual institutional relations of production and knowledge."[17] The "thrill of access" occluded the restrictive framing of that access.[18] At the same time, the program was good publicity for a Liberal government attempting to broaden its support in new non-party political movements.

Scott MacKenzie examines the work of *Société nouvelle*, established in 1969, for moving French production at the NFB past cinéma-vérité observation into the notion that media work could be "a catalyst for political action."[19] Like Marchessault, MacKenzie observes that although these films and videos were supposed to be self-erasing ephemeral texts to help constitute an alternative public forum, notions of process and interactivity ultimately "fell by the wayside."[20] Nevertheless, despite these recent analyses of the legacy of the *Challenge for Change/Société nouvelle* program, it is often comments like that of CBC stalwart Patrick Watson that circulate as assessments of the program. "Its purpose," said Watson, "is not the seduction of the eye and the ear. It is the enlargement of eye, ear and voice, through the film as an instrument for helping people in trouble get out of it. Get *themselves* out if it."[21] Gary Evans asserts that after *Challenge for Change*, "representing the unrepresented became an idea that is now welded to the Film Board's creative conscience."[22]

Challenge for Change/ Société nouvelle films were used in familiar ways to spark discussion amongst middle-class Canadians and to figure out how to mold social policy. Indeed, even more than previous films, the *Challenge for Change/Société nouvelle* films were incorporated into a communications loop between people and government meant to bring about consensus on social policy. The film's much-touted process orientation was a textual strategy as much as a community-organizing strategy. The highly vaunted "process" was a public performance about liberal democracy and an expanded public sphere as much as (if not more than) it was for the benefit of the film subjects. This is increasingly true, for while the social events the films document are receding into the distance, the films are still used to signal a radical moment in Canadian government filmmaking.

Challenge for Change and *Société nouvelle* are an important part of the NFB's international reputation for radical filmmaking. Even today, American commentators often seem incredulous about the possibility of the Canadian government's participation in creating such oppositional films.[23] Part of the reason for this reputation comes from the involvement of George Stoney in the first two years of *Challenge for Change*'s existence (1967–69). Stoney was a longtime progressive media activist whose professional roots extended back to the New Deal (where he worked with Lewis Hine)[24] and the British Documentary Movement. After he left the NFB he was invited by Leo Hurwitz, then head of New York Univerisity's graduate school in film, to head up the university's undergraduate program (reputedly as a strategy to help curb violent student activism).[25] He was instrumental in establishing New York's Alternate Media Center, a public access project with cable companies, and was a mentor to a generation of independent American media artists and activists, including some who went on to be involved in radical community media projects such as *Paper Tiger TV* and *Deep Dish*. By association, the *Challenge for Change* program is assumed to be a comparably radical institution, and its state funding therefore is considered incredible.

Stoney's association with public service filmmaking has a direct link to the NFB through Nick Read, a friend who worked for the NFB in the 1940s and then moved to Georgia to work for Southern Educational Film Production Services. Read hired Stoney to act as a community animator in bringing agricultural educational films to the rural communities of the southern United States.[26] After this experience, Stoney went to the NFB in 1948 and then to England, where he spent a year with "the documentary pioneers of the Grierson school," teaching adults through an Oxford University extension program.[27] In the 1950s and 1960s, Stoney taught at the Film Institute at City College, as well as at Columbia and Stanford Universities. One of his Stanford students, Bonnie Sherr Klein, was working at the NFB when Frank Spiller invited Stoney to be the executive producer of *Challenge for Change*, a fact that may explain his recommendation.[28] However, Stoney's invitation, like Grierson's almost thirty years before, came for a reason. The Canadian political situation was becoming unstable in Quebec as support for separatism grew. Once again, the National Film Board would be called on to help the national cause.

THE BILINGUALISM AND BICULTURALISM REPORT AND MULTICULTURALISM

Some of the most famous films in the NFB's history were made by the French unit during the late 1950s and 1960s. Such renowned directors as Denys Arcand, Claude Jutra, Michel Brault, and Pierre Perrault got their start making films for the NFB. Surreptitiously turning permission for documentaries into feature films such as *Le chat dans le sac* (Gilles Groulx, 1964), the French studio of the NFB reached a pinnacle of creativity during this period. The philosophy of immediacy that became cinéma-vérité was seen in its first exciting guises. Aesthetic innovation seemed to match political foment in the days of Quebec's Quiet Revolution. The NFB's presence in Quebec was an invitation for French-speaking artists, writers, and filmmakers to become involved in the national filmmaking project. Indeed, the move of the NFB's headquarters from Ottawa to Montreal was part of the federal government's attempt to infuse Quebec's creative fringe with federal allegiances.

The decision to move the National Film Board's headquarters to Montreal had been made years before it finally occurred in 1956. As early as June 1950, Robert Winters, Arthur Irwin, and Prime Minister Louis St Laurent had discussed a move to Montreal, though Winters was "doubtful whether it would be wise, either practically or politically, to proceed with Federal Government film activities in this area at a time when circulation of National Film Board pictures [was] being withheld by Cine-Photographie and other obstacles [were] being placed in the way of production of new National Film Board films in the Province of Quebec."[29] Nevertheless, in September 1950 Winters, in conjunction with Irwin, floated the idea past the cabinet. Winters considered that even though Toronto was a film and broadcasting centre, relocating the NFB there "would not have the immediate contact with French Canada which is necessary to operate effectively in the French language." Also, Montreal was closer to Ottawa.[30] When in 1954 Premier Maurice Duplessis of Quebec banned the use of NFB films in the province's classrooms, the federal government was not amused.[31] Quebec's distinctiveness represented an important bastion against American culture, and an increase in French-language production was good strategy for resisting sectionalism. The NFB had long made films about Quebec, from *Habitant Arts and Crafts* (1944) and the *Chants populaires* series (1943) onward. Now Quebecers were brought into the institution in unprecedented numbers to make films about themselves.[32]

In his study *Résistance et affirmation*, Pierre Véronneau highlights the irony of the National Film Board of Canada becoming a space in which Québécois nationalist aspirations could be pursued.[33] In this view, despite its aim to provide a federalist presence in Quebec, the NFB created a hotbed of nationalist filmmaking. However, one may also see this as a governmental strategy. While it is true that Quebec filmmakers made films that challenged the federalist agenda, their work was often about themselves as subjects challenging the federalist status quo. The move to

Roland Barthes's *Mythologies* was the inspiration for *La lutte* (1961, Michel Brault, Marcel Carrière, Claude Fournier, and Claude Jutra), a study of popular sport in Montreal.

Montreal may well have been an attempt to stimulate and facilitate film-making activity. Even oppositional activity fulfilled this mandate. Indeed, just promoting engagement with the NFB was an improvement over Premier Duplessis's policy of non-engagement with the federal film service.

The celebrated films of the late 1950s and early 1960s, in particular, show the social scientific logic at work in the study of Quebec society. In his study of Quebec cinema, Scott MacKenzie comments that many of these films scrutinized "rituals" of everyday life.[34] Significantly, MacKenzie notes the significance of the structuralist and poststructuralist social science of Roland Barthes on this vision of Québécois life. Not only was Barthes's essay on wrestling cited in the credits to *La lutte* (1961), but the French philosopher also consulted on the scriptwriting of Hubert Aquin's *Le sport et les hommes* (1961).[35] In some ways, the significance of the work of the French section during the late 1950s and early 1960s is related to the filmmakers' more attenuated relationship to the Canadian state as well as their attention to changes in social science. The result was a corpus of films over the 1960s that challenged both the national framework and national ways of filmmaking. However, they still to some degree fulfilled the criteria of government realism: they still focused on typical members and groups of the population and on the ethnographic study of rituals of everyday life. Films such as *Les racquetteurs* (1958) and *Pour la suite du monde* (1962) limned the connection between the traditions of the francophone population, often in rural areas, and the modernizing forces that were affecting their communities. In this regard they are of a piece with other work that was being attempted at the NFB. Because of the nationalist agenda of many of the young francophone filmmakers in Quebec in this period, they seemed to negotiate with greater tension the contradictions that Véronneau identified than many other filmmakers did. However, as we shall see in chapter 7, they would not be the last group to negotiate an ambivalent relationship to state policy through the National Film Board.

In 1963 Lester Pearson and his Liberal Party won the federal election on a campaign of linguistic duality, that same year the new government initiated the Royal Commission on Bilingualism and Biculturalism, a major study of the subject, which led to the Official Languages Act six years later. As Quebec asserted its post-Duplessis politics as a partially cultural project with the foundation of the Ministère des Affaires culturales, Pearson countered by making the Secretary of State, formerly a mostly symbolic office, into a cultural ministry; in 1963 it received responsibility for a wide range of cultural development.[36] It is widely believed that the move to place the Board of Broadcast Governors, the Canada Council, the CBC, the Centennial Commission, the National Film Board, the National Gallery, the National Library and Public Archives, National Museums, and the Queen's Printer under the mandate of a single federal agency was intended as a counter-thrust to Quebec's increasing resistance to federal cultural agencies.[37] G.G.E. Steele, under-secretary of state, commented in 1968 that in order to emphasize the "provincial" quality of Quebec culture, "the federal government must emphasize the national significance of cultural programs."[38] Federal funding for official language minorities was increased from $1.9 million in 1972 to $26 million in 1987.[39] This money sweetened the deal for federalism in the face of a growing sovereignty movement and the emergence of the Parti Québécois in 1968.[40] Only eight years later, the PQ would form the provincial government with support for the French language and Québécois culture as one of its central mandates.

Pour la suite du monde (1963, Pierre Perrault and Michel Brault) limns the connection between traditional life and modernizing forces in rural Quebec.

Out of this federal concern to counter Quebec's nationalist cultural project came initiatives to placate what might be seen as the New Left: "youth, linguistic, ethnic, and women's politics."[41] Following the American civil rights and student movements, the Canadian government determined to focus on issues of youth and poverty as well as on social control.[42] In 1966, in anticipation of the radical movements of the American New Left, Pearson launched the Company of Young Canadians – a Canadian version of the U.S. Peace Corps – to increase participation, decrease alienation, and sensitize middle-class university students.[43] The underlying theory was that increased participation in the affairs of government would alleviate feelings of alienation. Political scientist Leslie Pal writes:

By January 1970 the S[ecretary] O[f] S[tate], and in particular the citizenship and Social Action Branches, had a clear mandate to mobilize Canadian society on the linguistic and broader participatory front. In principle, virtually any social group or category could be eligible for help and guidance, though the mandate referred vaguely to the disadvantaged, which clearly included the core constituencies that the branch had cultivated and connected with over the years: immigrants, Natives, youth, and, most recently, official-language communities. But it could embrace the elderly, women, and virtually any group or organization struggling to participate in the political process either for the first time or against what then was referred to as "the establishment." And this is precisely what happened.[44]

In 1969 the Secretary of State established the Social Action Branch, whose mandate was to "attack ... mass apathy" in both a proactive and reactive fashion.[45] Citizen participation and communication were the new buzzwords in government, and the Liberals were committed to the appearance of open government.[46] According to Pal, the late 1960s marked a shift in philosophy from a passive to an active concept of citizenship: "Most of the groups dedicated to development of Canadian citizenship did not exist before the branch did. Far from responding to swelling demand by organizations and groups, the branch, and the state in the larger sense as forger of the concept of Canadian citizenship, created a 'space' – a new terrain of political practice – into which societal and organizational energies could flow."[47] In this "complex coupling of state and societal interests,"[48] the state became responsible for "wider and wider circles of societal activity."[49]

The organizations that grew out of the civil rights movements of the 1960s represented a new moment in political organization. These groups had longer-term goals and a "wider and looser membership" than traditional political organizations, and they championed "life-style issues."[50] Importantly, federal funding of these groups was couched in terms of "citizenship development and national unity."[51] Pal concludes that Canadian social policy of the period created a culture of government-supported advocacy.[52] Paradoxically, although putatively introduced to alleviate identity-based claims for recognition, federal policy since 1970 has institutionalized Canada's "perpetual identity crisis"[53]: "The S[ecretary] O[f] S[tate] funding of groups fragments rather than unifies national identity."[54] In Canada, the state has become a terrain upon which "societal issues get addressed, if not always resolved."[55]

Canada's multiculturalism policy, originally a late addition to the Commission on Bilingualism and Biculturalism, was officially announced in 1971 and has turned out to be one of the defining features of Canada's political landscape. As Leslie Pal puts it, "The combination of bilingualism and multiculturalism seemed to balance the need to accommodate Quebec without implying that there were simply two peoples – French and English – in Canada."⁵⁶ In 1967 Canada removed all reference to nationality and race from its immigration policies.⁵⁷ The NFB was commended in the commission's report for its work in the area of multiculturalism.

The National Film Board has certainly not ignored the contribution of other cultural groups in its productions, and whether or not it should have produced more films about them is a question of subjective judgment. It has also attempted not to focus unduly on the folklore or on any curious aspects of the lives of members of any specific cultural group, as group spokesmen have suggested, in spite of the difficulty of making the participation of members of other cultural groups in everyday Canadian life sufficiently dramatic for film-making purposes. Therefore, we commend the Board for its past work, and we recommend that the National Film Board continue and develop the production of films that inform Canadians about one another, including films about the contribution and problems of both individuals and groups of ethnic origin other than British or French, and that the National Film Board receive the financial support it requires in order to produce such films.⁵⁸

The NFB management did not miss this invitation to make itself increasingly relevant to the new government policy. Gary Evans notes that "on the practical level, multiculturalism was a shot in the arm for Film Board programming, and in the next few years there was a plethora of films on immigrants ... From 1972, Ottawa provided almost $2 million over five years to version its films into languages other than French or English for domestic consumption and to make films about the contribution and problems of ethnic groups."⁵⁹ In 1971, following the announcement of the multiculturalism policy, the NFB produced sixty films to promote the learning of the official languages. Three major series were *Toulmonde* [sic] *parle français, Filmglish*, and *Adieu Alouette*.

In a burst of governmental expansion, the Department of Manpower and Immigration grew to encompass human rights, Native migration to cities, citizenship development, bilingualism, and labour.⁶⁰ The Citizenship Branch was at the centre of a "revitalized federal commitment to fostering national unity"; its budget doubled between 1969–70 ($4.6 million) and 1970–71 ($8.1 million), and increased fivefold in 1971–72 ($44 million).⁶¹ As aboriginals, French-speaking people, and women organized, there was no indication of a widespread popular movement for multiculturalism. Its motive forces, argues Pal, were elite support from ethnic organizational leaders, politicians, and government agencies. Nevertheless, once these programs were established, they provided space for work that was not necessarily endorsed by the government:

For the people who had been mobilized, who had participated, who had talked and written and conferred and traveled and filmed and raised consciousness – these programs were vital in a way that the politicians and officials could only have dimly realized. Some groups limped and slipped and eventually lost their edge – students and youth, for example – but others, once their fingers and toes gripped the crevices of Ottawa's funding edifice, refused to let go. The programs, originally intended simply to enhance participation, became the foundations upon which key segments of Canadian society defined their identity: women, O[fficial] L[anguage] M[inority] G[roup]s, and ethnics. The state, pursuing an eminently statist strategy, had been ensnared by the fruits of its efforts. While the Citizenship Branch thereafter lost some of its élan, and the government as a whole lost interest, the roots of "citizen participation" among groups and organizations themselves were now firmly established.[62]

As the profile of immigrants changed to include people from Asia and the Caribbean, the discourse of immigrants became antiracism rather than cultural retention. This new focus was reflected in the striking of a House of Commons Special Committee on Participation of Visible Minorities in May 1983. This committee eventually became the Standing Committee on Multiculturalism, which released a report in 1987 that recommended the Canadian Multiculturalism Act, passed in 1988. As the Empire Marketing Board had earlier tried to substitute one meaning of empire for another, multiculturalism was the attempt of the Liberal government to replace the British crown as Canada's dominant symbol.

REPRESENTING POVERTY

Paralleling these shifts in social policy, films from the 1940s and 1950s about the dignity of labour were largely replaced in the 1960s and 1970s by films about the injustice of poverty. While this would appear to provide a more radical perspective on the socio-economic structure, the films usually served to reinscribe governmental identities that could be served by liberal welfare-state social policy. Government realist documentary films, even of the participatory variety, more often than not took the speaking position of privileged state workers' investigations of others' marginalization. A common trope in NFB films found the filmmaker standing in for state representatives, especially in the realm of welfare provision. As Rick Clifton Moore puts it, "In many ways, the war on poverty was an attempt to bring that problem (as culturally perceived or framed) under the gaze of social scientists and bureaucrats so that it could be controlled."[63]

Tanya Ballantyne's *The Things I Cannot Change* (1967), which led to the inauguration of the *Challenge for Change* program, is a good example of the NFB's 1960s approach to the welfare concerns of an administered society. *The Things I Cannot Change* is an hour-long profile of a destitute Montreal anglophone family, the Baileys. The production proposal for the film indicates the kind of story the filmmakers hoped to capture:

The style and structure of this film are in some respects dictated by the subject matter. The essence of this family's life, how its members behave with one another, the little problems which arise out of their contacts with the outside world, their hopes, their general despair will all be lost if any attempt is made to control or direct them beyond what is absolutely necessary. The approach will therefore be entirely candid. As an aid to structure and continuity, the director's off camera voice will ask questions, and make comments on situations and people throughout the sound track. The personality of the voice will have certain middle-class characteristics, a value system somewhat different from the Baileys, certainly a different frame of reference. It is hoped that this juxtaposition will reveal much about the relationship of rich and poor in this society.[64]

The film was shot in hand-held black and white, and the narrator explicitly promised an "undirected observation of the life of this family during a three week period." It begins with an interview with the parents, who have journeyed from Nova Scotia to Montreal in order to have a better life – but instead have found more poverty and violence. An authoritative male voice-over tells us that "Kenneth and Gertrude

The Things I Cannot Change (1967, Tanya Ballantyne) was poised somewhere between socially responsible filmmaking and filmic slumming.

Bailey have nine children, soon to be ten." From the perspective of a state employee, we see scenes of the family's rundown apartment. One camera follows Kenneth as he goes out to look for work in the morning; the other stays at home with Gertrude. Taking the perspective of a social worker, the off-camera interviewer asks Gertrude questions about the family's expenses and rent. This scene, establishing their costs, is intercut with Kenneth's unsuccessful quest for work.

A tired and worried-looking Gertrude goes in for her first prenatal checkup in her ninth month. She answers a battery of questions, including those about her children and their birth weights, and she is sent to a social and nutritional worker. This interview is intercut with a sequence of Kenneth being interviewed by the filmmaker in which Ballantyne performs the role of the social worker. Kenneth dreams of a bourgeois life; he expresses anger at the injustice of his situation. Gertrude has an obstetrics exam while Kenneth tries to collect money from someone and gets beaten up. When we see him again, he has been charged by the police and is desperate and suicidal. He finally goes to the police station and has an interview. The charges are dropped. Soon, Gertrude goes into labour. The camera crew stays with the kids when the parents go to the hospital in a police car. Upon returning to the apartment with the baby, Gertrude is despondent. Kenneth, however, is ecstatic.

In the final scene, Kenneth reads from a poem used at Alcoholics Anonymous that he finds in the kitchen cupboard: "God give me the strength to change the things I can, accept the things I cannot change, and the sense to know the difference." He vehemently disagrees with the sentiment, and the association of him with the poem in the film's title is misleading. Moreover, the excerpt of the poem used in the title ironically implies that the Baileys should not accept the things they cannot change – the system at large. By implication, the film associates passive acceptance with a society in which people seem unwilling to acknowledge that there are systemic inequalities. In the final shot, Kenneth looks adoringly at their new baby and says, "I won't let you suffer. If I have to steal I will." Rhetorically this shot suggests the need for social services to help the likes of the Baileys, who clearly do not have the wherewithal to raise ten future citizens. The film is critical of society at the same time as it reinforces, through its welfare state "voice," the provision of social minimums already in place.

The press release for the film's screening by the CBC on 24 April 1967 promised a trip into the exotic world of poverty: "This one-hour special takes the audience into the home of a family whose struggle for survival is a natural way of life. These are not actors. This family is not unlike hundreds of others in Canada and this is the alarming part of 'The Things I Cannot Change.' In a period of three weeks, this close-up of the other side of life provides more drama and pathos than most people experience in a lifetime." Promotional material was sent to eighty-thousand households in advance of the CBC screening.[65] According to Moore, the popular press and the government alike were pleased with the film's message about greater government intervention: "The film was in some ways a call for more government programs and thus not as an enemy of government policy but as an ally."[66] The film dovetailed with the Privy Council's War on Poverty program,[67] and before it was screened on television it received approval from the prime minister and the Privy Council.[68] Seventeen officials from the Department of Public Welfare attended the preview of the film before its broadcast. However, the Bailey family was not given advance notification of the screening and was shamefully exposed to its neighbours. The Baileys' existence as a type was more important than their ongoing reality. Moore observes, "In spite of their attempts to show the people of Canada the reality of poverty, what those people actually saw in the end was the view of Ballentyne and Kemeny, two white civil servants from Montreal."[69]

The framing of the film by the information and discussion guides that were put out is instructive about its relationship to the ultimately moralizing message of the Department of Welfare: "Made without comment other than what the Bailey's say or what other people – social workers, police, etc. – say to the Bailey's, this film says more about poverty in Canada today than has ever been said before. Its impression is that 'there but for the grace of God go I.' For that reason and others, all concerned Canadians will want to see and discuss it."[70] The discussion guide noted:

There is no narrative in the usual sense of the word, no real beginning and no ending. The family's existence has been much as it is portrayed before the film began, and there is no evidence to suggest that it is likely to change very much once the film is over. The purpose of discussion based on the film is fundamentally to explore why this is so, what causes people to live this way, and what might be done about it, if anything can or should be done. The value of the discussion will not be in further elaboration of the particular plight of this family, but in the development of audience responses to the family's position. The film is about the situation of one family, but it is also about the nature of poverty in Canada, and poverty is a fact both for those who endure it and for those who permit it to exist.

Some issues to address were listed: "Are there existing programs that could help this man or his family, e.g. retraining, family counseling?

How responsive do you think they would be to such methods?" Fifteen additional questions for the discussion guide were sent by David Gee of the Privy Council Office in October, including "What responsibility does Society have to children in poverty families (including so-called 'happy' poverty families)? How can the public and private resources and services which were available to this family, be improved (law, public welfare, public health, church charity, etc.)? Are the social services in your community and the administration of these services, adequate to serve the total poverty group? (e.g. clients – ethnic values, age groups, handicaps, etc; services and facilities – quality, quantity, location, hours of operation, etc.)" Significantly, although the destitute family was paid $500 for the intrusion of the film crew into their lives for three weeks, this seemingly salient fact was not mentioned in the discussion material.[71] The approach taken by the government and by many of the people who responded to the film by inquiring where they could send charitable donations was far from bringing about a systemic critique of poverty or a radical analysis of how Canada's welfare system could be made more effective.

PROCESS FILMS

Beginning in 1967, the Fogo Island project, managed by NFB stalwart Colin Low, was an experiment to use film to explore community decision making. Fogo was chosen because of its many social, economic, and educational problems and because government policy toward this area was being formulated.[72] But on a basic level it was chosen because of its representativeness. Fogo Island was seen to be a microcosm of Newfoundland, and it also stood for any isolated community that was having difficulty in modernizing. Several branches of the federal and provincial governments were consulted, and the Department of Extension at Memorial University was an active participant in the process.[73] An early report on the decision to choose Newfoundland made the following case:

There would be no attempt to foster a sophisticated film-making group but a self-help group, organized around film activities. Film activities would be a stimulus to and a focus for social change. The Board would withdraw after about a year (except for continuing local distribution assistance, advice and perhaps training arrangements) leaving behind, hopefully, an organization, a body of experience and a cadre of people to carry on. If the experiment proved valid, the experience thus gained would then be applied in other regions ... Obviously such explorations could not be carried out without active support from local representatives of federal departments and agencies; recommendations for film activities would have to be guided by their opinions in many cases.[74]

Premier Joey Smallwood was eager to relocate the Fogo Islanders, some five thousand people dispersed across the island, whose economy had collapsed with the fishery and 60 percent of whom were collecting welfare.[75] Many had taken government packages and left, but a "sizable portion of the community" still remained.[76] *Challenge for Change*'s native informant was Fred Earle. Born on Fogo and working for Memorial University's extension program, he had made various attempts to help the islanders modernize. "His main emphases were improving fishing techniques, being aware of useful government programs, and organizing the local community."[77] A small film crew shot twenty hours of material over five weeks and edited the material down to twenty-three films lasting approximately five hours in total. "The material covered such issues as fishing methods, welfare, education, and cooperatives. It also portrayed everyday events and unique qualities of Fogo Island life."[78] The crew included Randy Coffin, an islander who helped in selecting and interviewing the subjects.

Low has characterized the editing as vertical rather than horizontal. "In other words, the films were based on personalities discussing a variety of issues, rather than an issue incorporating a variety of personalities ... It was as valuable to highlight personalities as it was to present issues, since action would require leaders and community support for them. This method also avoids the obvious editorializing that occurs when personalities are juxtaposed by an editor. Furthermore, *certain people did embody specific issues* and horizontal editing was not needed."[79] The NFB representatives organized interviews, sorted the material into vertical films, and divided the films into the thirty-five screenings, which they showed to the islanders. They then facilitated discussion on the issues of welfare and self-sufficiency presented in the films. At least that was the plan. In the event, the islanders were just as interested in the filmmakers as the filmmakers were in them: "We soon became aware that we were the major topic of conversation on the Island."[80] Yet the pretence that the films were helping to crystallize the islanders' position on living in the island was maintained. The filmmakers even attempted to record the reactions at the screenings, but with little success.

Despite the rhetoric about process, the films were not made for the exclusive use of the islanders. They were also shown at Memorial University to members of the government. As NFB field organizer Bill Nemtin recorded, "The government did react honestly and constructively. However, we can only speculate on what might have been achieved had a Fogo delegation presented the material as their expression, their brief." An attempt to train student filmmakers to continue with this process in Newfoundland failed. Nemtin continues:

To insure success in this type of project, the film maker must be free to respond to the expressions of the people. One of the main reasons we were accepted in Fogo was the fidelity the films displayed in reflecting the views of the community. *Anti-government feeling, even when based on misinformation, must be allowed expression. This is essential for the community and for the government* ... We believe the government departments concerned with questions raised by the film material should be allowed to qualify the material by statements added to the films, but Government departments should not have the power to delete material before release. It may be that the department concerned may ask the University to delay release until an examination is conducted into a situation brought up by the material. A certain length of time may be agreed upon in order to allow time to investigate the situation but the decision to release the material should not be in the hands of the Government. This material should always be represented as the opinions of certain individuals and not the policy of the University or the NFB.[81]

A series of the films were released for general use as an example of using process videos in community organizing. Among other things, they helped establish the talking head as the favoured (anti)aesthetic of 1970s documentary filmmaking.[82]

Bonnie Klein's *VTR St. Jacques* (1969), a well-known film in the *Challenge for Change* series, is also telling about the role that film could play in government. Once again using a politicized middle-class perspective to interpret urban poverty (again in Montreal), the film documents the formation of a citizens' committee in the neighbourhood of St Jacques

In this scene from *VTR St. Jacques* (1969, Bonnie Sherr Klein) the filmmakers are shown to hand over the means of filmic production.

to address local needs, such as the need for a health clinic. Klein's husband was volunteering as a pediatrician in the clinic, and the overall theme of the film is the acceptable role of middle-class professionals in local struggles. In a report on the film's production, Klein noted the "advisability of *Challenge for Change* doing a French-language film, both in terms of our predominantly English audience and our administratively English nature."[83] Klein worked to facilitate self-documentation by the citizens' committee. In a moment iconic of the new theory of participant action research and community empowerment, Klein is shown handing over the filmmaking equipment to the "people." Nevertheless, in a meta-filmic style, Klein continues to film the people filming. Videotape recorders (VTRs) in hand, the citizens' group visits the local branches of government institutions, interviewing people as they come out of the social welfare office, the employment office, schools, and community centres. At the outpatient department of a local hospital, they are asked to erase their tape. Even though in VTR St. Jacques filmic representation is seen to stand in for, or complement, political representation, the filmmakers seem unconscious of the power relations that their film inscribes. The film's dominant "voice" is ultimately that of the NFB filmmakers and not the citizens' group.

Having been given the means of filmic production, the citizens' group chooses to address, or respond to, the government/film crew. For example, a voice-over says, "The government always talks about participation, but there isn't any. Using Video-Tape Recorders we can hear what people have to say." This statement implies that the video equipment provided by the "process video" community project of *Challenge for Change* facilitates the kind of representation that democracy does not. "When I look through the camera," says one participant, "I really see." The final scene of VTR St. Jacques is also the final moment of the existence of the citizens' committee: a community screening of the videotape in a school auditorium with groups of people gathered around several television monitors. Not only is the culmination of the project filmed by the NFB crew, but afterwards viewers and participants are interviewed by Klein. The discussion centres on social conditions. Klein ends with the voice-over directive, "What's important is to follow it up, to work face to face with people." Clearly, she is addressing not the members of the St Jacques citizens' committee but those in the audience who work with the "people." According to liberal citizenship discourse, the people are the poor and sick, those for whom the welfare state is not working. According to the logic of this film, which is organized around the bestowing of filmic attention on the underclass, what those at the bottom of the system need most is help from the liberal elite.

A caution appears on the information sheet circulated with the film which acknowledges the relationship of the filmmakers and the filmed: "Groups and individuals who wish to try this type of experience with VTR should seriously consider their long-term responsibilities to the people who will be affected. A short-term film or VTR blitz without adequate long-term social commitment can do more harm than good, as people get stirred up toward social action and are then abandoned before they are able to go it alone."[84] The NFB is clearly aware of its role as a stimulator of activity in the public sphere, as well as its ability to curtail such activity. But there is something patronizing at play here, where people's activism is seen as being coterminous with their access to state funds.

The difference between the scripted vision of ideal citizenship in, for example, *When All the People Play* (1948) and popular participation in the filmmaking process of *VTR St. Jacques* is actually less significant than their similarities as governmental narratives. In documentaries of the 1960s and 1970s we are shown a more complicated relation between citizens and film, but one that is no less tied to welfare state objectives. In *When All the People Play*, fitness and community recreation are seen to be the road to improved citizenship, whereas in *VTR St. Jacques* it is filmmaking itself that binds the community together. In both cases, community behaviour that promotes well-being is tied to governmentalized objectives of health and organization. Even the radical-seeming objectives of *VTR St. Jacques* are linked to organizing the neighbourhood into a lobby group that can articulate its criticisms to the government. The film is precisely about the production of legitimate lines of response about social policy. Tellingly, when the filmmakers go, so does the citizens' organization. In this way, Klein and her crew are not unlike the recreation directors of the 1940s – catalysts for the well-corralled expression of citizenship.

Challenge for Change championed public access to media as a tool for consciousness raising and process. Moore points out that *Challenge for Change* became caught up in its own rhetoric of media activism, connecting all social inequality to lack of access to the media:

Clearly for some *Challenge for Change* staff, the same problem could be visualized in communities all over Canada. Because of this, projects that were in the works for *Challenge for Change* were molded to fit this perspective. What were before seen merely as "social problems" to be attacked head on, were now part of a larger web. The "taking off" point for many *Challenge for Change* projects was now seen as the inability of common citizens to affect their environments. People had been alienated and made powerless by mass media that were unresponsive to their needs ... The media – used correctly

– was the answer to the media used incorrectly. In allowing common people to use channels of communication freely, the inhibitions and restrictions built up in the past were dealt with. People spoke freely of their problems and acted freely in solving them.[85]

For example, Klein argued that "the VTR project in Saint-Jacques is an attempt to extend to its logical conclusion the conviction that people should participate in shaping their own lives, which means among other things directing and manipulating the tools of modern communication necessary to gain and exercise that participation … Their experience with video – conceiving, shooting, editing and presenting their own programs – made the citizens particularly aware of the myth of objectivity in mass media reporting and sensitive to conscious and unconscious manipulation. They have become a less gullible public."[86] George Stoney included Klein's report when preparing material for presentation to the cabinet and showed the film to an interdepartmental committee in a quest for "supplemental funding" for the *Challenge for Change* program.[87]

As this examination of key Challenge for Change films has shown, the films were exercises in citizen building and social policy formation that fit well with state initiatives in citizen communication. George Stoney said "that Canadian government officials believe that Canadians understood the idea of government-sponsored subversion. It is an intelligent way to mobilize social revolution without violence."[88] Moore notes the highly normalizing aspect of the *Challenge for Change* as, to exercise power, all concerned must first submit to power: "they had to play within the rules of the dominant social structure and its requirements. Note that … gains were largely made on the playing field of the elites."[89]

FIRST NATIONS

Films about aboriginal people form their own subgenre at the NFB, showing the degree to which First Nations have provided both a barometer for the success of modernization and a tenacious spectacle of otherness. Laura Boulton was responsible for many of the early ethnographic films about native people. Like many anthropological photographs of the 1930s and 1940s, the images of native people in that period were often concerned with salvaging a traditional past that was seen to be rapidly disappearing. In the 1950s, by contrast, films such as *No Longer Vanishing* (1955) began to celebrate the modernization of the aboriginal people.

In the 1960s the citizenship status of First Nations was shifting again. In 1969 the Liberal government released a White Paper, *Statement of the Government of Canada on Indian Policy*, which argued for the dismantling of the federal bureaucracy of the Indian Act in favour of what was known as "termination" policy. Following the lead of the American government, which had introduced similar legislation in the early 1950s, the Canadian government proposed to close reserves and afford First Nations people complete citizenship through total assimilation. According to anthropologist Sally Weaver, "Indians responded to the policy with a resounding nationalism unparalleled in Canadian history ... With the press and other sectors of the public supporting the Indian indictment of the policy, the government came under heavy pressure to set the White Paper aside."[90]

According to political scientist Jeremy Webber, an important part of native politics in the 1960s was the retrieval of the language and culture of a vanishing heritage: "A step that clearly occurred in many Native communities in the 1960s, was to reclaim their cultures and languages and to rebuild their self-respect. Native Canadians, especially the youth, rejected [the mainstream Canadian] model with a vengeance, insisting on rediscovering their own identities and using those as the basis for engagement with the world."[91] Much of their anger was directed toward the Indian Act, according to which most native people were still wards of the state. However, because of its emphasis on culture as a private matter rather than an aspect of daily community, Prime Minister Trudeau's push to make aboriginals full and equal citizens rubbed many in the native community the wrong way.

On the heels of this policy dispute, the 1970s saw three crucial events in First Nations politics in Canada. The land claim of the Nisga'a people of northwestern British Columbia was taken to the Supreme Court, and although the specific claim was lost, the judgment "prompted the Liberal government to agree, at least in principle, to negotiate claims founded on aboriginal title."[92] The James Bay hydroelectric project in northern Quebec led to the first land claim settlement. Finally, the Berger Inquiry into a proposal for a gas pipeline down the Mackenzie Valley in the Northwest Territories provided a precedent for First Nations' rights to land. "In many ways, the questions posed by aboriginal peoples paralleled those of Quebec's Quiet Revolutionaries. Both struggled to reconcile the recognition of distinct societies with participation in Canadian society. Both believed that some decisions should be made in forums where their culture was the majority culture."[93]

The degree to which the aboriginal films of the *Challenge for Change* series were integrated into the welfare apparatus (and not in opposition to it) is clear in a letter which Freeman Compton, director of community development services in the Manitoba Department of Welfare, wrote to a member of the *Challenge for Change* team:

I'm writing this on my way to The Pas. On board with me are several Indian people en route to Cross Lake where the first round of consultations regarding the revision of the Indian Act are about to get underway ... My purpose of heading North today is to participate in a second round of discussion concerning reorganization of our Department and the integration of our Community Development Service into the new Department service delivery system which places major emphasis on prevention, rehabilitation and citizen participation. This is a major undertaking. Talk about change. Can you imagine the challenge inherent in this? I believe there is considerable merit in your suggestions that there be "further interim exploratory meetings – in each of the provinces" ... In our reorganized set-up, we have a Directorate of Research. It is headed by a fellow who for the last seven years has been with the United Nations as a consultant to several countries in setting up Community Development and Social Service programs.[94]

An aboriginal film training program was conceived in order to make *Challenge for Change* eligible for Company of Young Canadians funding.[95] Seven young people from a variety of First Nations across Canada were brought to Montreal to "receive training that would supposedly make them a voice for their people."[96] In Moore's view, "everything about the program was ethnocentric, in spite of its good intentions. The training of the youths was intended to lead the Indians to make white films, the organization of the project was restricting, and the evaluation of the program was entirely based on white ideals, not Native. The frustration revealed by the volunteers who made up the program stands as evidence of the difficulties it presented. Though eager to fight what they saw as the oppression of their people, they soon saw the danger of their course. To be totally effective in their battle, they would have to fight the enemy on its own ground."[97]

In the early 1970s the Supreme Court of Canada was considering the issue of aboriginal rights, and Hydro-Québec was building the James Bay Project.[98] Since the early 1960s, hydroelectric power had been an important component of Quebec's strategy to attain greater industrial independence from the rest of Canada.[99] In November 1973 the Cree and Inuit of northern Quebec obtained an injunction prohibiting work on the project until their "subsisting aboriginal title" was dealt with.[100] The resulting negotiations led to a "modern treaty," the James Bay and Northern Quebec Agreement. In 1972 Boyce Richardson, a columnist with the *Montreal Star* who had been critical of the Quebec government, was approached by Robert Cournoyer, chairman of the interdepartmental committee and a civil servant in the Privy Council Office, to propose a film on aboriginal life.[101] Although there was some support, the Prime Minister's Office advised that "the vibrations [were] bad, the timing was bad." A compromise proposal was drawn up whereby the NFB would produce four films under the rubric *Native People in Canadian Society*, "to be loosely based on the stories of four Native families in different stages of evolution." This was later modified to "traditional Indians, Urban Indians, Métis and Eskimo." Colin Low suggested a film on "Native people in Canadian Society" – much more in line with new multiculturalism language – rather than a project on aboriginal rights.[102] The resulting film, *Cree Hunters of Mistassani* (1974), was widely distributed and has become one of the most popular *Challenge for Change* productions.[103] Moore considers that the effect of the film on the Cree and the rest of the audience "aided the Cree in the battle against Hydro-Quebec. Though the film made no strong political statements against the utility per se, it did demonstrate what would be lost if it went ahead as planned."[104] This perspective worked effectively to condemn the Quebec sovereignty movement without apparently having any federalist bias.

At the research phase of the film, there were internal discussions about how to approach a film on native life, given the fact that the government had "taken an official stand on questions which would be raised by the project" and "delicate negotiations" were scheduled to take place.[105] The records indicate in 1972 that the film was made in the wake of a damning environmental impact report about the effect of the project on the native population.[106] In 1973 the NFB was trying to sell the film to the Department of Indian Affairs and Secretary of State.[107] Indian and Northern Affairs paid $25,000, the NFB $70,000.[108]

Cree Hunters begins addressing an outsider as it shows an arrival at a remote site. Aerial shots from a helicopter are accompanied by an anglophone male voice-over informing the outsider that we are going to the remote north of Quebec, where the Cree still maintain a traditional life on the land. Families pose in snapshot position before the camera. Each man and "his family" is identified in turn. Outsiders are then "invited" to travel with the families to "Indian land" in order to see First Nations' "life and problems." The remainder of the film consists of observing the everyday lives of the families over the course of the season. The outsider-filmmakers do not make their presence part of the situation; they are invisible. Recalling the connection between documentary film and social science, a 1974 report on the film gives statistical assurance that "this is a typical group."[109]

The film had extensive distribution in Quebec, mainly in the James Bay area. Screenings were accompanied by facilitators, and the filmmakers were often present to discuss the making of the film. Mark Zannis, one of the film's discussants, reported, "As a result of the work done there: 'Many Natives went off on a fishing trip after seeing the film and over the course of a few weeks began planning to return to the bush for winter trapping. Dozens of families, especially in the Fort George community, which is most affected by the Hydro Electric project, announced that they would return to the bush, as the film revived fond memories of what they knew and enjoyed about bush life' ... An object of the special distribution is to stimulate interest in the cause of the Cree people now engaged in a settlement with the Quebec government."[110] Zannis also showed *Cree Hunters* to a variety of "white people (students, teachers, environment groups, media people) in Montreal, Ottawa and Toronto." He explained:

Cree Hunters has been widely acclaimed as an excellent production and great historical document (it truly reflects the Cree way of life). "Cree" has exceptional educational value. (It fits in with Grade 5's study of Indians of Canada.) It has aroused a new awareness of the value and quality of Indian life not only for white people but for Natives as well. It is the first time the NFB organized the distribution of a particular film in the James Bay area. (The Natives were duly impressed – after being hounded by the media for 5 years,

Cree Hunters of Mistassani (1974, Boyce Richardson and Tony Ianzelo) was timed to crystallize outrage about the James Bay Project as the economic aspect of Quebec nationalism.

it was the first time anyone came back to show them something.) *Our Land Is Our Life* is now an historical film. It captures the problems of a people at a crucial time. It is important for the future – not to stop James Bay or others like it, but to make people aware of events and issues that will or may affect their own lives in the future.[111]

The film was linked closely to the land claim. In a 1974 memorandum, Ian Ball wrote to the regional distribution coordinators saying, "As you know, the negotiations between James Bay residents and the PQ government are underway now, and this is obviously the time to expose the film as widely as possible."[112] The final paragraph of voice-over narration regarding the impact of the James Bay Project on the Cree way of life was approved by Jacques Ouellet, a lawyer at the federal Department of Justice.[113] Part of the proposal for the project was to include it in the process of organizing the northern community to achieve consensus on the plan:

Clearly, there is a need for an effective means of communication so as to improve the chances of the affected Indian population to become fully aware of the effect of the project on their lives. Then there is a need to bring these people together to form a common front to defend their rights and have a voice in the decisions affecting their lives. The aim of the James Bay Communications project would be to fill those needs for communication between the Indians, and subsequently between Indians and Southern decision-makers. With the help of VTR equipment in the hands of Native social animators, information can be rapidly disseminated, exchanges of views with and between the communities aided, and awareness of problems and possible solutions can be accelerated. The Cree will then be in a position to communicate with the Southern Quebec Indians, with the James Bay Corporation and the Quebec Government, and with Ottawa and can use videotape as one possible means of supporting their views.[114]

Film presenters were to be selected from each of the major communities affected by the power project: "The animators must be well-respected members of these communities, with some animation background to enable them to cope with the necessary written reports as the project goes along. They must also have a firm commitment to provide a forum for discussion." The animators were not unlike the travelling projectionists of the rural circuits, gathering "quantitative and qualitative data ... [to] permit an assessment of whether the objectives have been reached and an evaluation of the impact of the film upon its audiences."[115] In their capacity as cultural mediators, they also resembled the local high school students who had been used by the rural circuits in immigrant communities in the 1940s.

Zannis proposed a six-week intensive training program for the facilitators. They would return to their communities and begin holding discussions and videotaping them. Tapes could then be circulated inside communities and between communities.

Three months could be devoted to exchanges of information and meetings and investigation while at the same time, the animators in each community are still stimulating discussions and generating proposals. By this time, the Indians would have reached a concensus [sic] on the solutions they propose to solve their common problems. They would then be ready to make tapes and written presentations in French and English to support their proposals. It is necessary that this stage begin after full consultations between the many communities comprising the Indian population. Presentations and representations would be made to the Quebec Indian Association with feedback to the Northern people. Presentation to the James Bay Corporation, the Quebec government, the Federal Government and feedback would be given to the Northern people and responsible communication would lead to responsible decision-making by all parties involved.[116]

As Moore suggests, the argument about process over product had come full circle: "Previously, *Challenge for Change* directors had implied that it was not sympathy that mattered in the filmmaking process, it was perspective, and that the only way to get the perspective of the powerless on film was to let them make the film. The new assessment was tremendously different. It stated that a sympathetic film made for the powerless would benefit them. In this light it was once again conceivable that a white, middle-class Canadian could make a 'sympathetic' (and thus beneficial) film about the poor, Native Americans, or any other disenfranchised group."[117]

In the end, filmmaking by professional filmmakers won out over filmmaking as a form of social work with amateurs. By late 1970s, "'access to the media' ... meant directing a film for a group of voiceless people, using the Fogo process as a supposed means of assuring validity. That process in its basest form had come to mean merely showing rushes to a group of citizens before putting together a finished product. In some cases it appears little effort was actually afforded to making sure the film was the 'peoples' voice.'"[118] The interdepartmental committee was becoming less sympathetic to *Challenge for Change*, and by 1978–79, all but the Secretary of State and Health and Welfare had discontinued funding for the program.[119] At this point, many *Challenge for Change* filmmakers moved to the New Perspectives program or to the newly formed women's studio, Studio D.[120] "Thus, in the end, little attempt was made to hear the voice of the people, or, as it was so often termed, 'the people's message to the government.' Apparently no consultation was made with any of the individuals from the various communities across Canada who had been involved in *Challenge for Change*. Film

Board staff members submitted their proposal for a new program based on what they wanted and what they thought the Treasury Board and the departments might approve. What 'the people' wanted was apparently of no consequence."[121]

The *Challenge for Change* initiative represented a new moment in government realism. Rather than basing documentary films on statistical data or quasi-sociological case studies, many of which were left open ended, these films were made as part of a process that targeted specific groups and made filmmaking a means to an end – namely, solving community problems. Yet the communities were chosen based on their need as seen in a population management perspective. As D.B. Jones has aptly observed, "The traditional sponsored film conveyed government's message to the people; the Challenge for Change films would convey messages from 'the people' (particularly disadvantaged groups) to the government, directly or through the Canadian public. Films would be like government briefs – expressions of citizens' opinions elicited by, and submitted to, the government, with the aim of directly influencing specific government policy, by criticizing it."[122] Unlike Jones's liberal perspective, however, I would position these experiments on a historical continuum of using documentary to represent and contain social problems. Very similar transformations were underway in the same period in qualitative social science. As new social movements presented new challenges to the state's governmental project, *Challenge for Change*'s direct approach seemed to offer new ways to deploy government realism.

STUDIO D

Although women's issues appeared in NFB films in the 1950s – for example, *Is It a Woman's World?* (1956) and *Women at Work* (1958) – they did not become the centre of much attention until the funding directives of the 1970s. In 1967 the government established the Royal Commission on the Status of Women to grapple with the demands of the international women's movement. After much lobbying, in 1974, just before the United Nations declaration of the International Year of the Woman, the NFB established a woman's studio, Studio D, and relegated much of its social issues filmmaking to the new unit. Long-time NFB filmmaker Kathleen Shannon was named head of the studio, and along with Margaret Pettigrew and Yuki Yoshida she

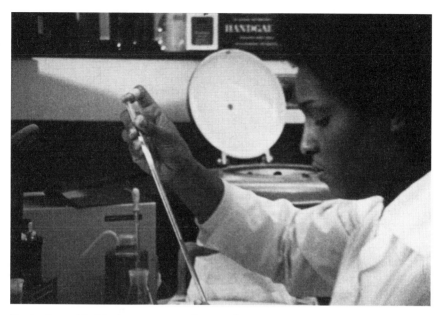

Beginning with *Mothers Are People* (*Working Mothers* series 1974, Kathleen Shannon), second-wave feminism makes its way to the NFB, paving the way for the foundation of Studio D.

inaugurated the women's production unit with a series of ten shorts, entitled *Working Mothers*. The films were used by five government departments for gender-sensitivity workshops.[123] Studio D was a direct outgrowth of *Challenge for Change/Société nouvelle*, which continued to be the rubric under which Anne Claire Poirier's *En tant que femmes* (1972), as well as the *Working Mothers* (1974) series, were produced. Film historian Elizabeth Anderson observes that these "early social realist documentaries can be viewed as visual representations of the popular and largely undocumented consciousness-raising groups of second-wave feminism."[124]

Achieving what Elizabeth Anderson calls an "unlikely alliance" between feminist filmmakers and a federal cultural institution, Studio D was founded in contradictory circumstances. Taking advantage of government initiatives in women's programs and multiculturalism, it received targeted funding to make dozens of films in the late 1970s and early 1980s. In its second year its budget was increased 600 percent to $600,000.[125] Anderson observes that many of the early films "focused

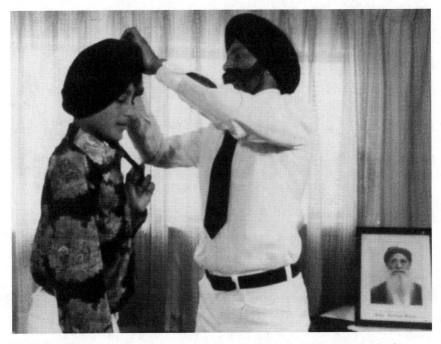

Facets of Canadian life are refracted through typical children in the high-profile series *Children of Canada*, which included *Gurdeep Singh Bains* (1977, Beverly Shaffer).

on individual women's lives, placing them in a larger socio-historical Canadian context."[126] Moreover, although the content varied widely, the "aesthetic form was fairly consistently didactic," distancing the studio even further from innovative work being done in the independent women's filmmaking community in this period.[127] The tactic of typicality was still in use.

Continuing in the government realism vein, between 1975 and 1981 Shannon produced a series of stories about Canadian children where the child's name was used to collapse distinctions between the person and the filmic profile. *My Name Is Susan Yee* (1975) is narrated by the film's subject, who describes her life in an immigrant family in Montreal's Chinatown. She and her family live in poverty, doing piecework at home. Nevertheless, Susan is being assimilated into Canadian society in the school system. *Kevin Alec* (1977) is an observational story about a Fountain aboriginal boy living in Lillooet, British Columbia. Different members of his family show him how to perform various traditional tasks – for the sake of the camera as much as for his education. *Gurdeep Singh Bains* (1977) is a film about a thirteen-year-old Sikh boy who lives on a dairy farm in Chilliwack, British Columbia. In voice-over he explains aspects of his life, both on a farm and as a Sikh. In one scene Gurdeep's father wraps his turban for him. "It's not easy to be different," he says in voice-over, "but I'm proud to be a Sikh and I'm going to keep my religion." *Julie O'Brien* (1981) profiles an eleven-year-old Newfoundland girl of the same name. In voice-over, Julie narrates her life's routines. Through her story, the viewer is introduced to the contradiction of modernization in Newfoundland as Julie participates in traditional religious and folk ceremonies and as she reads to her class her report on the modernization of her province.

All of these profiles collapse ethnic and regional identity into the figure of a typical child, who innocently explains his or her cultural identity for the benefit of an outsider. Although each of the films stands alone, when presented as part of the *Children of Canada* series they recall the trans-Canadian "national" films of the 1950s and 1960s, discussed above. Each region is encapsulated into a single figure of a child who typifies certain social or economic issues. Through the isolation of the profiled subjects from any historical or political analysis of Canadian society, the ways in which race, ethnicity, and region organize Canadian citizenship are naturalized onto the bodies of the children.

CONCLUSION

In most histories of the NFB, the film activity of the late 1960s and 1970s is presented as being a radical departure from the previously dominant Griersonian philosophy. In this chapter, I have tried to show how closely NFB policy and production was tied to new theories of citizenship and new moves in the social sciences toward self-reflexive practice, participant-action research, and progressive moves in anthropology and other social sciences about how subjects and objects of knowledge were connected in relations of power. These issues were particularly apt in depictions of First Nations people.

As the 1970s progressed, feminism provided the most powerful challenge to institutional social science, introducing methodological considerations such as the connection between researcher and subject, and challenging the division between subject and object, personal and political, reason and emotion. Consciousness-raising groups were transformed into the social scientific method of focus groups (in place of individual interviews), which aimed to foster group identity between subjects while downplaying the power imbalance between researcher and research subjects. In this atmosphere, the NFB became increasingly focused on questions of difference, a move that was also occurring outside the cultural institution in video art, alternative documentary practice and radical social science.

Historically, it is significant that as other mandates for nation building fell away, by the end of the 1970s, Studio D was seen to be the NFB's most important producing unit. Some of its films, such as *If You Love This Planet* (1982), a film about the dangers of nuclear war, and *Not a Love Story* (1981), about feminist responses to pornography, sparked controversial events wherever they were shown. *I'll Find a Way* (1977), a film about disability in the *Children of Canada* series, won an Academy Award for best short documentary in 1978. But the growth of alternative distribution sites, such as artist-run centres and film festivals, the expansion of cable television, and attempts to develop the feature film industry in the 1970s, were making the function of the NFB less clear. Interestingly, when the mandate was challenged in 1980–81, the NFB was not discarded but was reaffirmed as an important part of the use of film for public service. What this meant was that while arts policy turned toward the language of cultural industries over the next decade, the role of the NFB was confirmed as promoting the cultural policy of population diversity, an area which governmentality scholars have observed burgeoned in the 1980s and 1990s.[128] This outcome supports a reading of the National Film Board as part of the governmental apparatus of seeing the population through government realism – the statistical point of view – an important part of modern states and something that could apparently not be regulated in the feature film industry or left to the private sector.

SEVEN

Documenting Difference: The NFB in the 1980s and 1990s

Years ago the NFB not only led but was almost alone in the service of specialized audiences ... The challenge of the eighties is simply this: to discover new ways of reflecting the cultural maturity of our country using the new communication technologies so that the Board may continue to render a service to the nation as a whole by its traditional means of serving, separately and specially, the individual parts.
– National Film Board, *Annual Report*, 1979–80

A troubled Film Board seems to bear a close relationship with a troubled culture through the equally troubled medium of documentary. This unhappy triangle suggests that, although the Film Board's present difficulties could be analyzed conventionally, from a political, economic, or managerial perspective, they can be approached as well from an aesthetic perspective.
– D.B. Jones, *Movies and Memoranda*[1]

The *Challenge for Change* program petered out in the late 1970s. In many ways taking up the mantle, Studio D was a strong force for women's filmmaking through the late 1970s and early 1980s with such films as Anne Claire Poirier's *Mourir à tue-tête* (1979), *Not a Love Story* (Bonnie Sherr Klein, 1981), and *If You Love This Planet* (Terre Nash, 1982). However, the 1970s was a time of transition. Economic, social, and cultural shifts posed new challenges for epistemology in general and for documentary film in particular. The Canadian film and television industries were providing new opportunities for filmmaking outside the National Film Board, and spurred by public funding for alternative media practices, a number of video production and distribution centres, such as Video In, Videographe, and V Tape, were started across Canada, becoming flashpoints for alternative forms of cultural production and distribution.[2]

In *Brink of Reality*, Peter Steven identifies a shift in independent documentaries that occurred in the early 1980s. These "new documentaries," as he calls them, were at once opposed to mainstream media and "differ[ed] entirely from the prescriptive plans to develop better informed citizens, as set out by John Grierson at the National Film Board."[3] New forms of politics, especially the challenges of personal experience and difference within the left posited by feminism, linked new social movements to new forms of expression. As Steven puts it, "There is an awareness [among white producers] that the old ways of visual anthropology, no matter how well intentioned, will no longer suffice; neither neutral observation nor participant observation will continue unchallenged. Ethnographic media-making is on the defensive, and new visual languages for representing First Nations' people will soon dominate this documentary avant-garde formation."[4] Although the NFB was coming to represent an aspect of mainstream Canadian culture against which the independent film – and especially video making and left-wing communities – defined themselves, I would argue that this new ethos of filmmaking was felt strongly at the NFB as well.

Yet these changes were not taking place in a vacuum. The 1980s was also witness to a massive epistemological shift in the social sciences, when challenges felt since the 1960s were becoming increasingly mainstream. Work by James Clifford and Michael Taussig in anthropology, and Robert Rosenstone and Hayden White in history, among others, introduced questions of rhetoric and narrative into traditional disciplines.[5] Moreover, the role of the academic authority producing knowledge about the world was questioned. Film and media played a part in these debates about disciplinary integrity, especially on the question of popularizing knowledge. In fact, much of the fuss concerned the issue about the loss of the other, the subject of knowledge, which threw the social scientific project into crisis.[6]

This crisis of academic validity and legitimate knowledge dovetailed with a crisis of citizenship and the welfare state. The process of globalizing the world economy was well underway, and with the proliferation of new electronic technologies of communication, as well as shifting immigration policies, the notion of a located self and community became more abstract and arbitrary. In this period, the pressure to privatize cultural production that had previously been funded by the state became intense. As Michael Dorland notes, it was during the late 1970s and early 1980s that the discourse of cultural policy turned to the concept of the cultural industries, as signalled by Paul Audley's 1983 study of cultural institutions.[7] The notion of national culture endorsed by the Massey Commission in the internationalist moment of the cold war was being superseded by the notion of industry in a global marketplace.

AUTOBIOGRAPHICAL DOCUMENTARY

Although NFB films are not independent per se, they reflect the shifts in documentary form seen across the field of documentary in the 1980s, along with a consistent social science focus on the typical and the generalizable. In recent studies analysing this trend, Catherine Russell, Jim Lane, and Michael Renov all identify a shift toward the autobiographical in documentary production, which they term "experimental ethnographies," "autodocumentaries," and "domestic ethnographies," respectively.[8] These terms refer to a blurring of lines between personal and historical and often between straight and experimental forms as well. Russell notes that these forms are favoured by queer identity and ethnic or racial minorities and that themes of "displacement, immigration, exile, and transnationality are prominent."[9] Bill Nichols's analysis of "performing documentaries" of the 1980s also resonates with the turn toward the autobiography of the marginal subject. According to Nichols, performing documentary presents a distinct epistemological disturbance to ethnographic film.[10]

At the same time, there has been a turn toward the personal in social science writing. Michael Angrosino and Kimberly Mays de Pérez note that "traditional ethnographic reportage favored the supposedly objective third-person voice, emanating from the 'omniscient narrator'" and that "it was women and others previously marginalized by the academic world who first dared challenge orthodoxy by writing in the first person, a trend that ... has now entered the mainstream."[11] On the subject of focus groups in feminist research, Esther Madriz points out that they are well suited to women in general and women of colour in particular, since they increase the control of participants vis-à-vis the researcher, especially in unstructured sessions: "The collective nature of the group interview empowers the participants and validates their voices and experiences," breaking down barriers between individual and collective, reason and passion, personal and political, and self and other.[12] Similarly, in the domestic ethnographies that Renov identifies, the sharing of the camera between filmmaker and film subjects – usually the filmmaker's friends and family – destabilizes the power relationship between researcher/filmmaker and film subject.

NEW POLICIES

Despite the success of Studio D, in the early 1980s the future of the National Film Board was in question once more. Canadian cultural policy had shifted toward the funding of cultural commodities that could be traded, such as feature films, rather than non-theatrical films such as those produced by the NFB. As in the late 1940s and the early 1960s, the NFB was once more put in crisis. There was a review of cultural funding, and it was widely supposed that this would mean the end of the NFB. In 1980 the Federal Cultural Policy Review Committee (Applebaum-Hébert Committee) began deliberations, the first substantial review of Canadian cultural institutions and federal cultural policy since the Massey Commission. In 1981 there were hearings about the cultural industries in Canada, and in 1982 the *Report of the Federal Cultural Policy Review Committee* was published. In the study that preceded the policy, the authors were unsympathetic to the National Film Board, writing that the cultural benefits of the NFB to Canadians were obscure and that it was time for reassessment of the NFB mandate.[13] The report states: "It is impossible to imagine the history of filmmaking in Canada without the initial, nurturing presence of the NFB. However, today the NFB no longer occupies a central position in Canadian film … Even within the public sector, the NFB's mandate 'to interpret Canada to Canadians and other nations' has been increasingly assumed by the CBC's news and public affairs programming."[14] NFB films were no longer shown in theatres, on television, or in classrooms. "The Board's output of new work no longer represents a significant film experience for the Canadian public."[15] The report suggested that government film

needs should be handled privately and that the NFB should become a research and development laboratory for film technology, as well as a
training centre.[16]

But in the event, the new *National Film and Video Policy* released by
the minister of communications, Francis Fox, in May 1984 reaffirmed
the role of the NFB in no uncertain terms. The policy aimed to balance a
"more focused and more effective cultural and social role for the public
sector – and, in particular the National Film Board – in the film and
video area [with] a private sector thrust intended to assure the economic development of a strong private Canadian film and video industry."[17]
The public sector aspect of policy placed "particular emphasis on the
production by the public sector of high quality, distinctively Canadian
film and video productions which reflect our bilingual, multicultural and
regional reality and meet the distinctive cultural and social needs of minority and specialized audiences," a role different from and complementary to that of the private sector.[18] Acknowledging the critics, the policy
endorsed the defunct *Challenge for Change* program and Studio D and
lauded the "sense of social commitment, and a desire to articulate in film
the perspectives of Canadians [that had] been central to much of the
film-making at the NFB – especially in recent years at the board's Studio
D, the only permanent women's film-making unit in the world."[19] On
the strength of these recommendations, minor modifications to the National Film Act were tabled in 1985. The new act specified that the executive director of Telefilm, the revamped Canadian Film Development
Corporation, must be a member of the National Film Board, but otherwise it remained largely unchanged from the previous legislation.

What can be made of this reassertion of publicly funded, socially
committed filmmaking policy at the very moment when cultural policy
seemed most susceptible to the language and logic of the cultural industries? One factor to consider is the twin crises in documentary form and
the coherence of the state signalled by D.B. Jones in the quotation at the
head of this chapter. By hanging on to a state-run documentary filmmaking institution in the moment of crisis, it seems to indicate the overall importance of such an institution in the Canadian context. Where
broadcasting and the market-based film industry did not seem to be fulfilling the production of visual social science about the rapid changes in
Canadian society, there was still a need to have these changes monitored
and managed to whatever degree possible. And so, against the odds, in

the mid-1980s – a time of trade liberalization and government downsizing across the West – Canada retained the National Film Board to make an increasing number of films about aboriginal, women, and minority experiences in Canada.

The fact that the NFB was still seen to be an important cultural institution in this period of great uncertainty around the role of the state, the authority of documentary, and the place of social scientific knowledge may not be unrelated to the shifts in population underway at the time. The increased autonomy of First Nations communities, the 1980 referendum on Quebec sovereignty, and the increased attention to racism by immigrants from Asia, Africa, and the Caribbean meant that Canada's governance issues needed continued attention, if not management.

It seems significant that the endorsement of cultural policy in the early 1980s came enframed in the terms of diversity. This relates to Tony Bennett's analysis in *Culture: A Reformer's Science* (1998) that the expansion of the notion of cultural policy in the 1980s and 1990s toward diversity initiatives increased "the fields of activity which are now encompassed as objects of cultural administration."[20] Bennett argues that far from these policies effacing elite culture and cultural industries, the "hierarchical ordering of relations between different spheres of culture," with such goals as "empowering communities [and] promoting cultural diversity," are important aspects of the rethinking of cultural policy going on in this period.[21] The ground lost by the NFB as a film institution was seemingly made up for by its role as a conveyor of everyday life – culture in the anthropological sense. The need for film as a communicator of social scientific information about the population was reaffirmed.

NFB film commissioner Joan Pennefather put it succinctly in the 1989–90 annual report: "In these days of globalization, interdependent economies are distinguished by a nation's unique cultural characteristics." Women and minorities thus took a leading role in representing Canada's diversity in the 1990s. In 1989 the NFB declared its representational priorities to be children and youth, women, and special interest groups. Studio D was restructured to place an emphasis on women of visual minorities.[22] In 1991 Studio 1, the aboriginal studio, was opened in Edmonton in order to "provide Canada's aboriginal peoples with a greater opportunity to tell their stories and document their own lives on film."[23] At the same time, the NFB inaugurated the series *Meeting Place* to create portraits of immigrants. Following these diversity initiatives, in the next few years *Forbidden Love: The Unashamed Stories of Lesbian Lives* (1992) and *Out: Stories of Lesbian and Gay Youth* (1993) were notable successes.

In 1981, on the heels of the very active participation of the National Action Committee on the Status of Women in the constitutional negotiations in 1980–81, the government launched the Federal Women's Film Program, administered by Studio D in partnership with government departments, "with the purpose of producing films that reflect the point of view of women and creating an awareness of the real-life situation of women in Canada." The French women's studio, Regards des femmes, was established in 1985 under the direction of Josée Beaudet. By the end of the 1980s, according to Elizabeth Anderson, Studio D products were more or less indistinguishable from "typical" NFB products, relying on talking heads and voice-over narration.[24]

One example is Barbara Evans's *In Her Chosen Field* (1989), which focuses on female farmers who have to juggle childcare, farm work, and other jobs to make ends meet. The film provides a good example of how NFB documentaries continued both to rely on the depiction of typicality for their claims to significance and to depict citizens in contact with government. The climax of the film takes place when a group of farm women band together to apply for a federal government grant for childcare subsidies. This is a good example of the film depicting a normative narrative where community needs are met through government policy. While the film provides an exemplary narrative for other women in the same position, it also gives the administrator's view of citizens managing their affairs properly.

In 1990 Rina Fraticelli produced *Five Feminist Minutes*, an anthology of short films made by women. Widely viewed across the country, often in theatrical contexts, the film was a compilation of five-minute shorts chosen from hundreds of proposals submitted to an open call. The final film exemplifies the NFB's long standard of typification, which was upheld by Studio D. The mini-films include representative shorts from women from every region and from a range of ages, sexual orientations, and ethnicities. Without having to be sponsored by any particular department, the film enacts the long-standing role of the NFB as a federal producer

A compilation of sixteen short films made to
celebrate Studio D's fifteenth anniversary, *Five
Feminist Minutes* (1990, Mary Armstrong and
Nicole Hubert, producers) was a landmark production. This still is from the final segment uniting a
diverse range of women in song, *Let's Rap.*

for the array of representative groups. In the excerpt about poverty and
abortion, for example, women look directly at the camera and talk about
the welfare policies that affect them. And in the rap piece that ends the
film, women of different ethnicities and ages contribute their stanzas to
the overall chorus of "doing it the womanly way."

Since the Canadian Multiculturalism Act (1988) and in the wake of
the Canadian Charter of Rights and Freedoms (1982), NFB policy shifted
to reflect the citizenship struggles of multicultural Canada. After ten years

Five Feminist Minutes frames feminist issues by looking at
a range of representative women from across Canada. Issues
such as body image, occupation, and history all received
attention.

in the Department of Communications, in 1992 the NFB was moved to
the Department of Canadian Heritage, where it currently remains and
in which its citizenship mandate was again brought to the fore. Studio
D's production policy in the 1990s was dominated by New Initiatives in
Film (1991–96), a program aimed at providing opportunities for women
of colour and First Nations women. Sylvia Hamilton, a Nova Scotia
filmmaker who had worked for the Secretary of State in race relations,
was hired to work on designing and administering the program.[25] To
justify the program, Fraticelli argued that as Studio D is to the NFB, so
is New Initiatives in Film to Studio D.[26] Even the margins were becoming centres. Anderson notes that the program to bring diversity to Studio D and the NFB assumes that "women of colour and Native women
recognize that if their stories are to be heard and known they must 'gain

control' of the processes of representation."²⁷ The assumption is that these members of society must recognize their alienation from mainstream representation and believe that creating images is the way to address their social marginalization. Anderson concludes that "Studio D's attempts to give greater voice to marginalized groups and to produce more varied images of women were largely token efforts – token because they did not often lead to substantive structural change or to power sharing."²⁸ When Studio I was closed in 1996, it was replaced by the Aboriginal Filmmaking Program, which has been renewed every three years.

Films promoting multicultural citizenship in the tradition of *Peoples of Canada* and *Trans-Canada Journey* continued to be made. For example, *Canadian Portraits* (Siobhan Flanagan and Peter Williamson, 1988), sponsored by the Department of Multiculturalism and Citizenship, used the narrative strategy of a fictional teenager being given a classroom project to understand Canadian history. The student questions the emphasis on great men and decides to pursue a project about the "ordinary folk who really built the country." The filmmakers interview recent immigrants from Asia and South Asia and compare their stories with those of Canadians of African, Inuit, francophone, and Jewish descent. The film manages to exploit the documentary strategy of typicality while simultaneously questioning the traditional mode of history. The interviews with a range of new and old Canadians serves to reinforce the image of diversity without addressing difference. The anglophone filmmakers search out new Canadians and old Canadians of ethnic-minority status without putting themselves in the picture or questioning the idea of the "mosaic."

This is not so for Alanis Obomsawin, an aboriginal activist who was profiled in one of the original Studio D films, *Our Dear Sisters* (1975), and has become one of the NFB's most prolific and important filmmakers. Her series of films, spanning thirty-five years, often concern the state's clashes with aboriginal groups across Canada. From *Incident at Restigouche* (1984) to *Kanehsatake: 270 Years of Resistance* (1993), her films are often powerful indictments of the Canadian state's aboriginal policies. As a series, they have become a significant record of the landclaims battles and other social and political struggles of the past three and a half decades. The Obomsawin films participate in, and are acts of representation of, a dialogue within the Canadian state about the status

One of the most important directors of the NFB, Alanis Obomsawin (right) appears in *Our Dear Sisters* (1975, Kathleen Shannon) as the film's subject.

and plight of aboriginal peoples. In *Incident at Restigouche*, for example, the filmmaker interrogates an agent of the state, Lucien Lessard, the minister in charge of fisheries in Quebec, about his role in a violent raid on aboriginal fishers. Obomsawin's films are part of a process of negotiation of the rights and responsibilities of aboriginal and state actors.

In *Is the Crown at War with Us?* (2002), Obomsawin explores the traumatic experiences of the Mi'kmaq band at Burnt Church, New Brunswick, during a period of violent attacks by the RCMP on native fishers. Throughout the film, Obomsawin provides a powerful perspective on the erosion of the band's livelihood, land, and culture, not just in the recent past but stretching back over hundreds of years of contact with European powers. It is clear from many of the people interviewed the repeated physical and legal attacks (both of which are shown in the film) have worn down the community. Yet the message throughout is one of strength and survival. The attempt of the Canadian church and state to alter the Mi'kmaq way of life is repeatedly discussed as a relatively brief upheaval in the perspective of an ancient culture. As in all her films, Obomsawin puts recent clashes in a longer perspective and highlights the tenacity of aboriginal communities in the face of brutal policies of eradication.

Zuzana Pick notes that Obomsawin makes powerful use of the "insider voice" in her films; the interview becomes a way to make her presence felt: "The interview, used to shape point of view, becomes a valuable instrument to validate individual biography, make intelligible the ongoing struggles for Native self-definition, and contest Eurocentric narratives of First Nations history."[29] As a politicized aboriginal artist, Obomsawin brings a particular advocacy to her role as filmmaker; but since her films are made through the government agency, they also tacitly become part of the national dialogue about the place of aboriginal communities in Canadian society. The films themselves are important records of the contact between this segment of Canadian society and the state agents in charge of organizing them. In this way, her films are heightened versions of the NFB's recent work: filmmakers from identifiable communities are called upon to make films about the issues that face their communities in order to contribute to a larger government dialogue about the meaning and organization of a federal system.

In 1992 the NFB released First Nations: The Circle Unbroken, a compilation of films about First Nations made over the years at the NFB. Intended for classroom use, the seven-volume series presents a very sympathetic history of the NFB, the Canadian state, and the First Nations. As we have seen in the history of the representation of First Nations by the NFB, the images and narratives have changed from ethnographies and stories of modernization and progress to valorization of traditional ways of life and stories made by First Nations filmmakers about their communities. These differences are elided in the new packaging of the films into a series about the value of diversity.

The plethora of films made by and about First Nations since the 1990s production policies include Beating the Streets (Lorna Thomas, 1998), Forgotten Warriors (Loretta Todd, 1997), Hunters and Bombers (Hugh Brody, 1991), Is the Crown at War with Us? (Alanis Obomsawin, 2002), Lost Songs (Clint Alberta, 1999), Mi'kmaq Family (Catherine Anne Martin, 1995), Our Nationhood (Alanis Obomsawin, 2003),

Power (Magnus Isacsson, 1996), *Redskins, Tricksters and Puppy Stew* (Drew Hayden Taylor, 2000), *Totem: The Return of the G'psgolox Pole* (Gil Cardinal, 2003), *Yuxweluptun: Man of Masks* (Dana Claxton, 1998), and *Urban Elders* (Robert S. Adams, 1997).

Films made about white and First Nations relations are also part of this mandate to understand diversity. Nettie Wild's film *Blockade* (1994) is interesting in the way it sets up a dialogue between native and non-native perspectives in the face of disputes over the logging industry and land claims in British Columbia in the 1990s. Taking as its point of departure the McEachern decision that denied the authority of Gitksan and Wet'suwet'en oral history as evidence in land ownership, Wild interviews loggers, white and native, as well as a range of other people living in British Columbia's north. What she discovers is a more or less intractable situation where the imperative of the logging industry has everyone in its grip and there seems little hope of either resolving the land claims issue or saving the British Columbian forest.

After the demise of Studio D in 1996, its mandate was taken over in part by the *Reel Diversity* program, although the rearrangement lacked the symbolic presence of a women's program as such. *Reel Diversity* is the latest strategy for attracting "marginal" citizens to make films about their experiences, continuing to reinscribe Canadian "others" on film. Run as a competition in conjunction with the CBC, CBC Newsworld, and Vision TV, the program is restricted to "emerging filmmakers of colour" and places an emphasis on first-person experiences of race. Five winners are chosen from the five regions of Canada (Pacific, Western, Ontario, Quebec, and Atlantic), and a range of ethnicities are represented. Filmmakers are given lessons in video production and a maximum budget of $200,000 to make a forty-minute video in one year. The documentary treatment they submit is assessed on the basis of its social relevance, creative treatment, and broadcast potential. Winners have included *Raisin' Kane: A Rapumentary* (2000), which promises to take us "inside the Black male psyche"; *Black, Bold and Beautiful* (1999), which explores the issues surrounding black women's hairstyles; *Colour Blind* (1999), which explores teenage racial conflicts; and *Western Eyes* (2000), which explores Asian women's racial identities. The program restricts the filmmakers' projects to those dealing with race and identity, and thus it restricts filmmakers of visible minorities to the fact of their visibility as a marker of difference, without examining the *causes* of racism or issues of

Blockade (1994, Nettie Wild) explores 1990s
aboriginal land claims in British Columbia and
the challenges of diversity.

transnational migration, or the way in which racial difference and multicultural discourse function for dominant groups of white Canadians.
The program also follows closely on changes in the social sciences,
which have moved from participant observer to experiential and anec-
dotal. Nevertheless, the aspect of representativeness in both race and region – for filmmaker now as well as film subject – continues to form the
backbone of the much-reduced production policy.

Karen Cho's *In the Shadow of Gold Mountain* (2004) stages another
such dialogue about difference around the theme of Chinese Canadian

citizenship struggles. The film is presented from the viewpoint of Cho, who identifies herself as a mixed-heritage young Canadian. Over scenes of Canada Day celebrations in Ottawa, Cho says that she was "shocked" to learn about the past injustices done to her Chinese family members. This sets the scene for her investigation of these past wrongs and what is being done to compensate for them. She interviews family members as well as activists in the head tax redress movement. Using archival footage of the building of the Canadian Pacific Railway and of historic Chinatowns, Cho establishes the construction of the Chinese Canadian population as well as the historical injustices it has suffered. She also highlights the current debate within the Chinese community about the wisdom of the redress movement. Well-made and on a topic of significance, Cho's film seems exemplary of the type of filmic approach made logical by the NFB mandate. The film is made and narrated by an insider/outsider ethnographer who questions traditional ethnographic and state authority. Yet her presence in the film also serves to resurrect the very authorities that it would seem to destabilize – the state and documentary film's epistemological claims to reality.

CONCLUSION

A 1996 mandate review, *Making Our Voices Heard* (1996), affirmed the NFB as a production force on the Canadian scene: "Two things have made the NFB a unique Canadian institution. First, it has provided opportunities for new, emerging and established filmmakers to work in an atmosphere free from the constraints of the commercial marketplace. Second, the Board and its creative personnel have provided fresh and often iconoclastic perspectives on the rhythms of daily life in Canada."[30] And in 1998 the NFB annual report asserted, "We make it our particular mission to give voice to those Canadians whose voices are seldom heard – aboriginal people, people of colour, new Canadians from a variety of origins, Canadians from parts of the country seldom seen on the screen."[31] Yet Elizabeth Anderson posed a challenging question to Studio D which might be posed to the NFB overall: "Do images of diversity – what may be termed an aestheticized multiculturalism – substitute for the difficulties of actually working through and debating differences?"[32]

To the degree to which the National Film Board's production policies of the 1980s and 1990s provided an oppositional public sphere in which many activists and artists found funding and distribution, they also served to absorb and neutralize radical communities while enabling the projection of a tolerant state at home and abroad – or "aestheticized multiculturalism," in Anderson's phrase. At the least, in the NFB productions of this period we can see the contradictions at work of a liberal elite making films about members of marginalized groups for state scrutiny. In a gesture of flagrant federal nostalgia, one of the National Film Board's biggest successes in recent years, Catherine Annau's Genie-winning *Just Watch Me: Trudeau and the '70s Generation* (2000), provides a romantic portrait of the effects of Trudeau's bilingualism and biculturalism policy.

Significantly, the emphasis on aboriginal, queer, and minority filmmakers paralleled the shift during the same period to question the subject/object relations in social science. There were epistemological reasons for the shift toward autobiographical media and insider ethnography. Yet, arguably, when articulated to a state filmmaking organization, this way of seeing and knowing is still part of a governmental "politics of population." It still combines a cultural diversity mandate with social policy to create a space for a dialogue about the meaning of social difference. Even at the time of the National Film Board's greatest crisis – the 1980s push to privatization and free trade – its practice of documentary filmmaking about this aspect of the population was seen to be too valuable to eradicate entirely.

Since 2001, the NFB annual reports have been full of references to cultural diversity and liberalism. Thirty percent of the productions in 2003–4 were made by emerging filmmakers, and 73 percent of these were from aboriginal or visible minority cultures. This is equivalent to 25 percent of all NFB productions. Whereas the films of the 1940s and 1950s had situated ethnic and regional minorities in their relation to the whole nation, in the spirit of classical social science, and the films of the 1960s and 1970s had worked with disadvantaged groups, according to the participant action ethos of that period, today's cultivation of filmmakers from minority groups to make films about their experiences of marginalization and ultimate acceptance in wider Canadian society fits with a social science based on identity, voice, and the question of difference. Yet despite their differences, all three moments work toward a governmental project of consensus and citizenship training that has documentary film at its centre. And all three modes focus on documentary subjects as representative types in conveying a statistical point of view about the population.

Conclusion

Film constitutes ... a mirror of a period. By analyzing NFB *productions through the years one would notice that from time to time the emphasis was put on a particular type of film, as dictated by the course of events. The analysis would, however, also reveal that a definite continuity has been maintained all along.*
– National Film Board, *Annual Report,* 1958–59

In this book I have tried to indicate the ways in which the National Film Board of Canada might be understood as a cultural institution formed by the discourses and technologies of liberalism. Indeed, I have argued that in their large numbers and their presence in non-theatrical locations, many documentary films produced by the NFB have grappled with the formation and implementation of a variety of social policies. I have attempted to situate the NFB in relation to its contexts, including its role in government policy and in gathering social scientific information. My hope is that this study will contribute a new perspective on a film policy in dialogue with Canadian culture and philosophies of media, education, and nation building.

It seemed important to me that the NFB's establishment be reconnected to the imperial project from which it partly derived, especially as this connection was intentionally ignored by the cultural nationalist narratives of the 1970s. I also aimed to show that British imperial theories of governance emphasized decentralization and an attendance to local conditions while creating an overarching federation, something that seems to have guided the theory of cultural federation in Canada. I also wanted to think about how theories of modern communication were central to the project of nation formation in the twentieth century. Connected to theories of mass education and social science, documentary film was one of the technologies developed to bring this about.

I was intrigued to find the continuities of the NFB mandate throughout its existence. Where many histories distinguish between the early films and the later ones, I have placed some emphasis on the resemblances. Thus, I explored the question of how the apparent differences in film form masked continuities of educational theory, citizenship, and strategies regarding government information about the population. One of my interests in this project has been to sort out the excitement generated by the presence of a non-commercial film agency from other forms of instrumentality that may be present.

The history of documentary film at the NFB shows the degree to which storytelling and visual culture have been placed at the centre of social policy. Analyses of narratives and speech genres are political. Often politics comes in the struggle over meaning making that is sometimes factored into the decision to make films about particular subjects. But perhaps most important, the fact that there has been no mastermind at work does not minimize the persistence of a certain governmental and social scientific logic. Grierson is a convenient hook to hang the NFB philosophy on, but as I have tried to show, his views were interconnected with a dominant philosophy of the pragmatics of culture in liberal societies. These currents shaped Canadian domestic and foreign policy and linked Canada to Britain and the United States, which meant that Grierson's ideas found favour in many quarters in Canada. Not only was film funding a fortuitous loophole for federalists in a nation with regional schisms and provincially controlled education policy, but documentary film's association with education and non-theatrical screening venues seemed the perfect complement to American dominance at the movie theatre.

The National Film Board was born in a moment of crisis: the end of the depression and the beginning of the Second World War. With the vagaries of capital cycles, the cold war, myriad hot wars, labour and new social movements, and current fears of terrorism, arguably the crisis and insecurity have not let up since. It seems odd to suggest, as many do, that the scientific epistemology of modernity has only recently been challenged. If anything, this perpetual crisis *is* modernity. I thus propose that the current epistemological crisis of validity of documentary, along with the crises of state and citizenship, do not mark the failures of any of these projects so much as the site of their operation. Similarly, technological nationalism may be seen not as a failure of Canadian civil society, as Maurice Charland suggests, but rather as a certain sort of productivity. Part of the role of the NFB has been, in Grierson's words, to be the eyes of Canada. But all vision, like all knowledge, is mediated by culture and language. With the changes to visual knowledge production have come new forms of productivity. As Bruce Curtis has pointed out, this operation of representing or seeing the population, is productive.

I have also attempted to locate documentary in a new relationship to social science, at the heart of the epistemological debates of the twentieth century. Using versions of empirical data collection – interviews, direct observation, the analysis of artifacts, documents, and cultural records, the use of visual material, and personal experience – documentary and social science share more than a formal resemblance. Documentary form is not simply a reaction to previous documentary theory; it is also a response to shifts in theories of knowledge more generally. In its relation to social science, documentary is a discourse subject to objectives and truth claims that transcend film.

Like all cultural production, documentary must be connected to the context in which it is made. At the National Film Board, changes in documentary form have been connected to social policy. The resulting government realism has paralleled the development of social science and government policy alike and has shifted from profiling communities to asking for perspectives from those very communities. The similarity that obtains between early social science narratives depicting types and autoethnographic projects depicting a filmmaker's own perspective lies in the realm of context and generalizability.

The NFB is often characterized as a site of contradictions. A federalist agency fostering a nationalist Québécois cinema (Véronneau), a patriarchal institution funding a unique women's studio, a government film agency making groundbreaking work. Grierson himself was a man with a "penchant for contradiction," according to D.B. Jones, enigmatically reconciling seemingly incongruous influences.[1] In many ways, it would seem that ambivalence has been built into the institution's constitution, for the National Film Board represents a decades-long experiment in making films with and against an official agenda for education and visual knowledge production about the nation. Beyond the identification and description of government realism in this study, I also posit that the governmental project of the National Film Board has been the root of both its longevity and aspects of its creative success. The NFB has been the site of innovation in filmmaking and visual education, not in spite of but precisely because of its nation-building mandate. Much of its innovation has come in the form of creative rejection of its official mandate or in response to public ambivalence about its products.

Privatization and commercialization have always been anathema to the NFB's nation-building mandate. The NFB has gone from being a dynamic part of the process of imagining Canadian society to an archive of government in the welfare state. New technologies have grown up alongside transnational, transcultural perspectives on identity and affiliation, challenging old models of national cohesion. Tied to citizenship and nation building, the NFB's current crisis, shared to some degree by all national cultural institutions, stems from a lack of clear language on the meaning of citizenship. Even the CitizenShift aspect of the NFB's website demonstrates a lack of clarity about its own mission. Yet despite the fact that the market dominates the discourse of cultural funding, the NFB has proved that it is still essential for its ability to satisfy the language of cultural diversity currently favoured by international cultural agencies such as UNESCO.[2] Indeed, the question of the local in a global world is seen to be increasingly important in cultural policy discourse, and government realism is still unsurpassed as a mode of cultural expression in this realm.

Just as documentary form has changed over the past sixty-five years, the National Film Board also has not been just one thing. The National Film Acts are quite schematic and a little vague, but the way that documentary film has acted in Canada as a training ground for filmmakers, as a part of our educational system, and as a technology of liberalism has remained consistent. This book has attempted to supply another voice in the dialogue on the meaning of the NFB in particular and on the exploration of state-sponsored art and education more generally. My goal has been to open up an interpretive framework for the many projects about state culture in Canada and elsewhere that have yet to be undertaken. Film acts, both parliamentary and performative, are moments in a dialogue, a struggle over what culture – in all its senses – could or should be. The NFB archive of films about Canada are acts of government realism that can tell us a great deal about Canadian society and the discursive frames that have been used to interpret and direct it. James Coldwell's words in the House of Commons on 12 May 1944 have been prescient: "Twenty, thirty, fifty or one hundred years from now the library of films being built up, and the documents being collected to-day by the national film board, will be of supreme interst."

National Film Board of Canada Annual Budgets and Responsible Government Departments *

Year	Government department responsible for the NFB portfolio	Budget (exclusive of revenue)	As a figure in 2006 dollars†
1939	Trade and Commerce	$85,024	$1,214,629
1939–40		$142,126	$1,924,623
1940–41		$103,033	$1,300,417
1941–42		Not available	
1942–43	National War Services	Not available	
1943–44		$426,500	$5,133,796
1944–45		$257, 237	$6,206,825
1945–46		$1,145,965	$13,068,022
1946–47	Reconstruction and Supply	$2,290,148	$23,628,511
1947–48		$2,141,679	$19,334,602
1948–49		$992,854	$8,901,450
1949–50	Resources and Development	$2,122,854	$18,276,226
1950–51		$2,307,804	$17,858,007
1951–52		$2,662,333	$20,601,386
1952–53		$2,919,779	$22,593,528

1953–54	Citizenship and Immigration	$2,997,528	$23,057,908
1954–55		$3,211,060	$24,700,462
1955–56		$3,192,405	$24,128,642
1956–57		$4,960,143	$36,225,763
1957–58		$4,019,466	$28,710,471
1958–59		$4,258,905	$30,090,090
1959–60		$4,555,417	$32,011,038
1960–61		$4,866,930	$33,834,273
1961–62		$5,143,773	$35,380,449
1962–63	Secretary of State	$5,182,849	$34,910,382
1963–64		$5,536,300	$36,720,357
1964–65		$6,046,000	$39,103,483
1965–66		$6,485,200	$40,338,565
1966–67		$7,509,500	$44,781,422
1967–68		$8,662,800	$49,830,265
1968–69		$9,456,200	$51,869,451
1969–70		$9,891,300	$52,916,420
1970–71		$9,657,562	$50,019,245
1971–72		$11,355,236	$55,704,931
1972–73		$13,734,740	$62,213,108
1973–74		$16,218,646	$66,094,795
1974–75		$18,784,628	$69,375,047
1975–76		$20,410,161	$70,755,225
1976–77		$24,465,047	$78,143,885
1977–78		$28,692,961	$84,391,062
1978–79		$32,095,710	$86,207,486
1979–80	Secretary of State and Communications	$29,697,147	$72,026,663
1980–81		$40,790,806	$87,940,378
1981–82	Communications	$48,100,062	$93,889,010
1982–83		$52,786,817	$98,172,907
1983–84		$56,309,518	$100,968,790
1984–85		$60,528,426	$104,221,130
1985–86		$59,418,903	$98,275,539
1986–87		$63,272,631	$100,188,088

1987–88		$66,735,572	$101,469,290
1988–89		$71,068,664	$102,654,736
1989–90		$72,565,352	$100,570,317
1990–91		$75,349,259	$99,043,515
1991–92		$78,395,420	$101,710,624
1992–93	Canadian Heritage	$81,198,717	$103,488,560
1993–94		$81,389,506	$103,528,725
1994–95		$80,136,671	$99,691,552
1995–96		$77,257,388	$94,660,325
1996–97		$72,790,837	$93,167,536
1997–98		$60,716,124	$72,680,443
1998–99		$56,728,570	$66,200,306
1999–2000		$60,591,213	$68,853,651
2000–01		$61,531,277	$68,135,145
2001–02		$62,167,184	$67,291,706
2002–03		$66,382,163	$70,331,550
2003–04		$67,251,238	$69,997,285

*Source: NFB annual reports
†Conversion done on the inflation calculator provided by the Bank of Canada
(www.bankofcanada.ca/en/rates/inflation_calc.html), accessed 23 October 2006.
Figures rounded to the nearest dollar.

NOTES

INTRODUCTION

1 Documentary has not of course been the only type of film made at the National Film Board (NFB). Many animated films and a few feature films have also been produced over the years. However, the vast majority of the output of the board has been documentary films, and this is still the dominant association with the NFB.

2 Hunter, *Culture and Government*; Bennett, *Culture*; Miller, *The Well-Tempered Self*; Lewis and Miller, *Critical and Cultural Policy Studies*.

3 Foucault, "Governmentality," 87–104; Althusser, "Ideology and Ideological State Apparatuses," 127–88.

4 Lewis and Miller, *Critical Cultural Policy Studies*, 2.

5 Miller, *The Well-Tempered Self*, 20.

6 Dorland, *The Cultural Industries in Canada*, xii.

7 Hacking, *The Taming of Chance*, and Curtis, *The Politics of Population*.

8 Winston, *Claiming the Real*, 127–250.

9 See, for example, Beattie, *Documentary Screens*.

10 Fontana and Frey, "The Interview," 652.

11 Denzin and Lincoln, *The Landscape of Qualitative Research*, 3–4.

12 Nichols, *Blurred Boundaries*, 95.

13 Angrosino and Mays de Pérez, "Rethinking Observation," 688.

14 Gergen and Gergen, "Qualitative Inquiry," 1028.

15 Lincoln and Denzin, "The Seventh Moment," 1059.

16 Harcourt, "The Innocent Eye," 73.

17 Ellis and Bochner, "Autoethnography, Personal Narrative, Reflexivity," 741.

18 Ibid.

19 Charland, "Technological Nationalism," 197–8.

20 Acland, "Popular Film in Canada," 281–96.

21 Bakhtin, "The Problem of Speech Genres," 60.

22 Ibid., 69.

23 Kristeva, "Word, Dialogue, and Novel," 37.

24 Bakhtin, "Discourse in the Novel," 272.

25 Davis, *Fiction in the Archives.*
26 Ginzburg, *Clues, Myths, and the Historical Method* and *The Cheese and the Worms.*
27 One of Ginzburg's articles is called "The Inquisitor as Anthropologist." See also *The Cheese and the Worms.*

CHAPTER ONE

1 Nichols, "The Voice of Documentary," 18.
2 Curtis, *The Politics of Population,* 3.
3 *The NFB Film Guide,* published in 1991, posits that between 1939 and 1989 some 8,000 films were produced. Allowing for 100 or more films per year for the past fifteen years, a conservative estimate, the total has increased by at least 1,500. (Bidd, *The NFB Film Guide,* xiv.) The NFB website reports 6,500 English films and 4,500 French, for a total of 11,000, but the number includes films "versioned" into each official language and therefore is inflated. Also, the NFB catalogue contains information about films that it currently distributes, not all of which are NFB films.
4 Canada, "An Act to Create a National Film Board," *Statutes of Canada, 1939,* 103.
5 See Knight, *How the Cold War Began.*
6 Marjorie McKay, "History of the National Film Board," NFB Archives (NFBA).
7 Jones, *Movies and Memoranda,* 2.
8 Nelson, *The Colonized Eye,* 13.
9 Morris, "Backwards to the Future," "Re-thinking Grierson," and "Praxis into Process"; Elder, "The Legacy of John Grierson."
10 Marchessault, "Amateur Video and the Challenge for Change" and "Reflections on the Dispossessed"; MacKenzie, "*Société nouvelle*: The Challenge for Change in the Alternative Public Sphere" and *Screening Québec; Wide Angle* 21, no. 2 (1999); Anderson, "Studio D's Imagined Community"; Taylor, "Implementing Feminist Principles in a Bureaucracy; Stoney, "The Mirror Machine."
11 Leach, *Claude Jutra;* Clandfield, *Pierre Perrault and the Poetic Documentary.*
12 Babe, *Canadian Communications Thought,* 89–111. See also McInnes, *One Man's Documentary.*
13 Kristmanson, *Plateaus of Freedom,* 49–85; Waugh, "Monkey on the Back."
14 Pronay, "John Grierson and the Documentary," 229.
15 Ibid., 238.
16 Barry, Osborne, and Rose, *Foucault and Political Reason,* 8.

17 Gordon, "Governmental Rationality," 4–5.
18 Curtis, *The Politics of Population*, 24.
19 Ibid., 42.
20 Gordon, "Governmental Rationality," 35.
21 Barry, Osborne, and Rose, *Foucault and Political Reason*, 24.
22 Curtis, *The Politics of Population*, 3.
23 Starr, "Social Categories and Claims in the Liberal State," 166.
24 Hacking, "Making Up People."
25 Hacking, *The Taming of Chance*, 1.
26 Canada, Department of Trade and Commerce, *The Dominion Bureau of Statistics: Its Origin, Constitution and Organization*, 15.
27 Nichols, "The Voice of Documentary," 17–30.
28 Nochlin, *Realism*, 14.
29 For an important discussion of performance in documentary, see Waugh, "Acting to Play Oneself."
30 Nichols, *Blurred Boundaries*, 93.
31 Williams, *Keywords*, 255.

CHAPTER TWO

1 John Grierson Archive (JGA), G4:23:35, Grierson to Stephen Tallents, 9 November 1939, 3.
2 Grierson, "Documentary: A World Perspective," in *Grierson on Documentary*, 207.
3 Beveridge, *John Grierson, Film Master*, 137.
4 Backhouse, *Canadian Government Motion Picture Bureau*, 25.
5 Ibid.
6 Beveridge, *John Grierson, Film Master*, 135.
7 Library and Archives Canada (LAC), RG26, J1, vol. 223, Ross McLean, "Memorandum on the Use of Canadian Films in the United Kingdom," 20 March 1936, 1.
8 Ibid., 6. See also, Evans, *John Grierson and the National Film Board*, 33.
9 LAC, RG26, J1, vol. 223, Ross McLean, "Memorandum," 1.
10 Swann, *The British Documentary Film Movement*, 10.
11 Ibid.
12 "Exhibition within the Empire of Empire Films," 1926, 2–3, reproduced in Jarvie, *Hollywood's Oversea's Campaign*, 68–74.
13 *Imperial Conference, 1926. Appendices to the Summary of Proceedings*, 403.
14 Ibid., 404.
15 See Constantine, "Bringing Empire Alive," 192–231 and Meredith, "Imperial Images," 30–6, and Constantine, *Buy and Build*.

16 Constantine, "Bringing Empire Alive," 217.
17 Ibid.
18 Ibid., 218.
19 Tallents, *The Projection of England*, 39.
20 Swann, *The British Documentary Film Movement*, 34; See also Stollery, *Alternative Empires*, 140–71.
21 Grierson, "The EMB Film Unit," in *Grierson on Documentary*, 49.
22 *The Film in National Life*. See also, Druick, "Reaching the Multimillions."
23 *The Film in National Life*, 15.
24 National Archives, UK., (NAUK), ED121/285, S.A. Hammond, "Proposal for a Colonial Film Unit," read into the Minutes of the Dominions, India, and Colonies Panel of the Advisory Council, 6 March 1936, 2.
25 NAUK, ED121/285, Minutes of the Dominions, India, and Colonies Panel of the Advisory Council, 5 May 1934.
26 NAUK, ED121/285, "Draft Memorandum on the various agencies concerned with the promotion of imperial unity through the film."
27 Rodger, "Some Factors Contributing to the Formation of the National Film Board of Canada," 264.
28 *Imperial Relations Trust, Annual Report, 1938–39*, 5.
29 Ibid.
30 Swann, *The British Documentary Film Movement*, 148.
31 JGA, G3:5:4, John Grierson, "Canadian Film Activities," 3 July 1939, 4.
32 Ibid., 5.
33 Ibid., 10.
34 Ibid., 12.
35 Ibid., 1.
36 JGA, G4:4:10, "Report on the Distribution of Empire Films in Great Britain and of British Films in the Dominions and India," n.d., 2–3.
37 This was, in effect, a harbinger of the postwar policy of the Canadian cooperation project in weekly instalments. And, indeed, much of Grierson's work with Hollywood can be seen, pace Joyce Nelson, as his attempt to use the superior American distribution system for ends complementary with empire communication.
38 Jones, *Movies and Memoranda*, 36.
39 NAUK, BW4/19. The following quotations are all taken from the 52-page *Report on Canadian Government Film Activities* (abridged for circulation to the board of the IRT and members of the trust's film committee), submitted by Grierson in August 1938.
40 Canada, *Report of the Royal Commission on National Development in the Arts, Letters and Sciences*, 53–5.
41 Canada, "An Act to Create a National Film Board," *Statutes of Canada*, 1939, 103.

42 JGA, G3:6:2, "A Plan for a War-Time National Film Propaganda Service in Canada," 15 September 1939, 7.

43 Ibid.

44 JGA, G4:23:35, Grierson to Tallents, 9 November 1939, 2–3.

45 JGA, G4:21:13, John Grierson, "Canada's International Position," n.d., 7.

46 JGA, G4:23:71, John Grierson, Grierson to Tallents," n.d., 1.

47 Ibid., 4.

48 JGA, G4:27:12, John Grierson, Grierson to Tallents, 16 February 1943, 4.

49 Canada, House of Commons, *Debates*, 12 May 1944, 2876.

50 NAUK, STAT 14/931, correspondence between J.S. Garner, Office of the High Commissioner for the United Kingdom, Ottawa, and R.B. Pugh, Dominions Office, London, in October 1945.

51 The Arts Enquiry, *The Factual Film*, 228–37.

CHAPTER THREE

1 Library and Archives Canada (LAC), RG20, vol. 578, A581(2), John Grierson, "The Eyes of Canada" (CBC radio address), 21 January 1940.

2 Grierson, "The Course of Realism," in *Grierson on Documentary*, 78.

3 John Grierson Archive (JGA) G4:21:21, Grierson, "Confidential Memorandum," n.d., 6.

4 Grimshaw, *The Ethnographer's Eye*, 62.

5 Ibid., 59.

6 Ibid., 63.

7 Winston, *Claiming the Real*, 134.

8 Barry, *Welfare*, 40.

9 Ibid. See also Beveridge, *Social Insurance and Allied Services*.

10 Marsh, *Report on Social Security for Canada*.

11 Guest, *The Emergence of Social Security in Canada*, 112, 134.

12 Barry, *Welfare*, 7.

13 McLaren, *Our Own Master Race*. See also Valverde, *The Age of Light, Soap, and Water*.

14 Purcell, Jr, *The Crisis of Democratic Theory*, 160 (figures in U.S. dollars).

15 For a detailed discussion of the Rockefeller Foundation's reproduction of hegemonic scholarship in the social sciences, see Fisher, "The Role of Philanthropic Foundations in the Reproduction and Production of Hegemony." A note on the private donors: The Carnegie Corporation and the Rockefeller Foundation were interested in cultural relations and seemed particularly taken with the possibilities of new technologies for social improvement. Both organisations showed early interest in social science and remained heavily invested in education and culture broadly defined.

Historian Frank Ninkovich cites the establishment of the Carnegie
Endowment for International Peace in 1910 as marking the beginning of
the institutionalization of "cultural relations" tied "however tentatively,
to foreign policy objectives" (Ninkovich, *The Diplomacy of Ideas*, 9).
The Carnegie Foundation established lending libraries across Canada,
and both foundations were involved in the funding of Canadian universities, particularly on the East Coast, early in the twentieth century (Acland
and Buxton, *American Philanthropy and Canadian Libraries*, 1–46).
Edward H. Berman has written about the hegemonic function of these
foundations in perpetuating ruling-class ideology: "The foundations' location in the capitalist state leads them to support educational institutions –
particularly universities – at home and abroad to train individuals who
not only share their perspectives, but who will use their influence to 'sell'
it to others who are less convinced of its merits" (Berman, *The Ideology
of Philanthropy*, 13).

16 Gallup, *A Guide to Public Opinion Polls*, 26–9; Désrosieres, "The Part
   in Relation to the Whole," 217–44.

17 Stott, *Documentary Expression and Thirties America*, 153.

18 Ibid., 160.

19 Hardy, *John Grierson*, 59.

20 Thornton, "Introduction to Part One," in *The Subcultures Reader*, 11.

21 See Rockefeller Foundation, *Annual Reports*.

22 Purcell Jr, *The Crisis of Democratic Theory*, 17, 19.

23 Hardy, *John Grierson*, 31.

24 Grierson, "Propaganda and Education," in *Grierson on Documentary*,
   149–51.

25 Grierson, "The Russian Example," in *Grierson on Documentary*, 23–4.

26 Karl, *Charles Merriam and the Study of Politics*, 118.

27 Willey and Rice, *Communication Agencies in Social Life*, frontispiece.

28 Merriam, *The Making of Citizens*, 34.

29 Ibid., 42.

30 Ibid.

31 Ibid., 75.

32 Ibid., 327.

33 Ibid., 378.

34 Ibid., 380.

35 Ibid., 382.

36 Ibid., 204–5.

37 Hardy, *John Grierson*, 34.

38 JGA, G5:11:1, Grierson to Brooke Claxton, 12 November 1945, 2.

39 Shore, *The Science of Social Redemption*, 85–6.

40 Park, "Sociology and the Social Sciences," in Park, *Society*, 232.

41 Park, "The Problem of Cultural Differences," 3.
42 Ibid., 4
43 Ibid., 5.
44 Park, "Sociology and the Social Sciences," 235.
45 Ibid., 193.
46 Park, "The Problem of Cultural Differences," 4.
47 Park, "The City: Suggestions for the Investigation of Human Behaviour," 16.
48 Ibid.
49 Ibid., 26.
50 Ibid., 18.
51 Ibid., 22.
52 Shore, *The Science of Social Redemption*, 95.
53 Ibid., 105.
54 Evans, *John Grierson and the National Film Board of Canada*, 29, 35; Young, *Making the Truth Graphic*, 52.
55 Lippmann, *Public Opinion*, 39.
56 Ibid.
57 Lippmann, *The Phantom Public*, 189.
58 Grierson, "Education and Total Effort," in *Grierson on Documentary*, 139.
59 Young, *Making the Truth Graphic*, 14.
60 Ibid., 66.
61 Ibid., 65.
62 Young, "Chauvinism and Canadianism," 32.
63 LAC, RG53, vol. 1, "Meeting of the National Film Board," 8 June 1943, 1.
64 Ibid.
65 JGA, G4:23:70, Grierson to Stephen Tallents, n.d.
66 JGA, G4:23:35, Grierson to Stephen Tallents, 9 November 1939.
67 JGA, G3:6:2, "A Plan for a War-time National Film Propaganda Service in Canada," 15 September 1939, 2.
68 Canada, House of Commons, *Debates*, 14 July 1944, 4904.
69 Dreiziger, "The Rise of a Bureaucracy for Multiculturalism," 22.
70 These are categories exclusive of "resources and industry" and "current events." My thanks to Peter Morris for sharing this unpublished raw data with me.
71 See Low, NFB *Kids*.
72 Grierson used the term "peoples" as we would now use "cultures." See Robert McMillan, "Ethnology and the NFB," 68.
73 Driesziger, "The Rise of a Bureaucracy for Multiculturalism," 6.
74 Kirkconnell, *Canadians All*, 5.
75 Ibid., 7, 12.

76 NFB Archives (NFBA), A Man and His Job file, Alistair to Dallas Jones, 3 August 1942.

77 NFBA, A Man and His Job file, Phelan to David Petegorsky, 13 April 1943.

78 Whynot, "The NFB and Labour, 1945–1955," 14.

79 Hackett, "The National Film Society of Canada, 1935–1951," 149.

80 McInnes, "Teamwork for Harmony," 318.

81 Ibid., 323–4.

82 Ibid., 348.

83 Ibid., n 94.

84 Nichols, "The Voice of Documentary," 17–30.

85 NFBA, Labour Looks Ahead file, information sheet, April 1945.

86 NFBA, Labour Looks Ahead file, Stanley Jackson to F.R. Clarke, 9 November 1942.

87 NFBA, Labour Looks Ahead file, information sheet, April 1945.

88 NFBA, Coal Face Canada file, W.H. Cranston to Ross McLean, 15 October 1941.

89 NFBA, Coal Face Canada file, George Lebeau, "Confidential Report of Labour Conditions in the Coal Mines of Alberta," 6 May 1943.

90 NFBA, Coal Face Canada file, "Draft Memo on the Coal Film," n.d.

91 Ibid.

92 NFBA, Coal Face Canada file, "Moving Picture: Coal Production in Canada," n.d.

93 NFBA, Coal Face Canada file, McInnes to V.C. Phelan, Director of Information, Dept. of Labour, n.d.

94 NFBA, Coal Face Canada file, David Petegorsky to Ross McLean, "Industrial Morale Program in the Coal Mining Industry," 11 March 1943.

95 Ibid., 2–3.

96 NFBA, Coal Face Canada file, "Suggested Script Treatment for Coal Mining Film," n.d.

97 NFBA, Coal Face Canada file, Dan Wallace to Lt-Col. F.X. Jennings, Director of Public Relations, Army, 14 July 1943.

98 NFBA, Coal Face Canada file, Graham McInnes to Robert Edmonds, 10 August 1943.

CHAPTER FOUR

1 Library and Archives Canada (LAC), RG27, vol. 852, John Grierson, "Outline of Policy and Future Perspective for the Board," 28 September 1942, 3.

2 Kidd, *Pictures with a Purpose*, 11.

3 For an important exception, see Kristmanson, *Plateaus of Freedom*, 49–85.

4 Tippett, *Making Culture*, 180, 187.
5 Dowler, "The Cultural Industries Policy Apparatus"; Litt, *The Muses, the Masses, and the Massey Commission*.
6 Aside from Vincent Massey, the members of the Massey Commission were Hilda Neatby, a professor of history at the University of Saskatchewan; Georges-Henri Lévesque, dean of the Faculty of Social Sciences at Laval University; Norman A.M. MacKenzie, president of the University of British Columbia and member of the Wartime Information Board; and Arthur Surveyer, a civil engineer from Montreal.
7 Faris, *The Passionate Educators*, 121; Litt, *The Muses, the Masses, and the Massey Commission*, 20.
8 Description taken from the preface to Gwendolen Carter's Canadian Institute of International Affairs–issued book, *The British Commonwealth and International Security*. Through the Massey Foundation, which Vincent ran after his father's death, money was granted to the Canadian Institute of International Affairs in 1932 (Massey, *What's Past Is Prologue*, 57). See also Druick, "International Cultural Relations as a Factor in Postwar Canadian Cultural Policy."
9 Litt, *The Muses, the Masses, and the Massey Commission*, 21.
10 Massey, *What's Past Is Prologue*, 40. For more on the round table movement, see Faris, *The Passionate Educators*, 2–3.
11 Massey, *What's Past Is Prologue*, 85.
12 Massey, *On Being Canadian*. The book was originally called *Canada and the World*.
13 James, *Film as a National Art*.
14 Bertrand and Collins, *Government and Film in Australia*, 97.
15 Grierson, "Memorandum to the Right Honourable, the Prime Minister (1940)," 72–8; Hawes, "Grierson in Australia (1972)," 79–84; Dennis, *"The Tin Shed"*; Dawson, "The Grierson Tradition," 139–41; Bertrand and Collins, *Government and Film in Australia*, 94–118.
16 Hackett, "The National Film Society of Canada, 1935–1951," 148.
17 Tippett, *Making Culture*, 149. See also Vincent Massey Archives (VMA), B1987-0082/004, file 11, for correspondence and background information on this committee.
18 VMA, B1987-0082/032, file 6, McCurry to Massey, 27 September 1935.
19 Acland, "Patterns of Cultural Authority," 16.
20 Hackett, "The National Film Society of Canada," 162n42.
21 Buchanan, *Report on Educational and Cultural Films in Canada*, 20 (emphasis added).
22 Kidd, *Pictures with a Purpose*, 34. Kidd was formerly executive secretary of the Joint Planning Council as well as being Ned Corbett's assistant in the Canadian Association of Adult Education. See Faris, *The Passionate Educators*, 42–3.

23 Tippett, *Making Culture*, 144.
24 Faris, *The Passionate Educators*, 49. See also, Hackett, "The National Film Society of Canada," 135–68; Acland, "National Dreams, International Encounters," 3–26, and "Patterns of Cultural Authority," 2–27; Young, *Making the Truth Graphic*, 29.
25 Dreisziger, "The Rise of a Bureaucracy for Multiculturalism," 20–3.
26 This approach is exemplified in Gibbon's *Canadian Mosaic*.
27 Canada, House of Commons, *Debates*, 5 November 1941, 4104.
28 Fromer, "Canada's Rural Movies Building Citizenship," 19a.
29 McInnes and Gauthier, "Canada: Film Producer," 42.
30 Ibid.
31 There were similarities with the contemporaneous British Mass Observation project. See Pickering and Chaney, "Democracy and Communication," 41–56; Richards and Sheridan, *Mass-Observation at the Movies*; and Baxendale and Pawling, "Representing the People," 17–45.
32 Gray, *Movies for the People*, 26.
33 Ibid., 52.
34 Hemming, "Canada's National Film Board," 38.
35 Hackett claims 1942, but the NFB annual report for 1944–45 states that the circuits were launched in 1943 (Hackett, "The National Film Society of Canada," 149).
36 LAC, RG28 A, vol. 1/2, file 3-C2-1-3, "Industrial and Trade Union Circuits Report for January 1944," 3.
37 Ibid., 50.
38 NFB Archives (NFBA), Film and You file, Charles W. Marshall to T.V. Adams, 17 June 1948.
39 NFBA, Film and You file, Calais Calvert to Dave Woodsworth, 28 July 1947.
40 Ibid.
41 NFBA, Film and You file, "B.C. Co-operative Film Council Regional Convergence at Creston," 14 April 1947.
42 Ibid., 126.
43 Ibid., 90.
44 NFBA, Film and You file, Professor E. Bovard to Julian Biggs, 6 May 1953. Bovard was a strong advocate of unchaired, "conversational" discussions (Gray, *Movies for the People*, 92–3.)
45 Ibid.
46 NFBA, Film and You file, Vaughan Deacon, "Getting the Most Out of Your Film Screening" (draft report), 29 December 1952.
47 In British Columbia and Alberta the film was paired with the Frank Sinatra film, *The House I Live In*, causing at least one Alberta viewer to

note that *Everyman's World* "suffered more than otherwise by comparison." This evokes Joyce Nelson's analysis that the circuits were little more than attempts to avoid Hollywood's jurisdiction over theatrical distribution and served to keep Canadian shorts as handmaidens to American features. See also Gray's assessment that the film circuits were occasions for multiple types of entertainment and were often paired with magic shows, agricultural fairs, square dances, community business meetings, sporting events, and other forms of sociality (Nelson, *The Colonized Eye*, 89; Gray, *Movies for the People*, 48).

48 NFBA, Film and You file, official information sheet, n.d.

49 NFBA, Film and You file, "Let's Discuss it! A film Discussion Guide," n.d.

50 VMA, B1987-0082/346, file 2, NFB submission to the Massey Commission, 33.

51 NFBA, Film and You file, Don Fraser to Ross McLean, "Memorandum re: Film Council film project," 12 May 1947.

52 NFBA, V Is for Volunteers file, Tom Daly to Don Mulholland, "Memorandum, Re: Volunteers in Welfare" and Junior Leagues contract, 23 November 1950.

53 NFBA, V Is for Volunteers file, Meeting at NFB to discuss film on volunteer social workers, 20 October 1949.

54 NFBA, V Is for Volunteers file, Leslie McFarlane to Arthur Irwin, memo, "Script History of V is for Volunteers," 17 December 1951.

55 NFBA, V Is for Volunteers file, information sheet, n.d.

56 NFBA, V Is for Volunteers file, Norman Chamberlain to David Crawley, 23 November 1951.

57 Dufour, "'Eggheads' and Espionage," 189.

58 Ibid., 190.

59 Ibid., 196.

60 Whitaker and Marcuse, *Cold War Canada*, 252.

61 Ibid., 248.

62 Ibid., 253; Scher, *The Un-Canadians*, 85.

63 Canada, *National Film Board: Survey of Organization and Business Administration*; Special Committee on the National Film Board, *Minutes of Proceedings and Evidence*. H. Woods was on the executive of the Canadian Institute of International Affairs throughout the 1940s; Walter Gordon was the vice-chair in 1952–53.

64 Canada, House of Commons, *Debates*, 4 July 1952, 4278. For details of the relationship between the cold war and film noir at the NFB, see Druick, "Non-theatrical with Dreams of Theatrical."

65 Canada, "An Act Respecting the National Film Board," *Statutes of Canada*, 1950, 1: 569.

66 See Litt, *The Muses, the Masses, and the Massey Commission,* 50.

67 VMA, B1987-0082/345, file 4, 2, Ruth Cameron, "Submission from the Federation of British Columbia Film Councils," n.d.

68 Hackett, "The National Film Society of Canada," 154.

69 VMA, B1987-0082/380, file 26, Donald Buchanan, "Documentary and Educational Films in Canada, 1935–1950," 26.

70 VMA, B1987-0082/187, file 9, Donald Buchanan to Vincent Massey, n.d.

71 Canada, *Report on the Royal Commission on National Development in the Arts, Letters, and Sciences* (Massey Report), 246. The following references will be to the Massey Report.

72 Ibid., 246.

73 UNESCO, *Report of the Commission on Technical Needs in Press, Radio, Film,* 58, 60.

74 UNESCO, *Film and Cinema Statistics: A Preliminary Report on Methodology with Tables Giving Current Statistics,* 3.

75 UNESCO, *The United Nations Education, Scientific, and Cultural Organization: Final Act of the London Conference Constitution,* 5.

76 UNESCO, *Film and cinema statistics,* 3.

77 Tippett, *Making Culture,* 187.

78 VMA, B1987-0082/346(1), Submission to the Massey Commission from Canadian Council for Reconstruction through UNESCO, 28 July 1949.

79 Ibid.

80 Ibid.

81 See Evans, *John Grierson and the National Film Board,* 224–68; Jack Ellis, *John Grierson,* 229–39. There were six departments at UNESCO: education, natural sciences, social sciences, cultural activities, mass communication, and technical assistance (Laves and Thomson, *UNESCO: Purpose, Progress, Prospects,* 45.)

82 See Ellis, *John Grierson,* 229.

83 UNESCO, *Report of the Commission on Technical Needs in Press, Radio, Film,* 38.

84 Ellis, *John Grierson,* 232.

85 Ibid.

86 Kidd, "Canada's Stake in UNESCO," 249.

87 Cited in Ellis, *John Grierson,* 230.

88 VMA, B87-0082/346(2), 2, Ross McLean, NFB submission to the Massey Commission, n.d., 72.

89 Shea, *Culture in Canada,* 56. Albert Shea, a political scientist who worked for the Wartime Information Board during the war and wrote a synopsis of the Massey Commission's findings called *Culture in Canada* in 1952, went on to conduct a world survey of mass communications for UNESCO in the early 1950s (*Culture in Canada,* 6.)

90 Massey Report, 310.
91 LAC, RG2, 18, vol. 172, N13, "Press release from Department of Reconstruction and Supply announcing Irwin's appointment," 16 December
1949. From his new position as head of the Division of Film and Visual
Information at UNESCO, McLean wrote to Irwin requesting films for the
UNESCO library: "You will be able, I am sure, to judge this sort of thing
I have in mind. Among recently produced subjects which would be very
useful are the various psychiatric studies, *Science and Cancer* [sic], *Rising
Tide*, *Local 100*, *The World Is Our Town* [sic], the various films on con-
servation of resources, *Vegetable Insects* and good many of these you
are now putting into production – I hope all goes well with you and the
Board" (LAC, RG25, 3624, 2755-40-2, Ross McLean to Arthur Irwin,
8 March 1950).
92 Massey Report, 377.
93 Ibid., 310.
94 Robinson, "Falling into Line," 158–72.
95 LAC, RG25, 3624, 27555-A-40(1), Lester Pearson to Ross McLean,
7 June 1947.
96 Dowler, "The Cultural Industries Policy Apparatus," 329.
97 Ibid., 336.

CHAPTER FIVE

1 Vincent Massey Archives (VMA), B1987-0082/341, file 4, "His Excellency's
Remarks at the National Film Board," 27 January 1956.
2 McMillan, "Ethnology and the NFB," 68. One of the reasons Grierson
hired Boulton, a mediocre filmmaker, may have been because of her
University of Chicago credentials. She was registered in graduate study
of anthropology there from 1931 to 1935. See ibid., 69.
3 McDonnell and Depew, "Aboriginal Self-Government and Self-
Determination in Canada," 353.
4 Library and Archives Canada (LAC), RG26, vol. 143, 3-40-21, Department of Citizenship and Immigration, background paper, August 1955.
5 Pal, *Interests of State*, 91.
6 LAC, RG10, vol. 8813, file 1/12-11-3, Colonel H.M. Jones, "Report on
'Proposed Indian Film,'" n.d.
7 LAC, RG10, vol. 8813, file 1/12-11-3, Norman Klenman to Mr Reid,
Evelyn Horne, and Tom Daly, "Proposed Indian Film," 2 June 1954.
8 LAC, RG10, vol. 8813, file 1/12-11-3, E.B. Reid to Colonel H.M. Jones,
16 July 1954.
9 LAC, RG10, vol. 8813, file 1/12-11-3, letters from students at Wetmore
School, Regina, to Mrs Warden, 18 April 1956.

10 Driedger, *Multi-Ethnic Canada*, 53.

11 Whitaker, *Canadian Immigration Policy since Confederation*, 22.

12 LAC, RG26, vol. 143, 3-40-21, "Immigration Policy, Organization and Program," n.d.

13 LAC, RG25, vol. 6369, 2755-40(4.1), Minutes of Meeting between Officers of the Department and of the National Film Board to Discuss Policy in Film Distribution, 20 February 1952.

14 LAC, RG25, vol. 6369, 2755-40(3), Under-secretary of State, External Affairs, to Arthur Irwin, 25 October 1950.

15 Evans, *In the National Interest*, 20–3.

16 LAC, RG25, vol. 3624, 2755-40(2), Rogers to N.F.H. Berlis, 15 March 1950.

17 LAC, RG25, vol. 3624, 2755-40(2), Bellemare to N. MacDonald, 11 May 1950.

18 LAC, RG25, vol. 3624, 2755-40(2), Draft questionnaire sent by N. MacDonald to Bellemare, 16 May 1950.

19 LAC, RG25, vol. 3624, 2755-40(2), N. MacDonald to Bellemare, 22 March 1950.

20 LAC, RG25, vol. 3624, 2755-40(2), N. MacDonald to Bellemare, 18 March 1950.

21 LAC, RG25, vol. 6369, 2755-40(4.1), Confidential note for Mr Watkins from J.D.W., 18 February 1952.

22 NFB Archives (NFBA), The Newcomers file, information sheet, September 1953.

23 NFBA, The Newcomers file, "Report on the Distribution and Reception of Newcomers, produced for the Dept of Citizenship and Immigration 1953," December 1953.

24 Jones, *The Best Butler in the Business*, 122.

25 Ibid., 62–3.

26 Evans, *In the National Interest*, 75.

27 NFBA, Threshold: The Immigrant Meets the School file, Dorothy Macpherson to Guy Glover, memo re Immigration Integration, n.d.

28 NFBA, Threshold: The Immigrant Meets the School file, Len Forest to Gordon Burwash, 6 August 1958.

29 NFBA, Threshold: The Immigrant Meets the School file, Jean Boucher to Dorothy Macpherson, 4 December 1958.

30 NFBA, Threshold: The Immigrant Meets the School file, Dorothy Macpherson to Guy Glover, 4 March 1959.

31 NFBA, Threshold: The Immigrant Meets the School file, film evaluation report, 17 June, 1959.

32 Ibid.

33 Whynot, "The NFB and Labour, 1945–1955," 14.

34 Ibid.

35 Ibid., 20.

36 Canada, "National Film Board: Survey of Organization and Business Administration."

37 For more information on this topic, see Low, NFB *Kids*.

CHAPTER SIX

1 Magder, *Canada's Hollywood*; Dorland, *So Close to the States*.

2 NFB Archives (NFBA), Things I Cannot Change file, "Proposal for a Program of Film Activities in the Area of Poverty and Change," 16 February 1967, 1.

3 Evans, *In the National Interest*, 328–9.

4 Dick, "Regionalization of a Federal Cultural Institution," 107–33.

5 National Film Board, *Annual Report*, 1968–9, 1.

6 NFBA, Fogo Island file, Bill Nemtin, "Report on Challenge for Change," n.d.

7 Ibid.

8 NFBA, Fogo Island file, "Proposal for a Program of Film Activities in the Area of Poverty and Change," 16 February 1967.

9 Moore, *Canada's Challenge for Change*, 66.

10 Grierson, "Memo to Michelle about Decentralizing the Means of Production," 132–36.

11 James, *Film as a National Art*, 200.

12 Jones, *Movies and Memoranda*, 123.

13 Moore, *Canada's Challenge for Change*, 71.

14 Kurchak, "What Challenge? What Change?," 120.

15 Ibid., 123.

16 Marchessault, "Amateur Video and the Challenge for Change," 14–15. See also Marchessault, "Reflections on the Dispossessed," 131–46.

17 Marchessault, "Amateur Video and the Challenge for Change," 19.

18 Ibid., 22.

19 MacKenzie, "*Société nouvelle*," 68.

20 Ibid., 79.

21 Watson, "Challenge for Change," 112.

22 Evans, *In the National Interest*, xii.

23 See, for example, Engelman, *Public Radio and Television in America*, 222–35.

24 Jackson, "A Commitment to Social Values and Racial Justice," 31.

25 Boyle, "O Canada! George Stoney's Challenge," 57.

26 Boyle, "O Lucky Man! George Stoney's Lasting Legacy," 13–14.

27 Ibid., 14.

28 Boyle, "O Canada! George Stoney's Challenge," 49–50.
29 Library and Archives Canada (LAC), RG2, 18, vol. 172, N13, "Secret," Robert Winters to Louis St Laurent, 2 June 1950.
30 LAC, RG2, 18, vol. 172, N13, Robert Winters, "Secret Memo to the Cabinet: Submission on the Location of the National Film Board," 23 September 1950.
31 Evans, *In the National Interest*, 19.
32 Véronneau, *Résistance et affirmation*.
33 Ibid., 3.
34 MacKenzie, *Screening Québec*, 132.
35 Ibid., 126.
36 Pal, *Interests of State*, 98.
37 Ibid.
38 Ibid., 100.
39 Denis, "The Politics of Language," 157.
40 Handler, *Nationalism and the Politics of Culture in Quebec*, 9.
41 Pal, *Interests of State*, 101.
42 Ibid., 106.
43 Ibid., 109. See also Daly, *The Revolution Game*.
44 Pal, *Interests of State*, 109-10.
45 Ibid., 103–4.
46 Ibid., 105.
47 Ibid., 89.
48 Ibid.
49 Ibid.
50 For a contemporary description of how "deviance studies" became subculture studies, see John Irwin, "Notes on the Status of the Concept Subculture [1970]," in *The Subcultures Reader*, 66–70.
51 Pal, *Interests of State*, 244.
52 Ibid., 247.
53 Ibid., 255.
54 Ibid., 256.
55 Ibid., 278.
56 Ibid., 115.
57 Kelley and Trebilcock, *The Making of the Mosaic*, 351.
58 Canada, *Report of the Royal Commission on Bilingualism and Biculturalism*, vol. 4, 196.
59 Evans, *In the National Interest*, 210.
60 Pal, *Interests of State*, 94-7.
61 Ibid., 112.
62 Ibid., 122–3.

63 Moore, *Canada's Challenge for Change*, 240.

64 NFBA, The Things I Cannot Change file, "The Bailey Family: Eleven Going on Twelve: Proposal for a half hour 16mm black and white film to be produced for the Privy Council," n.d.

65 Moore, *Canada's Challenge for Change*, 54.

66 Ibid., 57.

67 Ibid., 56.

68 NFBA, The Things I Cannot Change file, "Notes of Interlock Screening of the Film, *The Things I Cannot Change*, 11:15 am, Dec 28, 1966, NFB 150 Kent St, Ottawa, T.V. Adams, Chief, Liaison Division."

69 Ibid., 98.

70 NFBA, The Things I Cannot Change file, information sheet, n.d.

71 Moore, *Canada's Challenge for Change*, 52.

72 NFBA, Fogo Island file, Colin Low, "Report on Fogo Island Project," 22 January 1968.

73 NFBA, Fogo Island file, Colin Low, "Factors Related to the Newfoundland Regional Film and Community Development Project," 22 January 1968, 1

74 NFBA, The Things I Cannot Change file, "Proposal for a Program of Film Activities in the Area of Poverty and Change," 26 February 1967, 4.

75 NFBA, Fogo Island file, Virginia Stikeman to R.L. Andres, Dept of Public Welfare, Newfoundland, 10 July 1968.

76 Moore, *Canada's Challenge for Change*, 79.

77 Ibid., 82.

78 NFBA, Fogo Island file, Bill Nemtin, "Report on Challenge for Change," n.d.

79 Ibid., (italics added).

80 Ibid.

81 Ibid., (italics added).

82 Marchessault, "Amateur Video," 16.

83 NFBA, VTR St. Jacques file, Bonnie Klein, "Report on Film and the Citizens Committee of St. Jacques," 6 December 1968.

84 NFBA, VTR St. Jacques file, information sheet, n.d.

85 Moore, *Canada's Challenge for Change*, 101–2.

86 NFBA, VTR St. Jacques file, Bonnie Klein and Dorothy Hénaut, "VTR in Community Organization: An Interim Report," n.d.

87 NFBA, VTR St. Jacques file, George Stoney to Frank Spiller, 3 January 1969; George Stoney to Lois Dooh, 8 September 1969.

88 Evans, *In the National Interest*, 167.

89 Moore, *Canada's Challenge for Change*, 243.

90 Weaver, *Making Canadian Indian Policy*, 5.
91 Webber, *Reimagining Canada*, 67.
92 Ibid., 70.
93 Ibid., 73.
94 NFBA, Fogo Island file, Freeman Compton to Don Duprey, 28 April 1969.
95 Moore, *Canada's Challenge for Change*, 129.
96 Ibid., 132.
97 Ibid., 264.
98 Ibid., 153.
99 Webber, *Reimagining Canada*, 71.
100 Ibid.
101 Moore, *Canada's Challenge for Change*, 151–2.
102 Ibid., 154.
103 Ibid., 157.
104 Ibid., 160.
105 NFBA, Cree Hunters file, "Report on Challenge for Change/Societé Nouvelle film on Aboriginal Rights," 31 May [no year].
106 NFBA, Cree Hunters file, Vic Adams to Chatwin "Re: James Bay Communications Project," 15 February 1972. Chatwin was executive producer of *Challenge for Change* after 1971.
107 NFBA, Cree Hunters file, Len Chatwin to Bob Verrall, 28 June 1973.
108 NFBA, Cree Hunters file, J. Walford Hewitson to Eleanor Ellis, 27 May 1974.
109 NFBA, Cree Hunters file, Mark Zannis, "*Cree Hunters of Mistassini* Report," September 1974.
110 NFBA, Cree Hunters file, Mark Zannis (May '74), cited in *Challenge for Change* report on *Cree Hunters*, 29 November 1974.
111 NFBA, Cree Hunters file, Boyce Richardson and Tony Ianzolo, "Report on *Cree Hunters*," n.d.
112 NFBA, Cree Hunters file, Ian Ball to Lynne Williams and regional distribution coordinators, 27 March 1974.
113 NFBA, NFB Cree Hunters file, Jacques Ouellet to Colin Low, 26 February 1974.
114 NFBA, Cree Hunters file, "The James Bay Communications Project," n.d.
115 NFBA, Cree Hunters file, "*Cree Hunters of Mistassini*, Distribution Plan," 24 September 1974,
116 NFBA, Cree Hunters file, "The James Bay Communications Project," n.d.
117 Moore, *Canada's Challenge for Change*, 165–6.
118 Ibid., 172.
119 Ibid., 179.
120 Ibid., 187.

121 Ibid.

122 Jones, *Movies and Memoranda*, 159.

123 Evans, *In the National Interest*, 174.

124 Anderson, "Studio D's Imagined Community," 44.

125 Ibid., 47.

126 Ibid.

127 Ibid., 48.

128 See, for example, Bennett, *Differing Diversities*.

CHAPTER SEVEN

1 Jones, *Movies and Memoranda*, 200.

2 Abbott, *Making Video "In."*

3 Steven, *Brink of Reality*, 8.

4 Ibid., 243.

5 Taussig, *Mimesis and Alterity*; Rosenstone, *Visions of the Past*; White, *The Content of the Form*; Clifford and Marcus, *Writing Culture*.

6 Lincoln and Denzin, "The Seventh Moment," 1050.

7 Dorland, "Cultural Industries and the Canadian Experience," 351; Audley, *Canada's Cultural Industries*.

8 Lane, *The Autobiographical Documentary in America*, 5; Russell, *Experimental Ethnography*, xi; Renov, *The Subject of Documentary*, 218.

9 Russell, *Experimental Ethnography*, 278.

10 Nichols, *Blurred Boundaries*, 96–7.

11 Angrosino and Mays de Pérez, "Rethinking Observation," 688.

12 Madriz, "Focus Groups in Feminist Research," 836, 8.

13 Canada, *Report of the Federal Cultural Policy Review Committee*, 263–4.

14 Ibid., 256–7.

15 Ibid., 263.

16 Ibid., 264–5.

17 Fox, *The National Film and Video Policy*, 8.

18 Ibid., 9.

19 Ibid., 11.

20 Bennett, *Culture*, 91.

21 Ibid., 92.

22 Canada, National Film Board, *Annual Report*, 1989–90, 14.

23 Ibid., 17.

24 Anderson, "Studio D's Imagined Community," 49.

25 Ibid., 51.

26 Ibid., 52.

27 Ibid., (italicis in original).

28 Ibid., 54.
29 Pick, "Storytelling and Resistance," 77.
30 Juneau, Murray, and Herrndorf, *Making Our Voices Heard*, 161.
31 Canada, National Film Board, *Annual Report*, 1997–98, 9.
32 Anderson, "Studio D's Imagined Community," 55.

CONCLUSION

1 Jones, *The Best Butler in the Business*, 124.
2 UNESCO, *Universal Declaration on Cultural Diversity*, November 2001.

FILMOGRAPHY

Beating the Streets (1998, Lorna Thomas)
Black, Bold and Beautiful (1999, Nadine Valcin)
Blockade (1994, Nettie Wild)
Building for Tomorrow (1947, David Bairstow)
By Their Own Strength (n.d., Evelyn Spice Cherry)
Canada from Sea to Sea (1956, Martin Bovey Films)
Le Canada: sa geographie (1974, Marc Beaudet, producer)
Le Canada: ses cultures (1974, Marc Beaudet, producer)
Le Canada: ses villes (1974, Marc Beaudet, producer)
Canada, World Trader (1946, Tom Daly)
Canadian Portraits (1988, Siobhan Flanagan, Peter Williamson)
Canadian Profile (1957, Allan Wargon)
Canadian Venture (1956, Caryl Doncaster)
Les canadiens (1959, Tom Daly)
Ce que femmes veut ... (1975, Robert Baylis)
The Changing City (1964, Kirk Jones)
Chants populaires, nos. 1–6 (1943, various directors)
Le chat dans le sac (1964, Gilles Groulx)
Citizen Discussions (1967, Colin Low)
The Clerk (1958, Morten Parker)
Coal Face Canada (1943, Robert Edmonds)
Colour Blind (1999, Ginder Oujla-Chalmers)
Common Concern (1947)
The Commonwealth of Nations – A Study in Thirteen Parts (1957)
Corral (1954, Colin Low)
Cree Hunters of Mistassini (1974, Boyce Richardson, Tony Ianzelo)
Democracy at Work (1944, Stanley Hawes, Fred Lasse)
The Department Manager (1958, Morten Parker)
Depressive States, part 1 (1951, Stanley Jackson)
Depressive States, part 2 (1951, Stanley Jackson)
Dues and the Union (1953, David Bairstow)
En tant que femmes (1972, Anne Claire Poirier)
Eskimo Arts and Crafts (1943, Laura Boulton)
Everyman's World (1946, Sydney Newman)

The Feeling of Rejection (1947, Robert Anderson)
The Feeling of Hostility (1947, Robert Anderson)
Film and You (1948, Jean Palardy, Donald Peters)
Fit for Tomorrow (1948)
Five Feminist Minutes (1990, Mary Armstrong,
    Nicole Hubert, producers)
Folie a deux (1951, Stanley Jackson)
Forbidden Love (1992, Lynne Fernie, Aerlyn Weissman)
Forgotten Warriors (1997, Lorna Todd)
Frontier College (1954, Julian Biggs)
Gaspé Cod Fishermen (1944, Jean Palardy)
The General Assembly (1962)
The General Foreman (1958, Morten Parker)
Getting Out the Coal (1943)
Getting the Most Out of a Film: Ballot Boxes
    (1946, Stanley Hawes, producer)
Getting the Most Out of a Film: Land for Pioneers
    (Stanley Hawes, producer)
Getting the Most Out of a Film: Now – the Peace
    (1945, Stanley Hawes, producer)
Getting the Most Out of a Film: Our Northern Neighbours
    (1944, Stanley Hawes, producer)
Getting the Most Out of a Film: A Place to Live (1946, Fred Lasse)
Getting the Most Out of a Film: Second Freedom (1945, Fred Lasse)
Getting the Most Out of a Film: Tyneside Story
    (1944, Stanley Hawes, producer)
Getting the Most Out of a Film: UNRRA – In the Wake of the Armies
    (1944, Stanley Hawes, producer)
Getting the Most Out of a Film: Veterans in Industry
    (1945, Fred Lasse)
Getting the Most Out of a Film: Welcome Soldier
    (1944, Stanley Hawes)
Getting the Most Out of a Film: Work and Wages (1946, Fred Lasse)
The Grievance (1954, Morten Parker)
Guilty Men (1945, Tom Daly)
Gurdeep Singh Bains (1977, Beverly Shaffer)
Habitant Arts and Crafts (1944, Laura Boulton)
He Acts His Age (1949, Judith Crawley)
Here Is Canada (1972, Tony Ianzelo)
High Steel (1965, Don Owen)
Hungry Minds (1948, Tom Daly)
Hunters and Bombers (1991, Hugh Brody)

I.L.O. (1947, Fred Lasse, producer)
I'll Find a Way (1977, Beverly Shaffer)
Iceland on the Prairies (1941, Radford Crawley)
If You Love This Planet (1982, Terre Nash)
Incident at Restigouche (1984, Alanis Obomsawin)
The Indian Speaks (1967, Marcel Carrière)
In Her Chosen Field (1989, Barbara Evans)
International Court of Justice (1964)
In the Shadow of Gold Mountain (2004, Karen Cho)
Introducing Canada (1956, Tom Daly)
Is It a Woman's World? (1956, Don Haldane)
Is the Crown at War with Us? (2002, Alanis Obomsawin)
Joe and Roxy (1957, Don Haldane)
Julie O'Brien (1981, Beverly Shaffer)
Just Watch Me (2000, Catherine Annau)
Kanehsatake: 270 Years of Resistance (1993, Alanis Obomsawin)
Kevin Alec (1977, Beverly Shaffer)
Labour Front (1943)
Labour Looks Ahead (1945, Stanley Hawes, producer)
La lutte (1961, Michel Brault, Marcel Carrière, Claude Fournier,
   Claude Jutra)
Lost Songs (1999, Clint Alberta)
Luckily I Need Little Sleep (1974, Kathleen Shannon)
Main Street, Canada (1945, Alistair Taylor)
A Man and His Job (1943, Alistair Taylor)
Manic State (1951, Stanley Jackson)
Man on the Assembly Line (1958, Morten Parker)
Maps We Live By (1948, Gudrun Parker)
Men of Lunenburg (1956)
Mi'kmaq Family (1995, Catherine Anne Martin)
Mothers are People (1974, Kathleen Shannon)
Movies for Workers (1945, Stanley Hawes)
My Name Is Susan Yee (1975, Beverly Shaffer)
Neighbours (1952, Norman McLaren)
New Horizons (1940, Evelyn Cherry)
The New South Asia (1953, Donald Fraser)
New Voices (1961, James Beveridge, Nicholas Bella, producers)
The Newcomers (1953, David Bennett)
No Longer Vanishing (1955, Grant McLean)
Not a Love Story (1981, Bonnie Sherr Klein)
Now – the Peace (1945, Stuart Legg, producer)
On a Day Off (1959, Erik Nielsen)

On Guard with UNEF (1959, A.W. Acland)
Our Dear Sisters (1975, Kathleen Shannon)
Our Land Is Our Life (1974, Boyce Richardson, Tony Ianzolo)
Our Nationhood (2003, Alanis Obomsawin)
Our Town Is the World (1950, Stanley Jackson)
Out: Stories of Lesbian and Gay Youth (1993, David Adkin)
Out of the Ruins (1946, Nicholas Read)
Overture (1958, G.L. Polidora)
Passport to Canada (1949, Roger Blais)
Paul Tomkowicz: Street Railway Switchman (1954, Roman Kroitor)
The Peace Builders (1945, Alan Field, producer)
The People Between (1947, Grant McLean)
People of the Potlach (1944, Laura Boulton)
Peoples of Canada (1941)
Peoples of the Skeena (1949, James Beveridge, producer)
Les peuples du Canada (1948, Jacques Bobet)
Polish Dance (1944, Laura Boulton)
Postmark UNEF (1965, Richard Gilbert)
Pour la suite du monde (1963, Pierre Perrault, Michel Brault)
Power (1996, Magnus Isacsson)
Prairie Profile (1955, Gordon Burwash)
Raisin' Kane: A Rapumentary (2000, Alison Duke)
Les raquetteurs (1958, Michel Brault, Gilles Groulx)
Redskins, Tricksters and Puppy Stew (2000, Drew Hayden Taylor)
The Road to World Peace (1950, Don Hirst)
The Security Council (1963)
September Five at Saint-Henri (1964, Hubert Aquin)
Sight and Sound (1954, Don Mulholland)
Sixteen to Twenty Six (1945, Crawley Films)
Shop Steward (1958, Morten Parker)
Skilled Worker (1958, Morten Parker)
Speak It! From the Heart of Black Nova Scotia (1992, Sylvia Hamilton)
Le sport et les hommes (1961, Hubert Aquin)
Stuff for Stuff (1948, Philip Regan, Michael Spencer)
Suffer Little Children (1945, Sydney Newman)
The Teens (1957, Crawley Films)
They Appreciate You More (1974, Kathleen Shannon)
The Things I Cannot Change (1967, Tanya Ballantyne)
Threshold: The Immigrant Meets the School (1959, George Bloomfield)
Thunder in the East (1950, D. Tundell)
To a Safer Place (1987, Beverly Shaffer)
Tomorrow Begins Today (1962, Terence Macartney-Filgate)

Tomorrow's Citizens (1947, Gordon Weisenborn)
Totem: The Return of the G'psogolox Pole (2003, Gil Cardinal)
Totems (1944, Laura Boulton)
Trans-Canada Express (1944, Stanley Hawes)
Trans-Canada Journey (1962, Graham Parker)
The Transition (1964, Mort Ransen)
The Trusteeship Council and System (1962)
Ukrainian Dance (1943, Laura Boulton)
U.N. in the Classroom (1959, Don Haldane)
Universities at War (1944)
UNRRA – *In the Wake of Armies* (1944, Guy Glover)
Up Against the System (1969, Terence Macartney-Filgate)
Urban Elders (1997, Robert S. Adams)
V for Victory (1941, Norman McLaren)
V for Volunteers (1951, Leslie McFarlane)
Vice President (1958, Morten Parker)
Volleyball (1966, Denys Arcand)
VTR *St. Jacques* (1969, Bonnie Sherr Klein)
The War for Men's Minds (1943, Stuart Legg)
Western Eyes (2000, Ann Shin)
When All the People Play (1948, Evelyn Cherry)
Why Canada? (1965, Edmund Reid)
Women at Work (1958, Gordon Sparling)
Working Mothers (1974, Kathleen Shannon, Margaret Pettigrew,
    Yuki Yoshida)
You are Welcome, Sirs, to Cyprus (1964, Richard Gilbert)
Yuxweluptun: Man of Masks (1998, Dana Claxton)

BIBLIOGRAPHY

MANUSCRIPT AND ARCHIVAL SOURCES

The John Grierson Archive, Stirling, Scotland
Library and Archives Canada, Ottawa
National Archives, Kew, United Kingdom
National Film Board Archives, Montreal
Vincent Massey Archives, Toronto

GOVERNMENT PUBLICATIONS

British
Constantine, Stephen. *Buy and Build: The Advertising Posters of the Empire Marketing Board*. London: Queen's Printer, 1986
Imperial Conference, London, 1926: Summary of Proceedings. London: King's Printer, 1927
Imperial Conference, London, 1930: Summary of Proceedings. Ottawa: King's Printer, 1931
Imperial Economic Conference at Ottawa, 1932. Summary of Proceedings and Copies of Trade Agreements. London: King's Printer, 1932
Imperial Relations Trust, Annual Report, 1938–39

Canadian
Bensimon, Jacques. NFB 2002–3 *Estimates: Report on Plans and Priorities*. Ottawa, 2002
Bidd, Donald W., ed. *The NFB Film Guide: The Productions of the National Film Board of Canada from 1939 to 1989*. Ottawa: National Film Board, 1991
Canada. "An Act to Create a National Film Board." *Statutes of Canada*, 1939, 101–5
– "An Act Respecting the National Film Board." *Statutes of Canada*, 1950, 1: 567–74
– "An Act Respecting the National Film Board." *Revised Statutes of Canada*, 1985, vol. 4, c. N8, 1–7

- Department of Trade and Commerce. *Catalogue of Motion Pictures Produced by Canadian Government Motion Picture Bureau.* Ottawa: King's Printer, 1930
- *The Dominion Bureau of Statistics: Its Origin, Constitution and Organization.* Ottawa: King's Printer, 1935
- House of Commons. *Debates,* 1939, 1941, 1943, 1944, 1949, 1950, 1952
- "National Film Board: Survey of Organization and Business Administration." *Parliamentary Papers,* 1950
- *Report of the Federal Cultural Policy Review Committee.* Ottawa, 1982
- *Report of the Imperial Committee on Economic Consultation and Co-operation, 1933.* Ottawa: King's Printer, 1933
- *Report of the Royal Commission on Bilingualism and Biculturalism.* Vol. 4. Ottawa: Queen's Printer, 1970
- *Report of the Royal Commission on Broadcasting.* Ottawa, 1957
- *Report of the Royal Commission on Dominion-Provincial Relations.* Ottawa: King's Printer, 1940
- *Report of the Royal Commission on National Development in the Arts, Letters and Sciences* and *Studies (1949–1951).* Ottawa, 1951
- Special Committee on the National Film Board. *Minutes of Proceedings and Evidence,* 8, 15, 22, and 29 May 1952. Ottawa: Queen's Printer, 1952
- *Statement of the Government of Canada on Indian Policy.* Ottawa, 1969
Dominion Bureau of Statistics. *The Use of Films and Slides in Canadian Schools.* Ottawa, 1937
Fox, Francis. *The National Film and Video Policy.* Ottawa, May 1984
Gray, C.W. *Movies for the People: The Story of the National Film Board's Unique Distribution System.* Ottawa: National Film Board, 1977
Hurd, Burton. *Origin, Birthplace, Nationality, and Language of the Canadian People.* Ottawa: King's Printer, 1929
Hurd, Burton, and T.W. Gindley, *Agriculture, Climate, and Population of the Prairie Provinces of Canada.* Ottawa: King's Printer, 1931
Juneau, Pierre, Catherine Murray, and Peter Herrndorf. *Making Our Voices Heard: Canadian Broadcasting and Film for the 21st Century.* Mandate Review Committee CBC, NFB, Telefilm. Ottawa: Minister of Supply and Services, 1996
Kirkconnell, Watson. *Canadians All.* Ottawa: Department of Public Information, 1941
National Film Board. *Annual Reports,* 1939–2004
Statistics Canada. *Seventy-five Years and Counting: A History of Statistics Canada.* Ottawa, 1993
The United Nations Education, Scientific, and Cultural Organization: Final Act of the London Conference Constitution. Ottawa: Canadian Council of Education for Citizenship, 1945

SECONDARY SOURCES

Abbott, Jennifer, ed. *Making Video "In": The Contested Ground of Alternative Video on the West Coast*. Vancouver: Video in Studios, 2000

Acland, Charles R. "National Dreams, International Encounters: The Formation of Canadian Film Culture in the 1930s." *Canadian Journal of Film Studies* 3 (Spring 1994): 3–26

– "Popular Film in Canada: Revisiting the Absent Audience." In *A Passion for Identity: An Introduction to Canadian Studies*, 3rd edn, ed. David Taras and Beverly Rasporich, 281–96. Toronto: ITP Nelson, 1997

– "Patterns of Cultural Authority: The National Film Society of Canada, 1938–1941." *Canadian Journal of Film Studies* 10 (Spring 2001): 2–27

Acland, Charles R., and William Buxton. *American Philanthropy and Canadian Libraries: The Politics of Knowledge and Information*. Montreal: McGill Graduate School of Library and Information Studies, 1998

Aitken, Ian. *Film and Reform: John Grierson and the Documentary Film Movement*. London: Routledge, 1990

– ed. *The Documentary Film Movement: An Anthology*. Edinburgh: Edinburgh University Press, 1998

Alexander, Donald. "Documentary Films." *New Statesman and Nation*, 14 August 1937, 246–7

Althusser, Louis. "Ideology and Ideological State Apparatuses: Notes towards an Investigation." In *Lenin and Philosophy*, trans. Ben Brewster, 127–86. London: New Left Books, 1971

Anderson, Elizabeth. "Studio D's Imagined Community: From Development (1974) to Realignment (1986–1990)." In *Gendering the Nation: Canadian Women's Cinema*, ed. K. Armatage, B. Longfellow, K. Banning, and J. Marchessault, 41–61. Toronto: University of Toronto Press, 1999

Angrosino, Michael, and Kimberly Mays de Pérez. "Rethinking Observation: From Method to Context." In *Handbook of Qualitative Research*, 2nd edn, ed. Norman K. Denzin and Yvonna S. Lincoln, 673–702. Thousand Oaks: Sage, 2000

Armatage, Kay, Brenda Longfellow, Kass Banning, and Janine Marchessault, eds. *Gendering the Nation: Canadian Women's Cinema*. Toronto: University of Toronto Press, 1999

The Arts Enquiry. *The Factual Film*. London: Oxford University Press, 1947

Audley, Paul. *Canada's Cultural Industries: Broadcasting, Publsihing, Records, and Film*. Toronto: Lorimer, 1983

Babe, Robert. *Canadian Communication Thought: Ten Foundational Writers*. Toronto: University of Toronto Press, 2000

Backhouse, Charles. *Canadian Government Motion Picture Bureau, 1917–1941*. Ottawa: Canadian Film Institute, 1974

Bakhtin, M.M. "Discourse in the Novel." In *The Dialogic Imagination*, ed. Michael Holquist, trans. Caryl Emerson and Michael Holquist, 259–422. Austin: University of Texas Press, 1981
– "The Problem of Speech Genres." In *Speech Genres and Other Late Essays*, ed. Caryl Emerson and Michael Holquist, trans. Vern W. McGee, 60–102. Austin: University of Texas Press, 1986
Bannerji, Himani. *The Dark Side of the Nation: Essays on Multiculturalism, Nationalism, and Gender.* Toronto: Canadian Scholars' Press, 2000
Barnouw, Eric. *Documentary: A History of the Non-Fiction Film.* 2nd edn. New York: Oxford University Press, 1993
Barry, Andrew, Thomas Osborne, and Nikolas Rose, eds. *Foucault and Political Reason: Liberalism, Neo-Liberalism, and Rationalities of Government.* London: University College London Press, 1996
Barry, Norman. *Welfare.* 2nd edn. Buckingham: Open University Press, 1999
Baxendale, John, and Chris Pawling. "Representing the People: The Documentary Film Movement and Mass Observation in the Thirties." In their *Narrating the Thirties*, 17–45. London: Macmillan, 1996
Beattie, Keith. *Documentary Screens: Nonfiction Film and Television.* Houndmills: Palgrave Macmillan, 2004
Bennett, Tony. *Culture: A Reformer's Science.* London: Sage, 1998
– *Differing Diversities: Transversal Study on the Theme of Cultural Policy and Cultural Diversity.* Strasbourg: Council of Europe Publishing, 2001
Berman, Edward H. *The Ideology of Philanthropy: The Influence of the Carnegie, Ford, and Rockefeller Foundations on American Foreign Policy.* Albany, NY: SUNY, 1983
Bertrand, Ina, and Diane Collins. *Government and Film in Australia.* Sydney: Currency Press, 1981
Beveridge, James. *John Grierson, Film Master.* London: Macmillan, 1978
Beveridge, William. *Social Insurance and Allied Services.* New York: Macmillan, 1942
Boyle, Deirdre. "O Canada! George Stoney's Challenge." *Wide Angle* 21, no. 2 (1999): 49–59
– "O Lucky Man! George Stoney's Lasting Legacy." *Wide Angle* 21, no. 2 (1999): 11–18
Brown, Robert C., and Ramsay Cook. *Canada 1896–1921: A Nation Transformed.* Toronto: McClelland & Stewart, 1974
Buchanan, Donald. *Report on Educational and Cultural Films in Canada.* National Film Society, 1936
– "Canadian Movies Promote Citizenship." *Canadian Geographical Journal*, March 1944, 120–9
Burchell, Graham, Colin Gordon, and Peter Miller, eds. *The Foucault Effect: Studies in Governmentality.* Chicago: University of Chicago Press, 1991

Carter, Gwendolen. *The British Commonwealth and International Security: The Role of the Dominions, 1919–39*. Toronto: Ryerson Press, 1947

Charland, Maurice. "Technological Nationalism." *Canadian Journal of Political and Social Theory* 10, no. 1–2 (1986): 196–220

Cinema Canada, June/July 1979. Special issue on the NFB

Clandfield, David. *Pierre Perrault and the Poetic Documentary*. Toronto: Toronto International Film Festival, 2004

Clifford, James, and George E. Marcus, eds. *Writing Culture: The Poetics and Politics of Ethnography*. Berkeley: University of California Press, 1986

Constantine, Stephen. "'Bringing the Empire Alive': The Empire Marketing Board and Imperial Propaganda, 1926–1933." In *Imperialism and Popular Culture*, ed. John MacKenzie, 192–231. Manchester: Manchester University Press, 1986

Curran, James, and Vincent Porter, eds. *British Cinema History*. London: Weidenfeld and Nicolson, 1983

Curtis, Bruce. *The Politics of Population: State Formation, Statistics, and the Census of Canada, 1840–1875*. Toronto: University of Toronto Press, 2001

Daly, Margaret. *The Revolution Game: The Short, Unhappy Life of the Company of Young Canadians*. Toronto: New Press, 1970

Davis, Natalie Zemon. *Fiction in the Archives: Pardon Tales and their Tellers in Sixteenth-Century France*. Stanford: Stanford University Press, 1987.

Dawson, Jonathan. "The Grierson Tradition." In *The Documentary Film in Australia*, ed. Ross Lansell and Peter Beilby, 139–41. North Melbourne: Cinema Papers, 1982

Denis, Wilfrid B. "The Politics of Language." In *Race and Ethnic Relations in Canada*, ed. Peter S. Li, 148–85. Toronto: Oxford University Press, 1999

Dennis, Jonathan, ed. *"The Tin Shed": The Origins of the National Film Unit*. Wellington: New Zealand Film Archive, 1981

Denzin, Norman K., and Yvonna S. Lincoln, eds. *Handbook of Qualitative Research*. 2nd edn. Thousand Oaks: Sage, 2000

– *The Landscape of Qualitative Research: Theories and Issues*. 2nd edn. Thousand Oaks: Sage, 2003

Désrosieres, Alain. "The Part in Relation to the Whole: How to Generalize? The Prehistory of Representative Sampling." In *The Social Survey in Historical Perspective, 1880–1940*, ed. Martin Blumer, Kevin Bales, and Kathryn Kish Sklar, 217–44. Cambridge: Cambridge University Press, 1991

Dick, Ronald. "Regionalization of a Federal Cultural Institution: The Experience of the National Film Board of Canada, 1965–1979." In *Flashback: People and Institutions in Canadian Film History*, ed. Gene Walz, 107–33. Montreal: Mediatexte, 1986

Dorland, Michael. "Cultural Industries and the Canadian Experience: Reflections on the Emergence of a Field." In *The Cultural Industries in Canada:*

Problems, Policies, and Prospects, ed. Dorland, 347–65. Toronto: Lorimer, 1996
– *So Close to the State/s: The Emergence of Canadian Feature Film Policy.* Toronto: University of Toronto Press, 1998
– ed. *The Cultural Industries in Canada: Problems, Policies, and Prospects.* Toronto: Lorimer, 1996
Dowler, Kevin. "The Cultural Industries Policy Apparatus." In *The Cultural Industries in Canada: Problems, Policies, and Prospects*, ed. Michael Dorland, 328–45. Toronto: Lorimer, 1996
Dreisziger, N.F. "The Rise of a Bureaucracy for Multiculturalism: The Origins of the Nationalities Branch, 1939–1941." In *On Guard for Thee: War, Ethnicity, and the Canadian State, 1939–1945*, ed. N. Hillmer, B. Kordan, and L. Luciuk, 1–29. Ottawa: Canadian Committee for the History of the Second World War, 1988
Driedger, Leo. *Multi-Ethnic Canada: Identities and Inequalities.* Oxford: Oxford University Press, 1996
Druick, Zoë. "'Ambiguous Identities' and the Representation of Everyday Life: Notes Towards a New History of Production Policies at the NFB of Canada." *Canadian Issues* 20 (1998): 125–37
– "Documenting Government: Re-examining the 1950s National Film Board Films about Citizenship." *Canadian Journal of Film Studies* 9 (Spring 2000): 55–79
– "'Non-theatrical with Dreams of Theatrical': Paradoxes of a Canadian Semi-Documentary Film Noir." *Canadian Journal of Film Studies* 12 (Fall 2003): 46–63
– "Framing the Local: Canadian Film Policy and the Problem of Place." In *Canadian Cultural Poesis*, ed. Garry Sherbert, Annie Gérin, and Shiela Petty, 85–98. Waterloo: Wilfrid Laurier Press, 2006
– "International Cultural Relations as a Factor in Postwar Canadian Cultural Policy: The Relevance of UNESCO for the Massey Commission." *Canadian Journal of Communication* 31 (2006): 177–95
– "'Reaching the Multimillions': Liberal Internationalism and the Establishment of Documentary Film." In *Inventing Film Studies*, ed. Haidee Wasson and Lee Grieveson. Durham, NC: Duke University Press, forthcoming
Dufour, Paul. "'Eggheads' and Espionage: The Gouzenko Affair in Canada." *Journal of Canadian Studies* 16 (Fall-Winter 1981): 188–98
Elder, Kathryn. "The Legacy of John Grierson." *Journal of Canadian Studies* 21 (Winter 1986–87): 152–61
Ellis, Carolyn, and Arthur Bochner. "Authoethnography, Personal Narrative, Reflexivity: Researcher as Subject." In *Handbook of Qualitative Research*, 2nd edn, ed. Norman K. Denzin and Yvonna S. Lincoln, 733–68. Thousand Oaks: Sage, 2000

Ellis, Jack C. "The Young John Grierson in America, 1924–1927." *Cinema Journal* 8 (Fall 1968): 12–21
– *John Grierson: A Guide to References and Resources.* Boston: G.K. Hall, 1986
– *The Documentary Idea.* Engelwood Cliffs: Prentice-Hall, 1989
– *John Grierson: Life, Contributions, Influence.* Carbondale: Southern Illinois University Press, 2000
Engelman, Ralph. *Public Radio and Television in America: A Political History.* London: Sage, 1996
Evans, Gary. *John Grierson and the National Film Board of Canada: The Politics of Wartime Propaganda.* Toronto: University of Toronto Press, 1984
– *In the National Interest: A Chronicle of the National Film Board of Canada, 1949–1989.* Toronto: University of Toronto Press, 1991
Faris, Ron. *The Passionate Educators: Voluntary Associations and the Struggle for Control of Adult Educational Broadcasting in Canada, 1919–52.* Toronto: Peter Martin, 1975
Feldman, Seth, ed. *Take Two: A Tribute to Film in Canada.* Toronto: Irwin, 1984
Feldman, Seth, and Joyce Nelson, eds. *Canadian Film Reader.* Toronto: Peter Martin, 1977
Ferguson, Barry, and Doug Owram. "Social Scientists and Public Policy from the 1920s through World War II." *Journal of Canadian Studies* 15 (Winter 1980–81): 3–17
Fetherling, Douglas, ed. *Documents in Canadian Film.* Peterborough: Broadview Press, 1988
Film and Cinema Statistics: A Preliminary Report on Methodology with Tables Giving Current Statistics. Paris, UNESCO Statistical Division, n.d.
The Film in National Life. London: Allen and Unwin, 1932
Fisher, Donald. "The Role of Philanthropic Foundations in the Reproduction and Production of Hegemony: Rockefeller Foundations and the Social Sciences." *Sociology* 17 (May 1983): 206–33
Fontana, Andrea, and James Frey. "The Interview: From Structured Questions to Negotiated Text." In *Handbook of Qualitative Resaerch*, 2nd edn, ed. Norman K. Denzin and Yvonna S. Lincoln, 645–72. Thousand Oaks: Sage, 2000
Forsyth, Scott. "The Failures of Nationalism and Documentary: *Grierson and Gouzenko.*" *Canadian Journal of Film Studies* 1, no. 1 (1990): 74–82
Foucault, Michel. "Governmentality." In *The Foucault Effect: Studies in Governmentality*, ed. Graham Burchell, Colin Gordon, and Peter Miller, 87–104. Chicago: University of Chicago Press, 1991
Fromer, Anne. "Canada's Rural Movies Building Citizenship." *Saturday Night*, 11 March 1944, 19a

Gallup, George. *A Guide to Public Opinion Polls.* Princeton: Princeton University Press, 1948

Gergen, Mary M., and Kenneth Gergen. "Qualitative Inquiry: Tensions and Transformations." In *Handbook of Qualitative Research*, 2nd edn, ed. Norman K. Denzin, and Yvonna S. Lincoln, 1025–46. Thousand Oaks: Sage, 2000

Gibbon, John Murray. *Canadian Mosaic: The Making of a Northern Nation.* Toronto: McClelland & Stewart, 1938

Ginzburg, Carlo. *The Cheese and the Worms.* Trans. John Tedeschi and Anne Tedeschi. Baltimore: Johns Hopkins University Press, 1980

– *Clues, Myths, and the Historical Method.* Trans. John Tedeschi and Anne Tedeschi. Baltimore: Johns Hopkins University Press, 1989

Gittings, Christopher E. *Canadian National Cinema: Ideology, Difference, and Representation.* London: Routledge, 2002

Gordon, Colin, "Governmental Rationality: An Introduction." In *The Foucault Effect: Studies in Governmentality*, ed. Graham Burchell, Colin Gordon, and Peter Miller, 1–52. Chicago: University of Chicago Press, 1991

Grierson, John. "The Film and Primitive Peoples." In *The Film and Colonial Development*, 9–15. London: British Film Institute, 1948

– "Memo to Michelle about Decentralizing the Means of Production." In *Canadian Film Reader*, ed. Seth Feldman and Joyce Nelson, 132–6. Toronto: Peter Martin Associates, 1977

– *Grierson on Documentary*, ed. Forsyth Hardy, revised edn. London: Faber, 1979

– *Grierson on the Movies*, ed. Forsyth Hardy. London: Faber, 1981

– "Memorandum to the Right Honourable, the Prime Minister (1940)." In *An Australian Film Reader*, ed. Albert Moran and Tom O'Regan, 72–8. Sydney: Currency Press, 1985

– "A Film Policy for Canada." In *Documents in Canadian Film*, ed. Douglas Fetherling, 51–67. Peterborough: Broadview Press, 1988

– "Flaherty's Poetic *Moana*." In *Documents in Canadian Film*, ed. Douglas Fetherling, 47–50. Peterborough: Broadview Press, 1988

Grimshaw, Anna. *The Ethnographer's Eye: Ways of Seeing in Modern Anthropology.* Cambridge: Cambridge University Press, 2001

Guest, Dennis. *The Emergence of Social Security in Canada.* 2nd edn. Vancouver: University of British Columbia Press, 1985

Hackett, Yvette. "The National Film Society of Canada, 1935-1951: Its Origins and Development." In *Flashback: People and Institutions in Canadian Film History*, ed. Gene Walz, 135–68. Montreal: Mediatexte, 1986

Hacking, Ian. "Making Up People." In *Reconstructing Individualism: Autonomy, Individuality, and Self in Western Thought*, ed. Thomas Heller,

Montron Sosna, and David Wellbery, 222–36. Stanford: Stanford University Press, 1986

– *The Taming of Chance*. Cambridge: Cambridge University Press, 1990

Handler, Richard. *Nationalism and the Politics of Culture in Quebec*. Madison: University of Wisconsin Press, 1988

Handling, Piers, ed. *Self Portrait: Essays on the Quebec and Canadian Cinemas*. Ottawa: Canadian Film Institute, 1980

Hannant, Larry. *The Infernal Machine: Investigating the Loyalty of Canada's Citizens*. Toronto: University of Toronto Press, 1995

Harcourt, Peter. "The Innocent Eye: An Aspect of the Work of the National Film Board." In *Canadian Film Reader*, ed. Seth Feldman and Joyce Nelson, 67–77. Toronto: Peter Martin [1964–65], 1977

Hardy, Forsyth. *John Grierson: A Documentary Biography*. London: Faber, 1979

Harris, Jonathan. *Federal Art and National Culture: The Politics of Identity in New Deal America*. Cambridge: Cambridge University Press, 1995

Hawes, Stanley. "Grierson in Australia (1972)." In *An Australian Film Reader*, ed. Albert Moran and Tom O'Regan, 79–84. Sydney: Currency Press, 1985

Hemming, A.E. "Canada's National Film Board." *Trades and Labor Congress Journal*, September 1945, 35–41

Hénaut, Dorothy Todd. "Films for Social Change: the Hammer and the Mirror." In *Studies in Canadian Communications*, ed. G. Robinson and D. Theall, 175–88. Montreal: McGill University, 1975

Herbst, Susan. *Numbered Voices*. Chicago: University of Chicago Press, 1993

Hill, O. Mary. *Canada's Salesman to the World: The Department of Trade and Commerce, 1892–1939*. Montreal & Kingston: McGill-Queen's University Press, 1977

Hogarth, David. *Documentary Television in Canada: From National Public Service to Global Marketplace*. Montreal & Kingston: McGill-Queen's University Press, 2002

Hood, Stuart. "John Grierson and the Documentary Film Movement." In *British Cinema History*, ed. James Curran and Vincent Porter, 99–112. London: Weidenfeld and Nicolson, 1983

Hunter, Ian. *Culture and Government: The Emergence of Literary Education*. Houndmills: Macmillan, 1991

Irwin, John. "Notes on the Status of the Concept Subculture [1970]." In *The Subcultures Reader*, ed. Ken Gelder and Sarah Thornton, 66–70. London: Routledge, 1997.

Jackson, Lynne. "A Commitment to Social Values and Racial Justice." *Wide Angle* 21, no. 2 (1999): 31–40

James, C. Rodney. *Film as a National Art: NFB of Canada and the Film Board Idea*. New York: Arno Press, 1977

Jarvie, Ian. *Hollywood's Overseas Campaign: The North Atlantic Movie Trade, 1920–1950*. Cambridge: Cambridge University Press, 1992

John Grierson and the NFB. Proceedings of a congress at McGill University, 29–31 October 1981. Toronto: ECW Press [1981]

Jones, D.B. *Movies and Memoranda: An Interpretive History of the National Film Board of Canada*. Ottawa: Canadian Film Institute, 1981

– "Assessing the Film Board, Crediting Grierson." *Historical Journal of Film, Radio, and Television* 9, no. 2 (1989): 301–8

– *The Best Butler in the Business: Tom Daly of the National Film Board of Canada*. Toronto: University of Toronto Press, 1996

Karl, Barry. *Charles Merriam and the Study of Politics*. Chicago: University of Chicago Press, 1974

Kelley, Ninette, and Michael Trebilcock. *The Making of the Mosaic: A History of Canadian Immigration Policy*. Toronto: University of Toronto Press, 1998

Kidd, J.R. *Pictures with a Purpose*. Toronto: Canadian Association for Adult Education, 1953

– "Canada's Stake in UNESCO." *Queen's Quarterly*, Summer 1956, 248–64

Kinsman, Gary, Kieter K. Buse, and Mercedes Steedman, eds. *Whose National Security? Canadian State Surveillance and the Creation of Enemies*. Toronto: Between the Lines Press, 2000

Knight, Amy. *How the Cold War Began: The Gouzenko Affair and the Hunt for Soviet Spies*. Toronto: McClelland & Stewart, 2005

Kristeva, Julia. "Word, Dialogue, and Novel." In *The Kristeva Reader*, ed, Toril Moi, 34–61. New York: Columbia University Press, 1986

Kristmanson, Mark. *Plateaus of Freedom: Nationality, Culture, and State Security in Canada 1940–1960*. Oxford: Oxford University Press, 2003

Kurchak, Marie. "What Challenge? What Change?" In *Canadian Film Reader*, ed. Seth Feldman and Joyce Nelson, 120–8. Toronto: Peter Martin, 1977

Lane, Jim. *The Autobiographical Documentary in America*. Madison: University of Wisconsin Press, 2002

Laves, Walter H.C., and Charles A. Thomson. *UNESCO: Purpose, Progress, Prospects*. Bloomington: Indiana University Press, 1957

Leach, Jim. *Claude Jutra: Filmmaker*. Montreal & Kingston: McGill-Queen's University Press, 1999

Leach, Jim, and Jeannette Sloniowski, eds. *Candid Eyes: Essays on Canadian Documentaries*. Toronto: University of Toronto Press, 2003

Lewis, Justin, and Toby Miller, eds. *Critical Cultural Policy Studies: A Reader*. Oxford: Blackwell, 2003

Lincoln, Yvonna S., and Norman K. Denzin. "The Seventh Moment: Out of the Past." In *Handbook of Qualitative Research*, 2nd edn, ed. Denzin and Lincoln, 1047–63. Thousand Oaks: Sage, 2000

Lippmann, Walter. *Public Opinion*. New York: Free Press, 1922

– *The Phantom Public*. New York: Harcourt Brace, 1925

Litt, Paul. *The Muses, the Masses, and the Massey Commission*. Toronto: University of Toronto Press, 1992

Low, Brian. NFB *Kids: Portrayals of Children by the National Film Board of Canada, 1939–1989*. Waterloo: Wilfrid Laurier Press, 2002

Low, Rachael. *Documentary and Educational Films of the 1930s*. London: Allen and Unwin, 1979

– *Films of Comment and Persuasion of the 1930s*. London: Weidenfeld and Nicolson, 1983

MacCann, Richard. "Documentary Film and Democratic Government: An Administrative History from Pare Lorenz to John Huston." PHD thesis, Harvard University, 1951

McDonnell, R.F., and R.C. Depew. "Aboriginal Self-Government and Self-Determination in Canada: A Critical Commentary." In *Aboriginal Self-Government in Canada: Current Trends and Issues*, 2nd edn, ed. John H. Hylton, 352–76. Saskatoon: Purich Publishing, 1999

McInnes, Graham. *One Man's Documentary*, ed. Gene Walz. Winnipeg: University of Manitoba Press, 2004

McInnes, Graham, and K.R. Gauthier. "Canada: Film Producer." *Canadian Forum*, June 1945, 39, 42

McInnes, Peter S. "Teamwork for Harmony: Labour-Management Production Committees and the Postwar Settlement in Canada." *Canadian Historical Review* 77 (September 1996): 317–52

MacKenzie, Scott. "*Société nouvelle*: The Challenge for Change in the Alternative Public Sphere." *Canadian Journal of Film Studies* 5 (Fall 1996): 67–83

– *Screening Québec: Québécois Moving Images, National Identity, and the Public Sphere*. Manchester: Manchester University Press, 2004

Mackey, Eva. *The House of Difference: Cultural Politics and National Identity in Canada*. Toronto: University of Toronto Press, 2002

McLaren, Angus. *Our Own Master Race: The Eugenic Crusade in Canada*. Toronto: McClelland & Stewart, 1990

McMillan, Robert. "Ethnology and the NFB: The Laura Boulton Mysteries." *Canadian Journal of Film Studies* 1, no. 2 (1991): 67–82

Madriz, Esther. "Focus Groups in Feminist Research." In *Handbook of Qualitative Research*, 2nd edn, ed. Norman K. Denzin and Yvonna S. Lincoln, 835–50. Thousand Oaks: Sage, 2000

Magder, Ted. *Canada's Hollywood: The Canadian State and Feature Films*. Toronto: University of Toronto Press, 1993

Marchessault, Janine. "Amateur Video and the Challenge for Change." In
    Mirror Machine: Video and Identity, ed. Janine Marchessault, 13–25.
    Toronto: YYZ Books, 1995
– "Reflections on the Dispossessed: Video and the 'Challenge for Change'
    Experiment." *Screen* 36 (Summer 1995): 131–46
Marsh, Leonard. *Report on Social Security for Canada*. Toronto: University
    of Toronto Press, 1975
Massey, Vincent. *On Being Canadian*. Toronto: Dent, 1948
– *What's Past Is Prologue*. Toronto: Macmillan, 1963
Meredith, David. "Imperial Images: The Empire Marketing Board, 1926–32."
    History Today, January 1987, 30–6
Merriam, Charles E. *The Making of Citizens*. Columbia: Teachers College
    Press, [1931], 1966
Miller, Toby. *The Well-Tempered Self: Citizenship, Culture, and the Post-
    modern Subject*. Baltimore: Johns Hopkins University Press, 1993
Moore, Rick Clifton. "Canada's Challenge for Change: Documentary Film
    and Video as an Exercise of Power through the Production of Cultural
    Reality." PHD thesis, University of Oregon, 1987
Moran, Albert, ed. *Film Policy: International, National, and Regional Perspec-
    tives*. London: Routledge, 1996
Morris, Peter. *Embattled Shadows*. Montreal & Kingston: McGill-Queen's
    University Press, 1978
– "Backwards to the Future: John Grierson's Film Policy for Canada." In
    Flashback: People and Institutions in Canadian Film History, ed. Gene
    Walz, 17–35. Montreal: Mediatexte, 1986
– "Re-thinking Grierson: The Ideology of John Grierson." In *Dialogue:
    Canadian and Quebec Cinema*, ed. Pierre Véronneau, Michael Dorland,
    and Seth Feldman, 24–56. Montreal: Mediatexte, 1987
– "'Praxis into Process': John Grierson and the National Film Board of
    Canada." *Historical Journal of Film, Radio, and Television* 9, no. 3 (1989):
    269–82
– ed. *The National Film Board of Canada: The War Years*. Ottawa: Canadian
    Film Institute, 1965
Nelson, Joyce. *The Colonized Eye: Rethinking the Grierson Legend*. Toronto:
    Between the Lines, 1988
Nichols, Bill. "The Voice of Documentary." *Film Quarterly* 36 (Spring, 1983):
    17–30
– *Blurred Boundaries*. Bloomington: Indiana University Press, 1996
Ninkovich, Frank A. *The Diplomacy of Ideas: U.S. Foreign Policy and Cultural
    Relations, 1938–1950*. Cambridge: Cambridge University Press, 1981
Nochlin, Linda. *Realism*. Harmondsworth: Penguin, 1971
Owram, Doug. *The Government Generation: Canadian Intellectuals and the*

State, 1900–1945. Toronto: University of Toronto Press, 1986
– "Economic Thought in the 1930s: The Prelude to Keynesianism." In *Social Welfare Policy in Canada: Historical Readings*, ed. Raymond Blake and Jeff Keshen, 172–200. Toronto: Copp Clark, 1995
Pal, Leslie A. *Interests of State: The Politics of Language, Multiculturalism, and Feminism in Canada*. Montreal & Kingston: McGill-Queen's University Press, 1993
Park, Robert. *Race and Culture*. Glencoe: Free Press, 1950
– "The Problem of Cultural Difference." In *Race and Culture*, 3–14. Glencoe: Free Press, 1950
– *Society*. Glencoe: Free Press, 1955
– "The City: Suggestions for the Investigation of Human Behavior in the Urban Environment." In *The Subcultures Reader*, ed. Sarah Thornton and K. Gelder, 16–27. London: Routledge, 1997
Pick, Zuzana. "Storytelling and Resistance: The Documentary Practice of Alanis Obomsawin." In *Gendering the Nation: Canadian Women's Cinema*, ed. Kay Armatage, Kass Banning, Brenda Longfellow, and Janine Marchessault, 76–93. Toronto: University of Toronto Press, 1999
Pickering, Michael, and David Chaney. "Democracy and Communication: Mass Observation 1937–1943." *Journal of Communication* 36 (Winter 1986): 41–56
Porter, Theodore M. *The Rise of Statistical Thinking, 1820–1900*. Princeton: Princeton University Press, 1986
Pronay, Nicholas. "John Grierson and the Documentary – 60 Years On." *Historical Journal of Film, Radio, and Television* 9, no. 3 (1989): 227–46
Pronay, Nicholas, and D.W. Spring, eds. *Propaganda, Politics, and Film, 1918–1945*. London: Macmillan, 1982
Purcell, Jr, Edward W. *The Crisis of Democratic Theory*. Lexington: University Press of Kentucky, 1973
Renov, Michael. *The Subject of Documentary*. Minneapolis: University of Minnesota Press, 2004
– ed. *Theorizing Documentary*. New York: Routledge, 1993
Richards, Jeffrey, and Dorothy Sheridan, eds. *Mass-Observation at the Movies*. London: Routledge and Kegan Paul, 1987
Robinson, Daniel. "Falling into Line: The National Film Board, Foreign Policy, and the Cold War." *National History* 1, no. 2 (1997): 158–72
– *The Measure of Democracy: Polling, Market Research, and Public Life, 1930–1945*. Toronto: University of Toronto Press, 1999
Rockefeller Foundation. *Annual Report*. New York, 1929
Rodger, Andrew. "Some Factors Contributing to the Formation of the National Film Board of Canada." *Historical Journal of Film, Radio, and Television* 9, no. 3 (1989): 259–68

Rosenstone, Robert. *Visions of the Past: The Challenge of Film to Our Idea of History*. Cambridge: Harvard, 1995

Rotha, Paul. *Documentary Film*. London: Faber, 1936

– *Documentary Diary*. London: Secker and Warburg, 1973

Russell, Catherine. *Experimental Ethnography*. Durham, NC: Duke University Press, 1999

Scher, Len. *The Un-Canadians: True Stories of the Blacklist Era*. Toronto: Lester, 1992

Scott, Joan. "Multiculturalism and the Politics of Identity," *The Identity in Question*, ed. John Rajchman, 3–14. New York: Routledge, 1995

Shea, Albert, ed. *Culture in Canada: A Study of the Findings of the Royal Commission on National Development in the Arts, Letters, and Sciences (1949–1951)*. Toronto: Core, 1952

Shore, Marlene. *The Science of Social Redemption*. Toronto: University of Toronto Press, 1987

Smith, Allan. "Metaphor and Nationality in North America." *The Canadian Historical Review* 51 (September 1970): 247–75

Starr, Paul. "Social Categories and Claims in the Liberal State." In *How Classification Works*, ed. Mary Douglas and David Hull, 154–79. Edinburgh: Edinburgh University Press, 1992

Steven, Peter. *Brink of Reality: New Canadian Documentary Film and Video*. Toronto: Between the Lines, 1993

Stollery, Martin. *Alternative Empires: European Modernist Cinemas and Cultures of Imperialism*. Exeter, UK: University of Exeter Press, 2000

Stoney, George. "The Mirror Machine." *Sight and Sound* 41, no. 1 (1971–72): 9–11

Stott, William. *Documentary Expression and Thirties America*. New York: Oxford University Press, 1973

Struthers, James. *No Fault of Their Own: Unemployment and the Canadian Welfare State, 1914–1941*. Toronto: University of Toronto Press, 1983

Sussex, Elizabeth. *The Rise and Fall of the British Documentary*. Berkeley: University of California Press, 1975

Swann, Paul. *The British Documentary Film Movement, 1926–1946*. Cambridge: Cambridge University Press, 1989

Tallents, Stephen. *The Projection of England*. London: Faber, 1932

– "Works of Canadian National Film Board: New and Vivid Links of Information." *Times* (London), 17 August 1946

Taussig, Michael. *Mimesis and Alterity*. London: Routledge, 1993

Taylor, Anita. "Implementing Feminist Principles in a Bureaucracy: Studio D, the National Film Board of Canada." In *Women Communicating: Studies of Women's Talk*, ed. Barbara Bate and Anita Taylor, 277–301. Norwood, NJ: Ablex Publishing, 1988

Thompson, John Herd, with Allen Seager. *Canada 1922–1939: Decades of Discord*. Toronto: McClelland & Stewart, 1985

Thornton, Sarah, and K. Gelder, eds. *The Subcultures Reader*. London: Routledge, 1997

Tippett, Maria. *Making Culture: English-Canadian Institutions and the Arts before the Massey Commission*. Toronto: University of Toronto Press, 1990

UNESCO. *Report of the Commission on Technical Needs in Press, Radio, Film, followiing the Survey in Twelve War-Devastated Countries*. Paris: UNESCO, 1947

– *Universal Declaration on Cultural Diversity*, November 2001

– *Film and Cinema Statistics*. Paris: UNESCO, n.d.

Valverde, Mariana. *The Age of Light, Soap, and Water*. Toronto: McClelland & Stewart, 1991

Véronneau, Pierre. *Résistance et affirmation: la production francophone à l'ONF – 1939–1964*. Montreal: Cinématheque québécoise, 1987

Watson, Patrick. "Challenge for Change." In *Canadian Film Reader*, ed. Seth Feldman and Joyce Nelson, 112–19. Toronto: Peter Martin, 1977

Waugh, Thomas. "Acting to Play Oneself: Notes on Performance in Documentary." In *Making Visible the Invisible: An Anthology of Original Essays on Film Acting*, ed. Carole Zucker, 64–91. Metuchen, NJ: Scarecrow Press, 1990

– "Monkey on the Back: Canadian Cinema, Conflicted Masculinities, and Queer Silences in Canada's Cold War." In *Love, Hate, and Fear in Canada's Cold War*, ed. Richard Cavell, 183–207. Toronto: University of Toronto Press, 2004

Weaver, Sally. *Making Canadian Indian Policy: The Hidden Agenda 1968–1970*. Toronto: University of Toronto Press, 1981

Webber, Jeremy. *Reimagining Canada: Language, Culture, Community, and the Canadian Constitution*. Montreal & Kingston: McGill-Queen's University Press, 1994

Wells, Clare. *The UN, UNESCO, and the Politics of Knowledge*. London: Macmillan, 1987

Whitaker, Reg. *Canadian Immigration Policy since Confederation*. Saint John: Keystone, 1991

Whitaker, Reg, and Gary Marcuse. *Cold War Canada: The Making of a National Insecurity State, 1945–1957*. Toronto: University of Toronto Press, 1994

White, Hayden, *The Content of the Form: Narrative Discourse and Historical Representation*. Baltimore: Johns Hopkins University Press, 1987

Whynot, Chris. "The NFB and Labour, 1945–1955." *Journal of Canadian Studies* 16 (Spring 1981): 13–22

Wiesner, Peter K. "Media for the People: The Canadian Experiments with Film and Video in Community Development." *American Review of Canadian Studies*, Spring 1992, 65–99

Willey, Malcolm, and Stuart Rice. *Communication Agencies in Social Life*. New York: McGraw-Hill, 1933.

Williams, Raymond. *Keywords*. Glasgow: Fontana, 1976

Winston, Brian. *Claiming the Real: The Documentary Film Revisited*. London: British Film Institute, 1995

Woodcock, George. *Strange Bedfellows: The State and the Arts in Canada*. Vancouver: Douglas & McIntyre, 1985

Young, William. "Making the Truth Graphic: The Canadian Government's Home Front Information Structure and Programmes During World War II." PHD thesis, University of British Columbia, 1978

- "Chauvinism and Canadianism: Canadian Ethnic Groups and the Failure of Wartime Information." In *On Guard for Thee: War, Ethnicity, and the Canadian State, 1939–1945*, ed. N. Hillmer, B. Kordan, and L. Luciuk, 31–51. Ottawa: Canadian Committee for the History of the Second World War, 1988

Zizek, Slavoj. "Multiculturalism, or, the Cultural Logic of Multinational Capitalism." *New Left Review* 225 (1997): 28–51

INDEX